rente, Vincent C. • Adkins, Anita • Adkins, Rebecca L. • Afful, James P. • Agha, Samer • Agli, Alfred A. • Ahee Sr., James Joseph • Ahmad, Sirajuddin • Ahn-Lee, Insun • Aiken, Mary
John C. • Alford Jr., Harold O. • Alford, Sundra J. • Allar, Kevin A. • Alldredge, David B. • Allen, Barbara Jean • Allen, Charles C. • Allen, Charles J. • Allen, Elizabeth • Allen, Joseph
Gregory T. • Altmiks, Henry • Altsman, Richard T. • Alvord, Joseph T. • Al-Yassi, Abdullah • Andary, Ajaj N. • Andejeski, Arthur Jo Robin Keen • Anderson, Theodora E. •
trong, Larry D. • Arneson, Susan R. • Arnold-Jessup, Brandon • Arnone, Lawrence • Arutoff, Alice M. • Ashby, Max R. • Ashraf, S Hernan A. • Atha,
, Rifat S. • Baar, Joanne • Baaso, Jeffrey E. • Bach, Jeanie M. • Bachler, Jeffrey S. • Bachman, Tanner J. • Backes, James M. J. Jonas,
oulos, George C. • Balan, E. Cheryl • Balde, Oscar Campos • Baldwin, Peter H. • Balian, Lisa A. • Balish, Jamie A. • Ballesteros ra J. •
David • Barden, Bonnie • Barger, Josephine • Barjaktarovich, Michael John • Barker, Eileen L. • Barkley, John Calvin • Barnes, ilip J. •
. • Bartos, Linda J. • Bartoy, Robert J. • Bas, Andrew M. • Bassett Jr., Arthur F. • Battles, Jennifer H. • Baum, Robert H. • Baum y M. •
r, Boris M. • Bedway, Joseph A. • Beeton, Philip E. • Begg, Kathleen M. • Behner, Victoria T. • Bell, Helen • Bell, Katheryn M. • buena,
Bensel, Heinz L. • Bently, Paulette • Berdenski, Nancy Ann • Berg, Howard K. • Berger, Glenn S. • Bergey, Arthur I. • Bergey, Charles Frank • Bergey, ert Eric
A. • Beverly, Thomas M. • Beydoun, Ali M. • Bhandari, Ashish • Bhattacharyya, Monjeera • Bhattacharyya, Sudharanjan • Biddy, Georgia H. • Bielecki, Waclaw Daniel •
dy L. • Blackstock, Herbert C. • Blackwell, Erica D. • Blair, Lucas R. • Blakey, Dwight Earl • Blanchard, Ryan James Valdez • Blank, Glenn Martin • Blaska, Robert J. • Blazevski, Kimberly
n, Robert Carl • Boccia, Mary • Bock, Erma June • Boe, Roger W. • Boehringer, Amy E. • Boermas, Thomas E. • Boersma, Gilbert R. • Boersma, Martin • Bogan, John K. • Bojanowski,
nie M. • Boram, Joan M. • Borders, Michael A. • Boscarino, Carl • Boskovic, Danilo • Botelho, Carolina • Botts, Aaron T. • Bou Younes, Fouad Y. • Bouey, Michael L. • Boufford, James
Braden, Michael P. • Bradley, Erica A. • Bradshaw, Clifford C. • Brain, Susan • Bramigk, Fred W. • Brand, Karl • Brandon, Kevin • Brashear, Ruth M. • Bratt, Leo B. • Braxton, Leroy D. •
y E. • Brisson, Victor G. • Britz, Dorothy • Broaddus, James E. • Broady, Harry W. • Brock, Lorieen T. • Bromley Jr., Walter G. • Broniak, Raymond T. • Brooks, Robert C. • Brooks, Vicky R.
own, Kenisha E. • Brown, Lloyd P. • Brown, Maureen • Brown, Michael J. • Brown Jr., William • Brownlie, Ian A. • Brueckner, Rosanna L. • Bruns, Gregory L. • Bruns, Maria R. • Bryant,
an D. • Bunce, William • Bunn Jr., Lynn L. • Burch, John K. • Burden Jr., Marcus B. • Burgess Jr., Henry T. • Burgess, Larry F. • Burke, Thomas E. • Burris, Bonita • Burris, James E. • Burton,
even C. • Byrnes, Margaret W. • Cadwell, Robert D. • Cain, Walter D. • Caladiao, Stephen A. • Calbeck, Mark M. • Calder, John Meek • Callas, John R. • Callis, Frank T. • Camada,
an, Gerald • Carlson, Verner C. • Carney, Lyster T. • Carr, Brian A. • Carr, Lois E. • Carrier, Gordon R. • Carter, Frederick David • Carter, Gary D. • Carter, Joy Elaine • Carter, Larry •
Castillo, Melejendo M. • Cavins, Terrance A. • Cenkush, Patrick A. • Cerreta, Dennis M. • Cervone, Evelyn • Chamberlin, Donald R. • Champagne, Judith E. • Chance, Susan A. •
ayne J. • Chow, Frank • Chranko, Joseph Edward • Christ, Deborah M. • Christensen, Daniel Frederick • Christensen, Nancy Lou • Christinson, Kenneth Earl • Christopher, Toni H. •
lapp, Howard M. • Clark, Charles O. • Clark, James A. • Clark, Keith • Clark, Rory K. • Clark, William B. • Clary, Laura A.R. • Claucherty, Douglas Gene • Clement, Amy • Clement,
rea, Aldo F. • Cole, John P. • Coleman, Donald E. • Coleman, Paul H. • Colina, Jose X. (Sonny) • Colletti, Mary • Colletti, Phillip • Collins (Kanyak), Nicole R. • Collins, Douglas Victor
onroy, Robert K. • Cooper, Danny R. • Cooper, Erika A. • Cooper, Steven D. • Cope, Louis • Copeland, Eric L. • Corcoran, Patrick Henry • Cornillaud, Chapin C. • Cornwall, Nellie •
erald L. • Courtright, Matthew D. • Cousins, Garnet R. • Cowen, Paul J. • Cox, Anne M. • Cox, Geraldine • Cox, James L.N. • Coyle, Mary Anne • Craft Jr., Milton • Craig, Grace A.
Romero M. • Cristofaro, Domenic • Critelli, Josephine • Crocker, Christopher, D. • Crockett, Lillie P. • Cronin, John T. • Cronovich, Milan • Cruciano, Michael A. • Cruz, Guillermo C. •
as, J. • Cushard III, Clifford G. • Cushing, Timothy J. • Czarnowski, Vincent A. • Dahlke, Donald • Dahoui, Karam K. • DallaVecchia, Violet Marie • Daltas, John P. • Danaher, Andrew
. • Das, Snigdha • Daskal, Joel Dennis • Daud, Suhel • Daud, Zafar • Daugherty, James Ronald • Davenport, Willie Mae • Davillies, Martin J. • Davis, Julie M. • Davis Jr., George L. •
chael W. • Dedic, Richard J. • Degnan, Frank J. • DeGregory, Thomas Joseph • Del Ben, Angelo A.• Del Corvo, Raymond A. • Delaney, Michael • Delaney, Tina M. • Demeulemeester,
DePaolis, Deloris Ann • DePersia, Ryan A. • DePotter, John E. • Deska, Eric Charles • Deskins, Jennifer L. • DeVaney, Sally Ann • DeVellis, Patricia M. • DeVor, Faith D. • DeWolf, John
o, Paul R. • DiGiovanni, Mark Anthony • Dillenbeck, Thomas M. • Dillon, Meryl L. • Dillon, Robert L. • Dilsworth, Blake W. • DiMaria, Charles A. • Dimitrijevic, Zoran • Dimond, Robert
• Dobbs, Thomas E. • Dobek, Debra Ann • Dobson, Gregory • Doering, Raymond M. • Dogan, Sharron M. • Doherty, Frank E. • Dombrowski, Christopher P. • Dombrowski, Jeffrey C.
drew M. • Donoghue, Steven M. • Doornbos, Jeremiah J. • Doran, Patricia Ann • Dorchen, Abraham Samuel • Dorda, Darryl J. • Dorsey, Edward Alan • Dowds, Thomas J. • Dowling,
Mark • DuBois-Holmes, Pamela • Duceatt, J. Robert • Duch, Michael • Ducharme, Gerald N. • Duff, Mable C. • Duffey, Heather Kay • Dugas, James T. • Dumlao, Violeta S. • Duncan
ard A. • Dye, Joshua S. • Dye, Rick S. • Dye, Stuart S. • Dyer, James Richard • Dysert, Marsha A. • Dziurlikowski, Katharine • Eady, Brian J. • Eardley, Edwin Huston • Earp, Robert H. •
Troy Buck • Edwards, Daniel S. • Edwards, Louis A. • Edwards, Thomas J. • Edwartoski, Daniel J. • Egan, John G. • Ehrmann, Frederick • Einberger, Franklin L. • Elayyan, Patricia M. •
et D. • Emdanat, Samir S. • Engler Sr., Charles • Enkemann, John E. • Epstein, Marcelo • Eriksen, Andrea L. • Esparza, David • Estwick, Keisha Elaine • Etchen, Edward A. • Eubank,
Fairbrother, Frederick • Fakih, Elham M. • Falcone, Rachel E. • Falconer, Eugene F. • Falzarano, Mark A. • Fang, Theresa Caihsum • Faour, Ahmad • Farley, Robert J. • Farrell, James
son, Thomas • Ferian, Natalia • Ferris, Deborah A. • Fidler, James A. • Fidler, Kevin W. • Figueroa-Ramirez, Uriel • Fill, Lawrence S. • Finch, Justin P. • Fine, Stuart • Fineburg, Keith S. •
G. • Fleming-Washeleski, Alicia • Flintoff Jr., Timothy R. • Flintoff-Ball, Ashley S. • Flores, Fernando A. • Flowers, Darrin • Flowers, Ricci L. • Floyd-Jackson, JonAnthony • Foland, Maynard
C. • Foxlee, Heather C. • Francis, Terrance L. • Francisco, Todd C. • Fraus, Adolph R. • Frederick, Daniel K. • Frederick, Marilyn A. • Frederick, Richard Harland • Fredericks Jr., Edward
rd A. • Fuhrer, Joseph W. • Fujivara, Fernando • Fuller, Cheryl E. • Fuller Sr., Roland A. • Fulmer Jr., David V. • Funderburg, Kurt K. • Furstenberg, Mark • Gabriel, Allan M. • Gadzinski,
Garcia, Rallo A. • Gardinal, Gerard J. • Gardner Jr., Joseph T. • Gardner, Robert L. • Gardzinski, Paul L. • Gargarello, Kaywana • Gargarello, Samuel L. • Garland, Philip J. • Garland,
D. • Geen, Donald J. • Gelff, Beldon • George, James O. • George, Theresa H. • Georgia, Erin L. • Geralds, Kevin T. • Gerdes, Jill • Gerencer, Alan P. • Gerig, Angelique • German,
ert J. • Gibson, Carolyn M. • Gienapp, Roger A. • Giertz, Jill K. • Gies, Randall D. • Gifford, Blake E. • Gilbert, Ray M. • Giler, Samuel • Gilkey, Julian D. • Gill, Inez • Gillespie, Larry S. •
Godbey, James D. • Godwin, Sylvia J. • Gofton, Sandra N. • Golla, Terri A. • Gooden, Sam • Goodhew, Terry J. • Gordon, Reginald S. • Gorman, Charles M. • Gossman, Frances •
Joshua N. • Gray, Patricia L. • Grecia, Jose Pepito N. • Green, Jennifer A. • Green, Terry W. • Greer, Kesiah L. • Gregg, Dean T. • Gregg, John W. • Grego, Tony L. • Gregory, William
iffiths, William A. • Grimm, Harry • Groat, Parke G. • Grochowski, Zbigniew • Grocki, Frank • Groen, Jeanette • Grosi, Jason M. • Grubbs, Alvin L. • Grujovski, Natasha • Grusenmeyer,
Gustafsson, Vernon M. • Guthard, Henry F. • Guthard, Sandra C. • Guy, Phillip A. • Gwin, Donald R. • Gwozdz, Daniel J. • Haas, Charles G. • Haas, Ryan P. • Haduck, Joseph J. •
Hamilton, Elizabeth • Hamilton, Margaret • Hammer, Harold N. • Hammoud, Nadim H. • Hamza, Majid • Handley, Frederick G. • Hanik, Irene J. • Hansen, Cody J. • Hansen, Richard
dy, Betty M. • Harenda, Conrad C. • Harlan, Joseph D. • Harman, Cynthia M. • Haro, John C. • Harp, Donnemeeco • Harper (Andrade), Esperanza C. • Harper, Jacqueline L. • Harris,
on • Hartel, Michael A. • Hartman, Elizabeth • Hartman, Ross A. • Hartman, Thomas Q. • Hartman, William J. • Harvey, Denise S. • Harvey, Dennis R. • Harville, Odis J. • Harwick, Rex
Hayden, William P. • Hayes, Donald A. • Haynes, Paula D. • Hazelhoff, Johnathan J. • Hazen, Scott Z. • Heaman, Jeffrey R. • Heath, Russell • Hedges, Timothy L. • Hegwood, Robert
D. • Hengesbaugh, Daniel J. • Henninger, Joseph R. • Henriksen, Kimberly A. • Henry, Edith G. • Hensel, Joerg • Herbart, Kenneth R. • Herman, Clarence P. • Hermann, Derek R. •
Hibbler, Ralph P. • Hickey, Lucile • Hicks, Jill Hursey • Hiddema, Wendy L. • Hilario Jr., Arsenio T. • Hill, Duane P. • Hill, Eric J. • Hill, John B. • Hill, Louis G. • Hill, Philip J. • Hillebrandt,
Hinterser, Cori E. • Hirami, Brian B. • Hirmiz, John • Hirt, Linda • Hitchcock, Jennifer • Hixson, Sondra A. • Hoag, Eugenia M. • Hoard (Jerry), Mayon J. • Hoare (Marsom), Ruby • Hodge,
William A. • Hoge, Robert D. • Hoig, Harry W. • Holcomb, Raymond B. • Holewinski, Chris E. • Holewinski, Daniel J. • Holley, Katherine L. • Hollier, Hubert • Hollinsworth, Galon • Holmes,
Garabed M. • Hopper, Kent H. • Horist, Ronald A. • Horn, Michael L. • Horn, Wilbur A. • Horner, Ronald P. • Horowitz, Kevin S. • Hoskins, Craig • House, Dorothy K. • Howard, Charles E.
d, Robert J. • Hubel, Robert W. • Hubner, Walter H. • Hudson, Kathleen M. • Hudson, Keith J. • Hudson, Mykal A. • Hudson, Richard C. • Hugh, Leighton P. • Hugo, Clarence • Hundt,
Innes, Gerald • Ireland, Robert C. • Ishii, Takaaki • Isner, Arnold • Issa, Jalal A. • Izadi, Mansour H. • Jackola, Thor A.M. • Jackson, Benard Carlton • Jackson, Kari L. • Jackson, Kevin
Jaeger, Shelli R. • Jahan, Mafruha • Jain, Prakash Chand • James, Michael H. • James, Stanley W. • Jamil, Raid G. • Jankowski Jr., Chester H. • Janowski, Janusz M. • Janowski Jr.,
ordon S. • Jennings, Larry • Jensen, Gustav Kurt • Jensen, Robert E. • Jesmore, David A. • Jeter, Billie W. • Jimenez, José Louis • Johnson (McMillan), Debra B. • Johnson, Delana C. •
Johnson, Olive G. • Johnson, Pamala D. • Johnson (Liggins), Phyllis • Johnson Jr., Roland • Johnson, Terdell C. • Johnson, Wayne D. • Jones, Abram • Jones, Arnold • Jones, Bethany
ard M. • Jones, S. Ruth • Jones, Theodore R. • Jones-Williams, Tawanesha • Jonsson, Maggi • Jordan, Larry T. • Jordan, Robert L. • Joseph, George Aloysius • Jubenville, Martin K. •
d • Kahn, William L. • Kalnas, Ralph G. • Kanipe, Lee Merrill • Karpala, Peter F. • Karr, Lisa M. • Karwan, Robert T. • Kasparek, Frank J. • Katz, Ralph • Kaufaman, Joyce A. • Kavanaugh,
rry • Kendall, William B. • Kenedi, Anna Fischer • Kennard, Frank • Kennedy, Alisha A. • Kennedy, Christine S. • Kennedy, Lawrence B. • Kennedy, Thomas R. • Kenny, William K. • Kent,
A. • Killion, Jim D. • Kim, Young Sung • Kimball Jr., James R. • Kincius, Stephen R. • King, Harry S. • King, Lydia • King, Sol • Kinner Jr., William G. • Kirby, Paul B. • Kirks, John E. • Kirkwood
Knight Pogue, Sandra • Knight, Raymond Lee • Knippenberg, Matthew P. • Ko, Alan C. • Koch, Timothy J. • Koehler, Harold A. • Koenig, Mark T. • Koeth, Caitlyn A. • Kohli, Surinder
ol • Kornbacher, Anna L. • Kosniewski Jr., John M. • Kostecke, Michael D. • Koster, Terry • Kovacs, Julius Steven • Kowalczyk, Rachel J. • Kowalski, Delphine • Kraemer, Maureen M. •
ul • Krupar, Stephen Stanley • Krupnick, Israel • Krysak Jr., David M. • Krzesimowski, John • Kuczajda, Robert • Kuhn, Joseph M. • Kuhn, Walter M. • Kukla, Dolores • Kulmaticki, Vladimir
Joseph S. • Lafontant, George G. • LaForce, Phillip J. • Lahey, Gary B. • Lam, Lawrence • Lamas, Ana M. • Lambert, Wayne E. • Lamer, Vaughn • Lanceta, Leonito L. • Land, Ruth V.
san • LaRuffa, August J. • LaSalle, Norman R. • Lashbrook, Nancy • Laskowski, Stephen • Lauer, Heather L. • Lauer, Matheus • Lauhoff, Michael J. • Lauhoff II, Michael J. • Lauri, Anna

The Art of Collaboration & Innovation

Albert Kahn Associates

Published by:
Visual Profile Books, Inc.
389 Fifth Avenue, New York, NY 10016
Phone: 212.279.7000
www.visualprofilebooks.com

Distributed by:
National Book Networks, Inc.
15200 NBN Way, Blue Ridge Summit, PA 17214
Toll Free (U.S.): 800.462.6420
Toll Free Fax (U.S.): 800.338.4550
Email orders or Inquires: customercare@nbnbooks.com

ISBN 13: 978-1-7330648-5-9

Library of Congress Cataloging in Publication Data: The Art of Collaboration & Innovation

Book Designer: Christina Chin

The Art of Collaboration & Innovation

Albert Kahn Associates

Caitlin Wunderlich

With Leslie Armbruster, Donald Bauman, Alan Cobb, John Cole,
Christo Datini, Katie Doelle, Rick S. Dye, Nancy Finegood, Jeffrey T. Gaines, John Gallagher,
Deirdre L.C. Hennebury, Grant Hildebrand, Michael H. Hodges, Gordon V.R. Holness,
Case Allen-Kahn Kittel, Peter G. Lynde, Chris Meister, Kimberly Montague,
Jamie Myler, Heidi Pfannes, Hank Ritter, Robert Sharrow, Michael G. Smith,
Greg Tasker, Stephen White, Gregory Wittkopp, and Claire Zimmerman

VISUAL PROFILE BOOKS, NEW YORK

TABLE OF CONTENTS

FOREWORD

"Now, when you write the story, credit it to Albert Kahn Associates (Architects) and Engineers, Inc., rather than to me, personally. After all, I am like the quarterback on a football team. Without the teamwork of my associates, I would be nothing."[1]

- Albert Kahn

Perhaps it was the foundation of Albert Kahn's family unit. Dedication, passion, mutual respect and collaboration are among the values the firm inherited from its founder. Despite his lack of formal education, Albert persevered and supported his siblings as they pursued advanced education and professional careers. He was dedicated, humble, and appreciated the unique talents of each person he met. He knew that architects and engineers could accomplish much more as a team than alone. This lesson has been passed on from generation to generation at Albert Kahn Associates (Kahn). We have always called Kahn a family, and supported one another as family members, encouraging each other's continued growth and creativity, and banding together to conquer any challenge.

Albert and his family were in the right place at the right time. His career began in Detroit; the city was an epicenter of innovation, novel technology, and new ideas to transform the world through mass production of the automobile. Through the various projects he had the good fortune to find, different challenges allowed him to collaborate with engineers, chemists, metallurgists, and inventors to solve the problems he faced. Using mock-up and testing, Albert and his brother Julius perfected a scientific method for designing reinforced concrete. He built a firm of architects, engineers, project managers, construction managers, and other disciplines that worked in concert with one other. That was the "great idea," organizing a way to bring the right talent, expertise, and passion to a client's challenge. Open collaboration integrated with the architectural design ideas and the detailed engineering solutions has been the key to our firm's success.

Albert was one of the most prolific and versatile architects, completing approximately 20,000 projects during his life for virtually every type of client. The Albert Kahn name is often linked with the development of industrial architecture, synonymous with the great industrial giants of the 20th century. He raised factory design to a legitimate level of architectural practice, recalling years later, "When I began, the real architects would design only museums, cathedrals, capitals, monuments. The office boy was considered good enough to do factory buildings. I'm still that office boy designing factories. I have no dignity to be impaired."[2] To Albert, all buildings deserved the consideration and skill of good design. He developed new ways of bringing natural light into buildings through skylights and glass curtain-walls. He set up businesses to fabricate well-designed steel sash systems for skylight and window systems. Using industrial spaces, he explored the relationship between the built environment, process, and wellbeing. He invented the concept of "Universal Space" that influenced later movements by contemporary architects such as Frank Lloyd Wright, Walter Gropius, Ludwig Mies van der Rohe, and Le Corbusier. This is only one part of the legacy. Albert's practice extended to corporate offices, civic structures, educational buildings, hospitals, social clubs, exhibition buildings, residential homes, and even tombstones for some of his long-term clients. Albert and the firm he founded mirrored the industrious spirit of the time, creating architecture that advanced their client's work and continues to inspire today.

Today, the Kahn firm design philosophy is rooted in the notion that few things in life touch us so powerfully, figuratively and literally, as architecture. All projects must be thoughtfully and carefully explored around the client's functional needs and goals, from educational and health care facilities to industrial and commercial structures. The Kahn design studio environment brings designers, planners, landscape architects, and engineers together in the same location, facilitating better communication, collaboration, integration, and ultimately, fostering design excellence. The smallest or most challenging large projects can yield the finest architectural and engineering solutions. Kahn has been committed to finding the most appropriate functional and aesthetic solution for every project. Having a complete understanding of the client's needs is key to a project's success.

A comprehensive integration of all building systems, creating a whole, is the fundamental principle in all of our work - a synthesis of architecture, engineered system and art, working together in sustainable unity with the site. Kahn is committed to creating intelligent solutions that look at long-term conditions relative to the limits of our natural resources. Sustainability in our work comes in many differing ways and levels. It can be as simple as considering the durability and longevity or recyclable content of materials chosen for projects, or as significant as a carbon-neutral solution.

The firm has survived many difficult times, including both World Wars, the Spanish Flu Epidemic, the Great Depression, the Cold War, the 9/11 Terrorist Attack, the 2008 Wall Street Crash, and the COVID-19 Pandemic. There are always unknowns that threaten success. Having a strong Strategic Plan and Company Goals, and being agile is extremely important in our business. A key to the firm's success has been our ability to lead the profession in multiple market segments and the ability to move from a slowing market to thriving market as the economy changes.

Clients have continued to hire our firm for many years (some over 100 years), because of the Kahn culture, ethics, and commitment. The Kahn culture of collaboration brings together internal and external team members, and our client's experience in a synergistic environment. With a thorough understanding, our design teams advance innovative solutions that realize efficiencies, and are flexible and adaptable to changes in the future. Kahn design teams are detail-oriented but do not lose sight of the big picture. We continue to amaze and delight our clients with our ability to deliver quality in a short time frame. That is "Speed to Market," because for many of our clients, "Time is Money."

I remember visiting the Fisher Building with my father, who worked for Fisher Body and General Motors, and being in awe of the integration of art and architecture. Perhaps, those trips to the Fisher Building and Fisher Theater were one of the reasons I wanted to be an architect. Albert Kahn was a master of his profession. He set an incredibly high bar for those who follow in the Kahn firm and the architectural profession, in general. Design and build, extremely fast, and measure how well your design meets the challenge – this process has inspired me throughout my career. It is a great honor to have been the 10th President and CEO of Kahn, and forever part of the Kahn family.

Alan Cobb, FAIA, Chairman & CEO, Albert Kahn Associates

THE LEGACY

The story of Albert Kahn as the great Industrial Designer – the Architect of Detroit – has been told. Often, this story recalls the incredible legacy of a revolutionary man who founded a firm that reached six continents.[3] What these stories haven't told you, however, is that this legacy hasn't stopped. It's not over. We, Albert Kahn Associates, Inc. (Kahn), are still here. We are still innovating.

Over the last 125 years, thousands of men and women have left their mark on this firm, shaping each project we have completed. This story is about the work that we have done and are currently doing, and the legacy we will continue to build in the future.

Albert's most innovative design was creating a collaborative Architectural and Engineering practice under one roof, which continues to this day from inside the Fisher Building in Detroit, Michigan. Julius Kahn, Albert's younger brother, joined the firm in 1902 to become chief engineer. Having served as an engineer for the U.S. Navy and the U.S. Engineering Corps, Julius brought technical expertise in structural design to the firm. This began Albert's ground-breaking establishment of a non-traditional, multi-disciplinary firm of designers, engineers, accountants, project managers, and field superintendents. With a diverse team of experts, the firm could provide the full range of design/build in-house, making construction more efficient and less costly for clients.

Albert spoke about the necessity of a collaborative practice on several occasions: "In this day of intricate problems and specialization there should be a very close relationship between the architect and the engineer, as each is dependent upon the other if the best interests of the client are to be served. Architecture, as we know it today, is in itself a life's study. Engineering, whether it be that of structural, sanitary, heating and ventilating, or electrical, is also a life's study. No one of us can live more than one life, consequently none of us can be proficient in all these professions."[4]

"It is true that the average architect can, with the assistance of the many hand-books published, design a frame-work for his building, which will be strong enough to support the structure; but the designing of a frame-work which is strong enough, and at the same time involves the least amount of structural material, requires the expert knowledge of a structural engineer."[5]

"A mechanical engineer, after preparing his process layout, can also in a fashion design a building to house the mechanical equipment; but it would be unreasonable to expect from him a plan which embodies the most suitable arrangement of departments, the best means of ingress and egress, the most practical location for stairways, elevators, toilet rooms; or the proper proportioning of these details."[6]

There is an artistry to both practices. When working together, they complement each other and create that spark of innovation that transforms the way we interact with the spaces we inhabit. Together, Architecture and Engineering is about designing an eloquent solution to propel our work and our lives into the next level of greatness.

ALBERT KAHN, THE ARCHITECT

Joseph and his wife Rosalie with their children Albert, the oldest on the far right, Julius, Felix, Louis, Gus, Moritz, Mollie, and Paula, Detroit, 1884.

With some cultural heroes, it can be hard to disentangle the woman or man from the myth. Not so with Detroit architect Albert Kahn. Stories about the German immigrant and his remarkable rise have surely puffed up a bit in the 80 years since his death, but key elements in both personal history and mythology synch up surprisingly well. Albert did rise from poverty to become one of the world's most-famous and successful architects. He was fired as a teenager from his first job at an architecture firm for smelling like the stables – the result of an early-morning job rubbing down a couple horses.

And his early 20th-century factories for Packard Motor and Henry Ford did, indeed, revolutionize American industry, temples of startling modernity that would be copied around the globe. Even more consequential – and largely overlooked by history – the 500-odd factories Albert Kahn Associates built across the Soviet Union in the early 1930s played a critical, if unforeseen, role in winning World War II for the Allies. Finally, in a profession dominated by towering egos, Albert appears to have been a true mensch – the Yiddish term denoting honesty, integrity and decency – which the architect had in abundance.

Albert was born in 1869 to Joseph and Rosalie Kahn in Rhaunen, Germany – a town some 60 miles west of Frankfurt, small enough that I have yet to meet a German who's heard of it. The family was cultured but not monied. Joseph, trained as a rabbi, never developed much of a gift for supporting a family. Perhaps reflecting this, when Albert was about seven, the Kahns left Germany and moved in with an aunt in the Duchy of Luxembourg, a decision likely driven by economic need. Ultimately, Joseph and Rosalie decided to bet everything on America, crossing the Atlantic in 1881 and making their way to Detroit. Albert, the oldest in a brood of seven, was just 12. (Incidentally, every other published source cites 1880 as the year the Kahns came to this country, but Albert's handwritten application for a U.S. passport some 10 years later clearly states they arrived in 1881.) The Kahns' early years in Detroit were marked by misfortune – a restaurant started with what little money they had caught fire in the middle of the night and burned down. For several years, thereafter – until Albert really got on his feet – the family, now with eight children, endured a tenuous, hand-to-mouth existence at poverty's edge common to many immigrants in those years.

Because of that, there was no question of Albert going to school. He went to work the moment he landed on these shores, and never attended another day of classes. After getting the boot from the John L. Scott firm ("I literally got on their olfactory nerves," he would explain in a speech some 40 years later), the teenager – all of about 14 – lucked into an apprenticeship with the well-regarded Detroit firm of Mason and Rice. It was unexpected good fortune, a turn that would set the young man on his life's course. If at the Scott firm Albert had done little but run errands, empty wastebaskets and grind ink, George Mason and partner Zachariah Rice could clearly see the promise beneath the rough outlines of an immigrant lad, and began to train their new hire in the architectural arts. In short order, Albert was making what must have seemed like a grand sum at the time – $3.50 a week. Just a few years thereafter, he was designing houses for prestigious clients all on his own.

The rising young star attracted notice, and in 1890 – when he was about 20 – Albert won a $500 scholarship (about $12,000 today) from a prestigious architectural journal to travel Europe for one year, sketching civilization's great buildings. In Florence, Albert bumped into another young architect by the name of Henry Bacon. Much wealthier and far-better educated than Albert, Bacon – a University of North Carolina graduate who 25 years later would design the Lincoln Memorial – took a liking to the Detroiter, and the two decided to travel together. Toward the end of Albert's career, the editors of Architectural Forum had a little fun at his expense, writing that in Italy the youngster "was so bewildered by the profusion of masterpieces that he didn't know what to do until Henry Bacon took him in hand." For his part, Albert always said the four months with Bacon constituted "my real education in architecture." Shortly after his return to Detroit, where Mason and Rice had held his job for him, Albert was named the firm's chief designer. He was all of 22.

In the years after his return from Europe, Albert took two momentous steps. He married his sweetheart Ernestine Krolik, and went out on his own with two other Mason and Rice architects to form Nettleton, Kahn and Trowbridge. The marriage to Ernestine in 1896 was a lifelong success, producing four children, but the newly minted design firm quickly went bust. In 1897, one partner left to head up the architecture program at Cornell University. Three years after that, the other succumbed to tuberculosis – which must have been awful for Albert personally, to say nothing of leaving him alone and swamped in a sinking firm. Kind as ever, George Mason threw his former apprentice a lifeline, and Albert returned to the office he had left with such high hopes. Finally, in 1902 Albert ventured out on his own again – this time with no untoward surprises. There commenced the long, upward trajectory that by the time of his death in 1942 had made Albert one of the century's most-famous and admired architects, mourned in newspaper obituaries worldwide.

Author: Michael H. Hodges, Author of *Building the Modern World: Albert Kahn in Detroit*

JULIUS KAHN, THE ENGINEER

Felix, Albert and Julius Kahn, 1931.

Though responsible for one of the most significant inventions of the 20th century, Julius Kahn (Albert's younger brother) is little known for his contributions. In 1902, Julius invented the first practical and scientific method for building with reinforced concrete.[7] He founded a company to market this and other construction technologies and quickly transformed concrete from a seldom used and little understood material into the basis for modern commercial and industrial architecture.

Julius earned a Bachelor of Science in civil engineering from the University of Michigan in 1896, largely paid for by Albert. For three years following graduation, he worked for several engineering firms, including the Navy Bureau of Yards and Docks in New York. After receiving his civil engineering degree in 1899 Julius accepted a position in Japan as chief engineer for a mining company. In 1902, Albert's partnership with George D. Mason was ending and Albert asked Julius to join him as a partner. Albert anticipated that having within his firm an engineer with strong industrial experience would pave the way for securing more of this lucrative work.

While working with Albert on buildings, such as the Palms Apartments (below), constructed with concrete floors, Julius recognized concrete's potential as a sturdy, low cost, and fireproof replacement for timber and steel frame construction. During the course of 1902, he devised a steel reinforcement bar that overcame the shortcomings of earlier attempts to combine the two materials. The bar Julius invented differed from others in that it had prongs extending up at a 45 degree angle. These prevented the reinforcement bar from being pulled loose from the concrete when the beam was under stress. The prongs also prevented vertical cracks from opening up and causing failure. Unlike other reinforcing methods, the maximum weight-bearing capacity of beams constructed with the "Kahn Bar" could be calculated with scientific certainty, making concrete buildings safe and economical.

To manufacture and market his reinforcement bars, Julius left the partnership with Albert and in October 1903 founded the Trussed Concrete Steel Company (Truscon), of which Albert was a partner. The biggest impediment to the use of reinforced concrete was the lack of trained engineers, so Truscon included engineering services for its customers in the form of plans showing where each reinforcement bar was to be placed. A lack of contractors experienced with concrete construction was another problem, so in 1904, Julius set up a construction subsidiary.

The first orders for the Kahn Bar were for the U. S. Army War College complex in Washington D.C., business that Julius secured through his meetings with the chief engineer of the U. S. Army. Julius and Albert collaborated on several jobs as Albert introduced reinforced concrete to his customers, including Burroughs Corporation, for whom Julius and Albert constructed in 1904 the first significant building to use reinforced concrete in Detroit.[8]

By the end of 1905, the Kahn Bar had become the most popular method of concrete reinforcement, used in buildings from the largest reinforced concrete structure in the world, Atlantic City's Marlborough-Blenheim hotel, to Albert's personal residence. In 1906, Truscon engineered over 600,000 sq. ft. of factory space for automobile manufacturing companies in three states (the vast majority of auto capacity built that year), facilitating a revolution in methods of mass production.[9]

A list of the buildings constructed with Truscon reinforcement during the early 20th century would include tens of thousands of the most important structures in the United States, Europe, and Asia. That's quite a legacy for a little known Detroit engineer.

Author: Michael G. Smith, Author of a forthcoming book on Julius Kahn

THE BEGINNING

For the last half-century, Albert Kahn Associates has attributed its start date to 1895 when Albert left Mason and Rice to start Nettleton, Kahn and Trowbridge with two of his colleagues. This date has been contested by numerous scholars and Albert Kahn aficionados throughout our history. With the opportunity to dig into our archives, we found that over the last 125 years, our materials, as well as those from outside sources, have listed 1894, 1895, and 1896 as founding dates of Nettleton, Kahn and Trowbridge. From what we can tell, the exact start date wasn't formally recorded, as businesses are today. Architects were not required to be licensed with the state of Michigan until 1915.[10] There are a handful of historical newspaper articles that hint at the recent start of the firm but do not list an actual start date. From our records, it seems that sometime between our 65th anniversary in 1959[11] and our 75th anniversary celebrated in 1970,[12] the date of our founding changed from 1894 to 1895. Other seminal accounts of the firm's history, such as W. Hawkins Ferry's *The Legacy of Albert Kahn*, and Grant Hildebrand's *Designing for Industry: The Architecture of Albert Kahn*, both published in the 1970s, note an official founding date of 1896, attributing the date to notes in George Mason's papers.

Albert speaks about the start of the firm in speeches he gave and articles he wrote during the 1920s and 1930s. In a speech at the dedication of George Mason's Masonic Temple in 1926, Albert recalls the incredible mentorship provided by Mason and his friendship with George Nettleton while at the firm of Mason and Rice – a friendship that led to a partnership in 1894.[13] In 1937, Albert described more about the early firm, "Our original firm was composed of three who after a period of years in a Detroit office decided to start on their own many, many years ago – in 1894 to be correct. A.B.T. (Alexander B. Trowbridge), the junior member, wrote from Paris in '93 suggesting our establishing ourselves jointly."[14] Albert notes a depression in 1894 and explains that the start of the company was rocky; projects included residential work, an occasional church building, schoolhouse, hotel, store or small office building.[15] Perhaps there was a period of overlap when the three men began planning for their firm, while still working with Mason and Rice.

Though it might not be possible to pin down the exact start date of the firm, we are able to trace when we began many of these early projects with our clients. A vital commission early on was Grace Hospital Nurses' home, which they won in a competitive process.[16] Still, the business was turbulent for those first years. Alexander B. Trowbridge took a job at Cornell University in 1897, and George W. Nettleton was diagnosed with tuberculosis and passed away in 1900. Albert notes that at the time he felt he was in a hopeless position, and to keep up with the work meant many evenings and Sundays at the office, "but encouraged by my (wife) who spent many evenings at the office with us, we carried on surprisingly well."[17]

Following the loss of Nettleton, Albert briefly partnered with his mentor, George Mason, to form Mason and Kahn. Newspaper accounts show that the partnership officially lasted one year,[18] but Albert's later speeches suggest that the two remained collaborative and cordial throughout their lives.[19] Together, they designed the Palms Apartments on Jefferson Avenue (1903), the Engineering Building for the University of Michigan (1904), the Belle Isle Aquarium and Horticultural Building (1904), and the Temple Beth El on Woodward Avenue (1903). Julius Kahn and Ernest Wilby joined the firm in 1902. The firm was referred to by several names at this time including Albert Kahn, Architect, Julius Kahn, Engineer, along with many variations thereof, as well as Albert Kahn, Architect, Ernest Wilby, Associate, which seemed to prevail until 1922.

Albert, on the left, in the office of George Mason, seated on the stool to the right, circa 1891.

PACKARD AUTOMOTIVE PLANT

DETROIT, MICHIGAN | DESIGNED 1903 OPENED 1905

Packard Motor Car Company played an important role in the early careers of both Albert Kahn, architect, and Julius Kahn, civil engineer. In January 1903, the two brothers were asked to design a factory for Packard, a job secured largely through the efforts of Joseph Boyer, who was responsible for the brothers' two previous factory commissions.

Julius and Albert's firm of Kahn and Kahn[20] was, at the time, the only architecture firm in Detroit offering engineering services, an approach they expected would secure lucrative work designing factories. The brothers had an exceptionally well-developed understanding of the requirements for industrial manufacturing facilities, an understanding that most architects of the era lacked. In designing the Packard factory, they focused on maximizing production efficiency, minimizing construction and factory maintenance costs, and reducing construction time. They lowered manufacturing costs by designing the complex around the most efficient flow of materials: "In planning these buildings the skill of the engineer has been drawn upon in order that there may be no time lost in handling the material from the time that it enters at one end of the plant, in the rough, until it is turned out at the other end a finished product."[21] Consideration was even given to the passage of employees to their workstations; the plant layout allowed workers to enter their department without passing through any others.[22]

Insurance was a major cost of maintaining a factory, and it was claimed that the Packard buildings were so well designed that fire insurance costs were reduced by 90 percent.[23] A coal-fired powerhouse provided electricity to motors throughout the plant that ran the machinery (by means of overhead shafting and belts). Each department had its own motor, so if one department needed to shut down, no other departments were affected.

Concrete was used for some of the floors depending on the work carried out within. One of the finishing buildings contained a reservoir in the basement. The floor above was concrete supported by reinforced concrete beams, each of which contained two reinforcement bars of a new type invented by Julius, but not yet patented. Within a few years, these bars would be extensively used throughout the world and this was their first use.[24]

The Packard buildings were of obsolescent mill construction and less advanced than the handful of concrete factories being built elsewhere, but they were designed to be constructed rapidly and inexpensively, permitting the owners to achieve production quickly, and at low cost. "Notwithstanding the unusual size of this establishment," reported one industry journal, "the buildings were erected in a very short time, only ninety days elapsing from the date on which the contract was signed."[25]

Their achievements with the Packard plant provided an opportunity for Albert and Julius to promote their firm's unique combination of architecture and engineering services. Even the building plans emphasized the collaboration: "Albert Kahn, Architect, Julius Kahn, Engineer."[26] The Kahn brothers' most powerful appeal to potential industrial customers was their understanding of, and attention to, the vital concerns facing manufacturers: production efficiency, operational costs, and speed of construction. Much of their future success resulted from remaining focused on these concerns throughout their careers.

Author: Michael G. Smith, Author of a forthcoming book on Julius Kahn

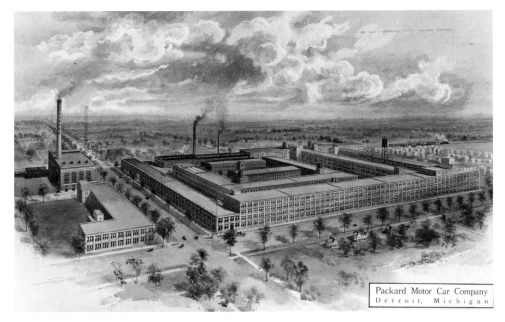

Packard Motor Car Company
Detroit, Michigan

TRANSFORMING INDUSTRY

Around 1902, Henry B. Joy bought into the Packard Co. of Warren, Ohio, and decided to locate the new factory in Detroit. Albert recalled, "I had just completed the alterations to Mr. Joy's house to his satisfaction. Shortly before I had done similar work for the late Mr. Joseph Boyer, president of the Chicago Pneumatic Tool Co., which he brought here from St. Louis. So when a new factory for the Packard Co. was decided upon, both Mr. Joy and Mr. Boyer recommended me for the architectural work. With practically no experience in factory building, it was with much trepidation that I undertook the work."[27] Albert and Julius, used the newly refined reinforced concrete system, catching the attention of other industrialists. Reinforced concrete factories were more fireproof, minimized vibration from machinery, allowed greater spans between columns to create more flexibility on the floor, and larger openings for windows to bring in more natural light and ventilation for workers. This design revolutionized factories as well as healthcare, corporate, educational, and many other spaces around the world.

The Kahn firm went on to design iconic manufacturing complexes for Ford Motor Company, General Motors, and Chrysler, to name but a few, with one-of-a-kind solutions that supported and improved the way a client mass-produced its product. These designs were driven by purpose – the form followed its function – and were a result of consistent collaboration with the client and their in-house engineers to incorporate process flow, accommodate machine placement, and provide flexibility for future product changes or building additions. In addition to well-known automotive factories, the firm also produced manufacturing facilities for clothing, textiles, food, cigars, cement, and countless other products.

"Though we specialize in industrial work, our commissions are of all sorts. Indeed, few firms deal with so many different problems," Albert explained during a later speech to the Cleveland Engineering Society, "Factory buildings of all kinds, power plants, steel mills, newspaper plants, storage warehouses, banks, office buildings, school houses, auditoriums, hospitals, prisons, asylums, even a residence now and then, all have had our attention and service. It is this variety which makes our work so interesting. We attack all problems in much the same way. As we tell our clients, we like to do so in the manner of solving an industrial layout, where the raw material enters at one point, passes through various operations and is delivered ready to ship at another. This principle is applicable to practically every problem and makes for straight-line operation, whether it be a hospital where we consider the patient the raw material, and the cured the finished product; or a club house or hotel in which the proper correlation of various departments is just as important as in the most complex manufacturing scheme. At the same time, we lay particular stress upon the matter of design and devote the closest attention to it. It need cost no more to have an attractive building than an unattractive structure. It is not expensive and elaborate decoration which makes a structure architecturally good; but rather proper mass and proportion, which as a rule require no additional outlay of money, but additional study and skill."[28]

User experience, whether that was in the factory, office, classroom, or home, has always been paramount to the firm. Kahn factory designs radically improved the health and safety conditions of workers through the incorporation of clerestory glass and roof monitors to bring in natural light and adequate ventilation. This notion extended to other facilities such as General Motors' new 15-story office building (1922) which was one of the largest office buildings in the world at the time (right). Designed with four wings that intersect a central corridor, each office had direct access to natural light and fresh air.

Kahn's expertise across an array of markets, unmatched efficiency in both design and execution, and the revolutionary structure of a multidisciplinary practice set the Kahn firm apart from the competition. The early collaboration between Albert, the architect, and Julius, the engineer, paved the way for a firm that would take on any challenge. The firm melded engineering advances across industries with the aesthetic of the client to create technologically advanced, efficient, and inspiring spaces regardless of the type of building. Numerous buildings and renovations across the University of Michigan campus, for instance, integrate the latest engineering innovations with elements from the history of design and regional materials to create a new academic campus.

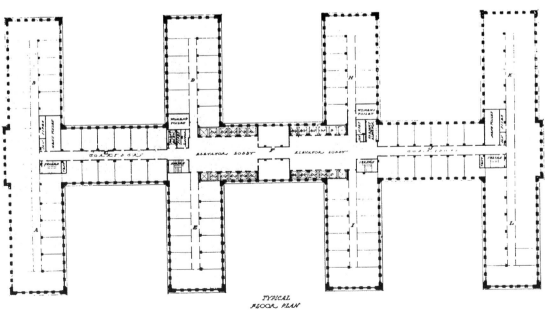

TYPICAL
FLOOR PLAN

WILLISTEAD AND WALKERVILLE

As a resident in the City of Windsor, you cannot help but be introduced to the works of Albert Kahn. While working at Mason and Rice, Albert began designing the iconic Hiram Walker executive offices located on Riverside Drive – an architectural jewel in the Walkerville District. This relationship with Hiram Walker, the Canadian Club Founder, led to many residential commissions and other buildings to support both the distillery business and the community employed by the distillery. These buildings included the town hall, bank, commercial buildings, rowhouses, and many executive homes that establish themselves along the tree-lined streets of Walkerville. One of the most iconic residences in the city is located in the heart of Walkerville: The Willistead Manor.

Commissioned by Edward Chandler Walker, the second son of Hiram Walker, the manor was named after his brother Willis, who passed away at an early age. This 36 room mansion was designed for Edward and his wife Mary, who were married later in life. Designed in a sixteenth-century Tudor-Jacobean Style, the manor sits on a fifteen-acre park, formerly the gardens of the estate. Constructed of gray limestone by Scottish stonemasons, the superior craftsmanship carries through the exterior and interior of the home. Marble fireplaces, rich wood paneling, and beautifully detailed hand carving provided a backdrop for the fine furnishings and art collection of the Walkers.

When Edward died, Mary donated the property to the City of Windsor. The manor served as the Walkerville Town Hall, the Library, and an Art Museum until it was closed to the public because of disrepair. A group of preservationists came together in the 1980s, and through their tireless volunteer effort, The Friends of Willistead have continued to raise funds for the restoration.[29] Today, Willistead Manor and the park are open for holiday tours and rented for special events. Maintained by the city and protected by The Friends of Willistead, the manor hosts the annual Art in the Park festival. For more than 40 years, the estate has hosted artisans from around the region to exhibit their art in a beautiful outdoor festival, encouraging visitors and residents to enjoy all that the town has to offer.

Stroll through Walkerville and you are greeted with one Albert Kahn project after another. His work supported the daily lives and activities of the community. Even the Ford Powerhouse, a large industrial facility, is an impressive piece of architecture. Kahn's architectural works have a positive impact on the district's character, creating a neighborhood that, to this day, is a desirable neighborhood to call home and supports one of the region's thriving areas of restaurants and eateries.

Author: Stephen White, ASLA, VP & Director of Landscape Architecture and Urban Design, Albert Kahn Associates

PRESENTATION OF A FOUNTAIN TO THE TOWN OF WALKERVILLE BY HIRAM WALKER & SONS LTD
JUNE 22nd 1897

WEST FRONT ELEVATION
SCALE 1/4 INCH = 1 FOOT

RESIDENCE FOR
MR. E. C. HANDLER WALKER
WALKERVILLE ONT.
ALBERT KAHN ARCHITECT
DETROIT MICH.
JOB NO. 210 JULY 20 1904

COLLABORATE WITH THE CLIENT

"This should be the creed of every business architect today: To plan carefully so as to save waste and with a view to the future to make possible expansion when necessary; to construct economically without resorting to cheap materials which in the end prove costly; to encourage the development of new materials and make use of such after careful investigation; to design logically so as to gain maximum aesthetic results; to serve the owner's interests to the best of one's ability and in a thoroughly business-like manner; to see to it that the owner obtains that to which he is entitled; to treat both owner and contractor fairly; and to have in mind at all times the aesthetic and practical welfare of the community."[30]

"To be sure, every owner prefers to have his building of good appearance, but this is only incidental. The plant must be economically designed. First and last, it must serve as an investment, not as a monument to the designer. And there is the rub. The very title 'Architect' which implies the building of the beautiful, fill the owner with fear that more attention will be paid the exterior to decorative details, than to the many practical features so vastly more important to the problem."[31]

"Service, satisfaction at all costs, sustained interest in the work at hand, strict attention to the detailed requirements of the client, a quick grasp of his needs, a prompt acceptance of his viewpoint, and a sincere desire to co-operate and to solve his problem for and with him: these are what he expects. And yet, how often is the owner served otherwise, and his viewpoint entirely ignored."[32]

"This brings me to a point which so often makes for distrust of the Architect – the eternal disposition of many to occupy a pedestal of exalted importance and superiority. It is their intent to make up by an air of profound wisdom for what they lack of actual knowledge. Educate the client is their cry, and while they are attempting to educate him in something he knows more about than they, some saner man rightfully walks away with the work. This attitude is particularly offensive to the builder of an industrial plant, who, as a rule, has definite ideas of what he wants.

"I have yet to find a single client unwilling to be advised, but in the proper manner, if you show him both that which he has in mind, and at the same time a better scheme, ten chances to one he will accept yours. But neglect to show him on paper his own ideas and submit merely yours, and you are doomed to failure."[33]

Author: Albert Kahn

Albert Kahn during construction of the First National Building, circa 1920.

Albert Kahn, Henry Ford, Glenn Martin, and Charles Sorenson, 1942.

UNIVERSITY OF MICHIGAN LIBRARY

ANN ARBOR, MICHIGAN | DESIGNED 1916 OPENED 1920

The University of Michigan was one of the first long-term clients for the Kahn firm – our records date back to 1901 with the Engineering Building designed by Mason and Kahn. Kahn's ability to quickly deliver cost-efficient and well-designed buildings won them multiple contracts from the regents. In 1916, Kahn designed the new General Library to replace an old library building which was deemed unsafe by the regents for the wood used in its roof and frame.[34]

At the opening of the University's new library, now known as the North part of the Harlan Hatcher Graduate Library, Albert gave this speech:[35] "The building which it was our privilege to work up involved a most interesting though difficult problem. It had to be designed so that it might be built in two parts, completing one section for temporary occupancy and the other and larger part later. The old book stack being of fireproof and otherwise satisfactory construction, was to be saved and made part of the new structure. The new Library was, therefore, built around the existing stack and in such a manner as to permit of adding not only now to the book stack space, but in the future should the need arise.

Provision for expansion is of prime importance in the modern Library building. Of equal importance is adequate room, light and air for the staff. Too often all effort is expended on the public rooms and the work rooms suffer in space, and light and air so necessary for the best results from the workers and for their health. It has been the particular aim in this building to properly provide for these. Then there are the necessary reading rooms, private study and seminar rooms, all planned to co-ordinate and function properly...Its cost including stacks, but not including other equipment, was approximately $525,000, or 25 (cents) per cubic foot. The cost of the plainest sort of factory work today is 25 (cents) and over per cubic foot."[36]

"Before the day of print, architecture served to express the thoughts of men. These are now recorded in books housed in libraries. Architecture, however, would not be equal to its opportunities today if it failed to express a thought. May the new Library tell the story of a sincere desire on the part of the officers of the University and their Architect to provide for the students and the State a structure which will inspire nobler aspirations, more enlightenment, greater tolerance and increased wisdom among the men and women who will enter its doors."[37]

The firm returned to the general library multiple times to complete renovations and additions, including the significant stacks addition (1970), behind the original Kahn-designed library.[38]

SPEED AND EFFICIENCY

Kahn employees on the roof of the Marquette Building, Detroit, 1924.

Innovation demands speed, efficiency, and brilliance. As the Kahn firm continued to grow with draftsmen, engineers, and administrative staff, Albert refined the practice, clearly influenced by the mass production processes and clients with which they were working. Louis Kahn, Albert's other younger brother, joined the firm around 1910 and was principally in charge of managing the office.[39] Louis led the administrative functions of the office, refining processes, tracking, and reporting to create an extremely efficient and orderly office.

Drawings from the early 1900s suggest that teams of architects and engineers worked on sections of a drawing simultaneously, each with their own specialty, which were then grouped to create a complete plan.[40] Albert had developed a new type of architectural office where technical engineers designed the mechanical and electrical systems. They produced standardized details of building elements that could then be combined in various ways to create a new complete package of drawings more quickly. This evolution toward standardization was one way the firm was able to quickly meet project goals, becoming a design powerhouse.

In 1917, the firm expanded and moved to the top floor of the Marquette Building, where they rented office space for more than a decade. Prior to this move, both Albert and Julius, and their respective companies, had rented space within the Trussed Concrete Steel Building (1907), which both firms designed and engineered.[41] Within the build-out of the Marquette Building, it is clear how organized and collaborative the Kahn firm had become. Floor plans indicate two large drafting rooms, one located near a structural engineering room, and the other near a mechanical engineering room. Specification writing and typing rooms were located near the vault that stored drawings and specifications, while filing rooms, estimating rooms, accounting rooms, as well as space for chief and field superintendents, were mapped out along the floor.[42] Related departments were placed near one another to improve communication. There were multiple entrances from the elevators, including one for clients, one for contractors, and a third for employees. Along one side of the building were the executive offices and conference rooms, where potential clients entered for consultations. Samples of all sorts of building materials could be easily pulled from the sample room nearby. The lobby and conference rooms were paneled in oak with ornamental plaster ceilings, and one of the conference rooms featured built-in bookcases that housed Albert's library.[43]

George C. Baldwin wrote an article about the office at the time, noting, "Mr. Kahn's office is particularly successful in combining two ideals that must characterize any successful office. The dignity and art aspect of the architectural profession are fully represented, and to no less a degree is the business structure upon which harmonious professional relations depend recognized."[44]

The firm streamlined their processes and its reputation for speed and efficient designs spread. When the United States entered World War I in 1917, Kahn was busy working on a variety of war-related projects for clients in Detroit and around the United States. The firm had already been working on a number of military bases and airfields in Virginia, Ohio, California, and Texas for the U.S. Signal Corps, a branch of the U.S. Army. In Detroit, plants began shifting production to the war effort. The Packard Plant, for instance, began producing airplane engines, and Ford had plans to mass produce the Eagle Submarine Chaser at the Rouge Plant, which was under construction. According to Edgar Kahn, Albert's son, Albert requested that the firm's fee be cut in half for the work they did during the war.[45]

Around the same time, the firm picked up more projects abroad. An early project in Europe was for a group called Norsk Maskinindustri A.S., in Norway. Kahn was tasked with designing an office building in Kristiania, now part of Oslo, in 1918 for a consortium of manufacturers that had partnered to better manage, produce, and market products after World War I ended.[46] The following year, Ford Motor Company also took the firm abroad to Argentina and other parts of South America to set up Service Buildings, Factories, Hospitals, and Hotels, and then on to Europe, Mexico, and Japan to expand its operations.[47]

The firm's reputation for delivering efficiently designed buildings on-time and often under-budget resulted in the office growing to 400 staff members by 1920, and bringing in more than $1,000,000 worth of work a week.[48]

Albert and Louis Kahn, circa 1935-40.

LANGLEY AIR FORCE BASE

HAMPTON, VIRGINIA | DESIGNED 1916 OPENED 1917

Established in 1916, Langley Field, now called Langley Air Force Base, Joint Base Langley-Eustis, is the longest continually active air force base in the world. Hosting the organizations that eventually formed into the U.S. Air Force and NASA, Langley quickly became one of the world's premier research and development facilities in aeronautics and aviation. Albert Kahn played a pivotal role in developing the general master plan for Langley and designing nearly three dozen of the base's original structures, including aircraft hangars, laboratories, and administration buildings. To help with the war efforts, "Kahn took on the design work at Langley for half of his usual commission," said David Jennings, 633rd Civil Engineer Squadron environmental engineer. "He also designed the original roadway that is still relatively intact," that acts as a regal entrance gateway into the base.

Albert Kahn designed the airfield's original buildings with ornate brickwork and intricate tile patterned accents (right). The officer's quarters and administration offices were designed in a traditional Tudor style, typical of many upscale residential properties Kahn designed around the country. While the research facilities at Langley have been modernized to meet the needs of the military, many original Kahn buildings remain in use and continue to give the base its iconic and strikingly classical appearance, uncommon to many modern-day military bases.

Langley Field and the Albert Kahn-designed research facilities were instrumental in the rapidly evolving American air defense throughout both World Wars. During World War I, Langley served as a testing facility for the development of balloon photography techniques and acted as a vital defense station along the east coast. Leading up to World War II, Langley Field became the primary proving ground for the future of aviation advancements in the United States – developing aircraft components that would prove essential to the mass production of aircraft such as the B-24 Liberator and B-17 Flying Fortress constructed in the many Kahn-designed factories around the country. Critical bombing training missions tested some of the first experimental B-17's which paved the way for America's air bombardment arsenal during the war. Additionally, engineers at Langley developed state-of-the-art wind tunnels and anti-gravity chambers, which were integral in deploying America's first jet-powered aircraft and spacecraft of the future.

For over a century, Langley has contributed heavily to America's wartime efforts and technological advancements, from testing torpedoes to training astronauts that have walked on the moon. Currently, the joint base acts as a research and command center, responsible for organizing, training, and maintaining rapid combat-ready deployable forces around the world.

Albert Kahn designed structures and other support bases for the U.S. Navy located around the world in Hawaii, Alaska, Midway (above), and Puerto Rico as well – but none were as striking or stately as his designs for Langley. Kahn envisioned a unique character and longstanding sense of authority for the base with the original Langley buildings. The prominent buildings that remain at Langley today are a reminder of how Albert Kahn's grandeur and attention to detail created an epicenter worthy of pioneering aviation accomplishments which allowed the United States' role in military democracy to flourish.[49]

Author: Case Allen-Kahn Kittel, Engineer and Great-Grandson of Albert Kahn

INDUSTRIALIZING THE SOVIET UNION

A delegation from the Amtorg Trading Corporation, fiscal agents for the Soviet Union, came to Detroit to meet with the Kahn firm in 1929. They wanted the firm to design a tractor plant in Stalingrad for $4,000,000.[50] Design work took place in Detroit, and the Stalingrad plant, designed with a 1300-foot-long assembly area to produce 40,000 tractors a year, was constructed in a record six months. On January 17, 1930, as the plant was nearly complete, newspapers across America announced that Kahn had just signed a significant contract to design and engineer many more factories as part of the Soviet Union's Five-Year Industrialization Program. For the next five years, the Soviet Union anticipated spending more than $10,000,000,000, with improvements to existing industrial plants for another $1,900,000,000.[51] Within that plan, eight farm-related factories were planned and four other large plants for automobiles, trucks, and motorcycles.

"We started with an enormous tractor plant at Karkhoff in Southern Russia," remembered Albert, "We had some twenty-five of our men in Moscow, Leningrad and Kiev, for two years, designing buildings and teaching a thousand or more young Russians – both men and women – in the methods employed by us."[52] Between 1930 and 1932, Moritz Kahn, Albert's third brother who was then the vice president of the firm, led an architectural and engineering office based in Moscow. The plan was for the Kahn team to advise the Soviets on how to assemble a larger bureau of approximately 4,500 architectural and engineering designers – the majority of these to be Soviets, but other American engineers and specialists from other countries also joined these ranks.[53] The firm produced approximately 500 tractor, steel, auto, airplane, and chemical plants, which was the largest architectural design project for the firm.[54] The tractor factories at Stalingrad (above) and Cheliabinsk (next page) were two of the largest plants built under Kahn's supervision.

Following a meeting with Albert in Dearborn in 1929, Henry Ford also signed on to work in the Soviet Union.[55] He agreed to $30,000,000 in products and the plan to produce a factory, where Ford staff will instruct Soviet technicians in Ford production.[56] An article from August 1931 reports that 47 American firms and around 1,500 American engineers and technicians were helping the Soviet government.[57]

Albert believed this commission was the first of many – that the firm might be called upon to design entire cities.[58] At the time, the United States had not formally acknowledged the existence of the Soviet state. Albert was noted as saying that their politics did not concern him, he was contracted for a specific project. Clippings saved by staff at that time suggest that this was a controversial decision. Several articles discuss the tumultuous political climate in the Soviet Union and even mention executions of professors and officials.[59] A decade later, the sentiment seems to have changed with the public. The unyielding structure of the Stalingrad factory played a part in the pivotal battle of Stalingrad, where the Soviets were victorious over the Germans and turned the tide of World War II.

The work in the Soviet Union was cut short, and in March of 1932, the firm returned home to Detroit. According to articles at the time, contract negotiations broke down when the Soviets wanted to pay the firm in their currency rather than Gold.[60] Employees in the Soviet Union experienced a number of other challenges including inefficiencies, red tape, and at times, an unwillingness to allow Kahn to design the systems in the "American method of planning everything, including power, heating, water and the like, as a unit."[61] Construction was also difficult as materials were scarce, meaning that materials had to be ordered from America and elsewhere. Transportation to remote areas like Stalingrad was inadequate, and at times construction equipment the team was used to simply wasn't available – wheelbarrows, apparently, were unheard of.[62]

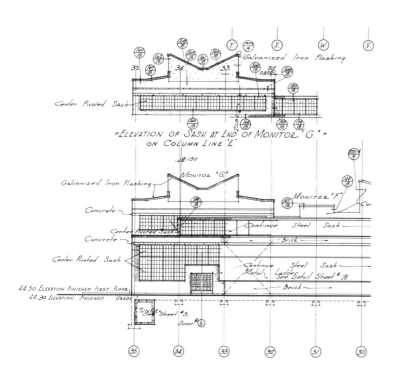

Signing the contract for the Soviet Union work. Albert is at the lower left and Moritz is in the center, 1929.

Moritz and Albert Kahn circa 1935.

Moritz Kahn, center, with Kahn employees accompanied by their spouses on the way to the Soviet Union, 1930.

33

NEW HOME AND ORGANIZATION

As the Great Depression hit Detroit in 1929, part of the Kahn firm was busy working in the Soviet Union, but many projects in the United States came to a standstill. Ambitious projects such as the Fisher Building, never reached their original designed size – stopping at the smaller of the three proposed towers. As projects stalled, the firm needed to temporarily downsize.

In September 1930, the Fisher Brothers announced that they were going to construct a new building adjacent to the Fisher Building. [63] The New Center Building (1931), a ten-story office building, was set to extend the new center area and boost employment in Detroit. Designed to complement the Fisher Building, the structure used materials that were already ordered for the additional towers of the Fisher Building. The New Center Building was designed as a mixed-use building with office space, retail space, and a grocer on the first floor. In 1931, the firm relocated their offices here, where they remained for the next 87 years. In 1988, the New Center Building was renamed the Albert Kahn Building.

Shortly after they moved into the New Center Building, the firm expanded again with numerous industrial projects and more staff, causing them to expand their footprint within the building as well. By 1938, the volume of Kahn's work reached 19% of all architect-designed U.S. industrial buildings. Architects around the country wanted to work for the firm.[64] Competition was fierce. Architects and engineers assimilated into the practice, and those that couldn't keep up with the pace of the firm were sent back home. Each project that entered the office was completed by the firm – a collective group of specialists – rather than one individual. Albert often acknowledged this and insisted that credit should always be given to the firm, for he was the 'coordinator' that unified the team.[65]

One employee, who joined the firm during World War II, recalled, "When I joined the Kahn office, the staff consisted of 450 architects and engineers. I was assigned to Frederic A. Fairbrother's drafting room, where approximately 40 architects worked. Several days after I was there, Fairbrother spoke to me about the lettering I was placing on my drawings. He said: 'You will have to use Kahn lettering on your drawings. All our 450 architects and engineers must letter the same way. We want each set of drawings to look like it was made by one man, even if 30 or 40 men produced it.' Then he asked me, 'Do you write to your wife every day?' 'Yes.' "I suggest that you stop writing. Use Kahn lettering instead.'"[66]

As Albert was getting older, his plans turned to succession. Along with his wife, Ernestine, and his brother Louis, they incorporated the firm, Albert Kahn Associated Architects and Engineers, Inc. on March 7, 1940. Initial officers were Albert as President, Ernestine as Vice President, and Louis as Secretary and Treasurer. On July 18, 1940, twenty-five key employees became shareholders of the company. This share in the ownership of the company built onto a program Albert had started in 1922,[67] when he promoted a group of hardworking employees as principals, who would then lead respective projects. This leadership structure ensured that the firm would continue after he was gone.

REPUBLIC STEEL STRIP MILL

It was unheard of for a consulting architect to design and engineer a steel mill facility. With Kahn's breadth of experience designing and engineering a wide variety of industrial complexes, it is not surprising that the firm became the first independent architecture firm to design a strip mill in the United States.[68] Republic Steel engineers had completed the initial drawings for construction of the strip mill, and when they were released to the firm, Kahn architects and engineers found a way to save 1,200 tons of steel. This project demonstrated that an independent firm can bring added value to the industrial client,[69] with the additional advantage of leaving the company's staff free to concentrate on process layouts and the placing of equipment.

"The Republic Steel Corporation's new mill at Cleveland, Ohio, embodying 21 acres of buildings, is claimed to be the world's most modern hot and cold strip mill. It is a maze of automatic machinery for rolling steel. The three-strand tandem continuous cold reduction mills can roll strip, 98 inches wide, down to 24 gauge. The thickness of the strip is measured as it comes out of the cold mill at a speed of 2,120 feet per minute by a sensitive micrometer which registers on a large dial variations in thickness as little as one thousandth part of an inch. Steel strip is gauged as it passes from the run-out table across the transfer table to the hot mill finishing department.

A truss, 30 feet high and 216 feet long, has been provided over the transfer table to carry the weight of the huge traveling cranes which operate overhead on either side of it. This truss is the largest steel-frame member used in the construction of the mill. The ten massive stands in tandem comprise the 98 inch hot mill. These stands weigh 425 tons each – are 22 ½ feet wide and 29 feet above base."[70]

In addition to the strip mill, Kahn designed other buildings on site including an office building, a welfare building, a machine shop, and a water and filter house. According to an article in *Architectural Forum*, speed was another key factor in this project: "The Republic plant is perhaps the most dramatic example of the speed with which the Kahn organization can function: eleven days after sketches were started, working drawings were sent out for steel fabrication."[71]

UNIVERSAL SPACE

A long-held tenet of the Kahn design philosophy has been flexibility. From its earliest structures, Kahn architects and engineers pushed the bounds of technological innovation to create wide-open spaces that could accommodate various equipment upgrades, process changes, and future expansions. Decades later, this idea was given a new name, "Universal Space," and made famous by Ludwig Mies van der Rohe, a modern architect who Albert Kahn influenced.

Universal Space describes a long-span, single-volume, flexible structure that can be broken up into small sections of use or used whole for any number of functions. The Kahn project that became an icon of this concept and inspired Mies van der Rohe was the Glenn L. Martin Company's Aircraft Assembly Building (1937). In his lectures at the Illinois Institute of Technology, Mies van der Rohe created collages over photographs of the building's interior to propose creating a more intimate concert space within this type of flexible building shell.[72] This flexibility was integral to industrialists to keep up with the rapid development of technology. It was now taught to future generations of architects who would go on to design structures for all markets around the globe.

The Glenn L. Martin Company was a leading producer of airplanes for international commercial enterprises and United States defense efforts, including the early Martin Bomber planes completed during World War I. Martin needed to enlarge its plant to accommodate future airplanes' larger wingspans and other aerospace transportation.

On February 3, 1939, Glenn Martin called Albert again, this time requesting a continuous manufacturing unit of approximately 450,000 square feet ready for use by May 1 – an impossible three months. Ten days later, Albert, his associates, and the contractor began construction on the site. More than 400 men worked in three shifts around the clock.[73] All skills of the firm, architects, engineers, estimators, and contract administrators, were utilized to the fullest. The building was completed within 77 days, three days ahead of schedule.

The facility Kahn designed was approximately 340 x 680 feet with no interior columns and a full basement.[74] The building was supported by 300-foot trusses, which at the time, were the longest flat-span trusses ever used in a building.[75] Rather than fabricating these trusses in the typical fashion for industrial buildings, teams of designers and engineers turned to bridge design to create a more economical and lighter weight design to accommodate the great expanse.

At the time, the building could fit about forty planes inside. The trusses extend the roofline of the facility, and a pair of trusses create a roof shed covered in glass that can be opened and closed as needed. These sheds along the roofline create a unique shape on the building's exterior and allow for plenty of natural light and ventilation for workers inside.

Today, Lockheed Martin still occupies the same facility.[76] Universal Space and its flexibility have carried through the work of the firm, whether it be industrial, healthcare, or other types of projects. A significant number of these structures still exist and have been able to be adapted to remain usable.

THE ARSENAL OF DEMOCRACY

As World War II raged on, the Kahn firm was building the "Arsenal of Democracy" on the homefront. Industrial plants were rapidly retooled, and new plants seemed to emerge overnight to produce virtually every material or product for the war. The firm was dominated by the war effort, employed by both the U.S. Government and independent corporations, and the staff grew to 600 employees to manage the workload of more than 800 projects. In 1941, Albert wrote, "Speed and more speed is the watchword of the Defense Program."[77] The firm needed to swiftly produce simple designs that could be constructed quickly and efficiently, "within a week's time, or even less, structural steel drawings for plants costing millions must be ready for placing contracts."[78] Seven days a week and twenty-four hours a day, the office remained open for the constant flurry of employees.[79]

Standardization was key to maintaining this momentum, but rarely could an entire building be reproduced. Instead, the firm would create standard details that could be inserted and combined to suit the specific need of the client. Producing scale models and adjusting with client feedback was impractical during the war years – the industrial architect needed to be right the first time. "He must be able to interpret the client's wants – vague as they often are – then to coordinate the work of the many assistants, specialists, contractors and subcontractors."[80] Each architect and engineer needed to work quickly, checking themselves along the way, "a detail such as locating a pipe where it will interfere with the swing of a door, for example, is an unpardonable sin."[81] In 1942, amidst the flurry of defense projects, the firm had to cope with the death of its founder, Albert Kahn. Louis Kahn then became president, leading the firm through the war.

Projects included countless aircraft and bomber plants, engine plants, ammunition and weapon plants, tools and machinery plants, aluminum forge plants, steel and magnesium foundries, chemical plants, and numerous air bases for the U.S. Navy, among others. One significant project at the time was the Chrysler Tank Plant (1941) (left and below). The U.S. Army contracted with Chrysler to build the Detroit Arsenal and Tank Plant on 113 acres of farmland in Warren, Michigan. This was the first plant constructed in America to mass-produce 28-ton medium tanks on this scale. Once Chrysler committed to manufacturing tanks, approximately 200 engineers worked around the clock to develop processes and machines on paper, dissecting the plans into sections for production. These plans were shared with Kahn, enabling design to begin in mid-August 1940. By February 1941, Chrysler engineers began working on a pilot tank in one of the completed sections of the building. In April, the entire plant, including the main manufacturing building, heating plant, administration building, personnel building, and garage, was complete and ready for production.[82] Streamlined in operation, materials flow through the production process until the fully assembled tanks are lifted onto the railcars for transit.[83] The Chrysler Tank Plant remained in use after World War II and continued to produce tanks for later war efforts.[84]

During the war, there was a shortage of structural steel, copper, and other materials, which radically changed the way these manufacturing plants were engineered. Alternative materials were used, and new designs and methods developed. For example, engineers developed thin-shell concrete roofs using retractable movable forms, or an arch-rib concrete roof in the case of the Dodge Chicago Plant (1944), to overcome the shortage of structural steel (next page). Some plants constructed for the government were designed for possible blackouts to deter enemy aircraft. Windows and roof monitors were eliminated, and flat roofs introduced. As these buildings were in use 24 hours a day, fluorescent lights and packaged heating and cooling units were installed, which created factories that were constructed quicker and more evenly lit and ventilated. These structures became the forerunners of today's large enclosed buildings with controlled environments.

Albert's son Edgar recalled, "In the emergency, with the demand for speedy erection of defense plants on the one hand and the scarcity of materials, particularly steel, on the other, many notable contributions toward the discovery of alternative methods and materials were made by the firm. None of these discoveries were ever patented; they were made freely available to other architects and engineers engaged in war-plant construction."[85]

Many of these plants were designed as five-year plants, meaning that they were designed and built to be in production for five years. They were not designed to be retooled after the war, as the expense would be exorbitant. In 1944, Louis Kahn explained, "In designing these plants, every possible short cut was taken to save time, costs and materials and still have plants entirely adequate for their intended job. They were 'streamlined' to the ultimate degree. An example is lighting. We knew that the plant would operate around the clock, on an all-out basis, so there was no need to take the time and materials to wire each individual bay for lighting. Whole departments were hooked up to one master switch."[86] After the war, new plants were needed. Instead of being driven by emergency, these plants were created with a longer life span.

The firm also designed several Navy air bases during this period of rapid defense projects, including bases on Midway Atoll, Puerto Rico, Alaska (below), Hawaii, and Rhode Island. The design for these bases were a collaborative effort between the firm and the Bureau of Yards and Docks, part of the U.S. Navy. Schematic designs and general layouts were prepared by the Bureau, then given to the firm to develop the architectural design and engineering plan for each structure on base.[87] Each base featured administration buildings, barracks, dining facilities, officers' quarters, and support facilities for sewage, water, power, etc. Drawings were sent from the firm to the builder daily, and these bases were designed and occupied in less than a year.[88] With bases located in the Atlantic Ocean, the Pacific Ocean, and the Caribbean, construction materials and labor were often shipped directly to the sites. In 1943, the firm received an award of excellence from the U.S. Navy for their part in the war effort.[89]

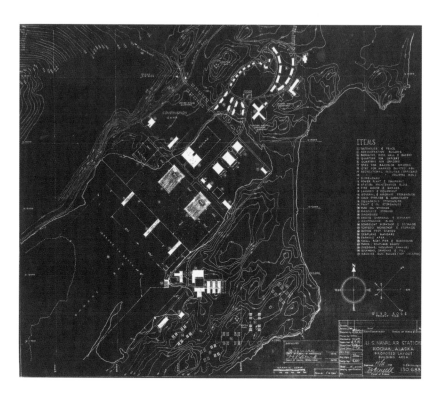

The firm's role in designing and constructing factories for the US aircraft industry leading up to WWII are among the most complex and least well understood projects on which Albert Kahn Associated Architects and Engineers, Inc., (Kahn) embarked before the 1942 death of the founder. The decentralized character of the aircraft industry meant that airplanes were often fabricated in an array of different plants, in different subassemblies, and by different firms. Car companies collaborated with aeronautics firms who collaborated with engine makers, and on occasion, formerly competing automakers would manufacture airplane engines for Curtiss Wright, Pratt & Whitney, or Rolls Royce. At the remarkable Dodge Chicago plant (above), the Kahn firm developed a novel building construction system in reinforced concrete, due to steel restrictions during wartime. There Chrysler built engines designed by Wright Aeronautics for Boeing B-29s and B-32s, but also nose sections and other airplane parts for a range of different uses and clients, including the army and navy.[90] In addition, the plants where components were produced were widely distributed, in part to guard against the possibility of aerial attack during WWII. Many of them were shuttered or demolished after 1945, making their historical footprint hard to trace.

The clearest line in the Kahn aircraft plant production story may be that of one of the firm's repeat clients, the Glenn Martin Company. During WWII, Martin himself was still running the firm, and his rapport with Albert Kahn and the firm as a whole was generative. Kahn did multiple projects for Glenn Martin during Albert's lifetime, beginning with a 1937 addition to Martin's manufacturing complex at Middle River, Maryland, that remains one of Kahn's best-known industrial projects. Albert and Martin together decided to make a building with a 300-foot clear span – even though the planes that would be produced there would have a wingspan no more than 200 feet. After the completion of the massive Plant 1, Kahn moved on to build Plant 2, just over a mile away, for the production of B-26 bombers. Plant 2 is one of the first buildings in which the typology of the aircraft manufacturing plant was clearly developed, with its characteristic human-centered program housed underneath the machine-scaled main hangar level. In other words, the entrances, kitchens, canteens, locker rooms, first aid stations, and other facilities were housed underneath a vast open floor that could be configured as necessary for plane production, and through which planes moved upon completion to a nearby runway, through giant hangar doors. Regular access points from the partly submerged human level below the main production floor kept humans and planes from crossing paths unnecessarily – similar to the principle that governs major airports today.[91]

While constructing Plant 2 in Maryland, Martin and Kahn also embarked on another massive airplane factory near Omaha, Nebraska (below).[92] Both of these massive buildings – Maryland's Plant 2 covers over one million sq. ft. and the main manufacturing building in the Nebraska plant over 540,000 – were completed between spring and fall of 1941, the Omaha building coming on line in October, and the Maryland plant in November. It was the former that produced the specially outfitted planes that dropped two atomic bombs on the Japanese cities of Hiroshima and Nagasaki in August 1945, after which the war officially ended, as the Japanese quickly surrendered.[93]

These plants, like other wartime plants, were owned and financed by the Defense Plant Corporation (PLANCOR), but operated by industrial vendors with the option to buy after the war. They were joined by Curtiss-Wright plants near Buffalo and Cleveland, Pratt & Whitney plants in Connecticut, and the massive plants built by automakers in commissions such as Dodge Chicago and Willow Run. All of these were intertwined with one another, and with the Boeing Corporation on the west coast, producing an extraordinary array of large aircraft for the war effort. The military-industrial complex, highlighted in a famous speech by President Eisenhower in 1961, had taken physical form in Kahn buildings much earlier. It remains an active force in global history and in the world of construction today.

Author: Claire Zimmerman, Professor of Architectural History and Theory, University of Michigan

THERMO-CON HOUSE

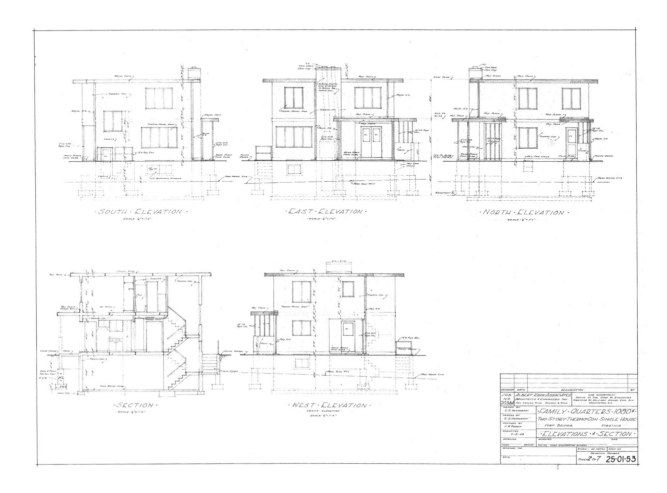

During World War II, as the United States experienced steel and timber shortages, Kahn developed unique engineered systems to produce the buildings their clients and the government needed. Concrete was often used instead of structural steel and was just one of the materials that the firm continued to employ in novel ways throughout its history. Following the war, there was a housing shortage across the United States. As industry and mass production accelerated, new approaches to solve this housing need were pursued; houses needed to be produced quickly, affordably, and at record numbers. This shortage extended to military bases as well.

In 1948, the Department of Defense worked with Kahn and Higgins Industries to develop a prototype house that could be mass produced to meet the Army's housing shortage.[94] Higgins had been designing and mass-producing amphibious landing craft for the war effort and patented a curious type of concrete called Thermo-Con Cellular Concrete. Thermo-Con was used to construct the walls, floors, and roof. It contained cement, water, and a patented mineral formula, which was then mixed in a Higgins patented generator and pumped into a form, where it remained to rise and set for 45 minutes.[95] As it set, the mixture expanded two and a half times its original size, and about one-third the weight of traditional concrete.[96] Not only did this concrete mixture grow, but apparently, it could also float, insulate, and be shaped with a handsaw.[97]

Prior to design, Kahn conducted a series of structural tests on the new concrete. These tests revealed, "a superior resistance of Thermo-Con cellular concrete walls against racking, impact and transverse loading, it appears that these walls are especially adapted to locations where those actions occur, in sections of the country subject to earthquake shocks."[98] This was not a prefabricated system, instead forms were designed to be modular, allowing the finished sections to be arranged in ways determined by the designer.

According to the historical plaque out front of the house, "The renowned industrial architects, Albert Kahn & Associates, designed the prototype in the International Style and the 410th Engineer Battalion (Construction) completed the building in 1949. Due to its innovative design and construction techniques, the house was placed on the Virginia Landmarks register in 1997. In 2000, the Army renovated and returned 'Thermo-Con' House to use as distinguished visitor housing." Though it was never mass produced, this prototype home speaks to the partnership between industry and engineers at Kahn, and the consistent experimentation that has occurred throughout Kahn's history.

POST-WAR BUILDING

Following the war, the firm answered the call of post-war America, Kahn continued the rapid design and engineering of industrial plants to manufacture everything from household goods and automobiles to foundries that cast the metal used in production. George Miehls, an engineer who had been with the firm and risen through the ranks, became the third president in 1945. During this period, Kahn was producing many plants with a 50-year lifespan, quite a contrast to the 5-year war plants.[99] To conserve cost, many of these structures were designed without windows; instead, they used the building systems implemented in the blackout plants of the war. The firm also made significant engineering advances in environmental technology such as developing waste treatment facilities to avoid polluting the natural environment near plants that lacked municipal facilities for sewage and industrial waste disposal.[100]

Aircraft plants around the country saw dramatic expansion, perhaps more than any other industry.[101] No longer was the firm building huge aircraft assembly plants such as Willow Run and others built during World War II. These new plants were broken up into three main types of aircraft manufacturing – engines, propellers, and air frames – each requiring machining and assembly plants, a variety of test cells, storage for parts, fuel, and other hazardous materials, and a hanger where the final airplane is stored. Following the war, there was more time for Kahn engineers and architects to experiment with building design and spans. Aircraft hangars, for example, utilized rolling walls instead of canopy doors, and a deluge sprinkler system was implemented to deliver vast quantities of water quickly to protect the aircraft in case of a fire. Engineers also developed several hangar styles including the Nose Hanger, which protected the front of the plane, the Complete Hangar, with rolling doors on two sides, and a Round Hangar, proposed with rolling doors that form a semi-circle in the front of the building.[102] With the advent of the jet engine, which was becoming more popular in aircraft production, the firm began engineering the jet engine test cell. This complicated building type demanded that architects and engineers research the latest in materials, acoustics, and structure to create highly technical spaces that could test these powerful engines. The firm produced many jet engine test cells and plants for Pratt and Whitney, Sikorsky, Chrysler, and United Airlines, among others.

In the 1950s, the firm returned to working with its broader base of clients, taking on more civic, educational, and commercial structures in addition to their constant stream of industrial projects. This period saw a more balanced approach to the type of work the firm was doing, and progression in both creative design and engineering disciplines. A few key projects include the National Bank of Detroit (1958), which was recognized for architectural excellence and the winner of multiple design awards, the Undergraduate Library for the University of Michigan in Ann Arbor (1956) (left and below), additions to Henry Ford Hospital (1957) and the new Sinai Hospital (1953), both of which the firm continued to renovate over the years.

In 1958, Sol King, an architect who started with the firm before World War II, became the fourth president of the firm. King and the leadership set out to restructure the firm, focusing on the unique specialties within the practice, and emphasizing these talents to its broad network of clients. A document from 1958 describes the specialties of the firm:

> "Every one of the associates, and nearly every one of the 250 workers comprising the organization, has particular training and peculiar experience fitting him for some one of the myriad phases of industrial, institutional, and commercial design and construction in which the firm has won a world-wide reputation over a span of sixty-four years.
>
> There are architects, civil engineers, mechanical engineers, electrical engineers – degree men in lighting, heating, ventilation – specialists in every profession and industry have to do with modern building design and construction. There is even an expert on parking lot surfaces.
>
> These specialists are required by the very nature of their work to be as skilled in their own fields as any other men in the world. Each hews to the line of his own specialty; and to expect any one of them to give you a quick picture of the overall plan of any one project on the boards would be no more logical than to expect an eye doctor to diagnose a stomach ailment.
>
> The Kahn organization plans a new structure much as the automobile industry normally plans a new model. Just as the chief engineer lays out the broad objectives of the new car, and assigns to a dozen or more engineers the details on frame, brakes, carburetors, etc., so the Kahn co-ordinator parcels out the work on a new project, within the limits laid down by the owner, for detailed solution by those best qualified for each assignment. A broad background of experience and technical skill enables the co-ordinator to blend individual efforts into architectural teamwork expressed in Kahn-designed buildings on six continents."[103]

NATIONAL BANK OF DETROIT

DETROIT, MICHIGAN | DESIGNED 1957 OPENED 1959

Designed during the height of Modernism in Michigan, the National Bank of Detroit embraces a sleek and precise design for its headquarters which was to be part of Detroit's larger initiative to redefine its financial district. Around the world, modernists preached "Form Follows Function," a concept that Albert Kahn infused into his practice from the beginning and is most readily seen in early industrial buildings.

As a result of refined construction technologies, the glass curtain wall system was becoming popular to convey a sense of "newness" throughout cities. This building was one of the first to employ a staggered curtain wall design that incorporates alternating panels of glass and white marble. The marble was chosen to harmonize with surrounding structures. Applied ornamentation was foregone as elements of the structure are exposed to create the key elements of the design. Steel, marble, and glass make up much of the exterior, in fact, 170 tons of steel were used in the exterior alone.[104]

Set back from the street to form a pedestrian-friendly space, the 14-story rectangular building is perched on structural columns faced with marble creating a sheltered walkway under the cantilevered edges of the building. This attention to the human experience on the ground level makes the building less imposing. Inside the colonnade is a grand lobby encased in large vertical panes of glass. The interior of the lobby was originally designed by W. B. Ford Design Associates, and featured a continuation of the marble and rich wood accents through the main banking hall.[105]

Seated on the former site of the city's first high-rise building, the Hammond Building, the National Bank of Detroit building was part of a series of new buildings designed and constructed to shape the city. At the dedication of the new structure on October 4, 1959, the firm chose this opportunity to celebrate its 65th anniversary.[106] A significant commission for the firm, the design also garnered worldwide attention with models of the building toured through Europe and publications in Japan covering the building's modern design.[107] Back in Detroit, the building won numerous awards, including an award of excellence from the Detroit chapter of the American Institute of Architects. Through the years the building has undergone various name changes and interior renovations by the firm, including the installation of one of the first building-wide computerized energy management systems in metropolitan Detroit in 1981.[108] Today, it is known as The Qube, part of the Quicken Loans umbrella.

BALANCED DESIGN

Perhaps the firm's strongest advantage throughout its history has been its interwoven culture of engineers, architects, project managers, field representation, and support staff. Operating under one roof, all disciplines work together from initial planning through to construction to serve the client. This balance between the creative and technical teams has resulted in well-designed, technologically advanced structures that, in their design, materials, and systems are safeguarded against premature obsolescence.

During the 1960s and 1970s, the firm received numerous architectural and engineering awards for institutional, commercial, and industrial work, demonstrating the flexibility and diversity of its practice, while continuing the legacy of design excellence. Among the buildings recognized were: a Laboratory and Office complex at Springdale, Ohio (1966), and Southeastern Branch Facilities at Atlanta (1969), both for Avon Products, Inc.; and a Parking Structure for the Henry Ford Hospital, which received an architectural award, and a "citation for its innovative and economical design from the Institute of Civil Engineers in London, England."[109] The firm was also recognized for designing one of the "Top Ten Plants" in the United States with the Automotive Assembly Plant in St. Louis, Missouri, for Chrysler Corporation.

The 1960s marked several important events in the life of the firm, such as the creation of the profit sharing and pension plans which came about in 1964, the creation of senior associate and associate categories in 1969, and the shortened name of the firm, from Albert Kahn Associated, Architects & Engineers, Inc. to Albert Kahn Associates, Inc. The firm also implemented a computer division in the 1960s, which allowed them to increase capacity in planning, cost estimating, and other aspects of project management.[110] And, in 1971, the firm received the Architectural Firm Award from the American Institute of Architects, for consistently producing distinguished architecture. An element of this, of course, is producing architecture that anticipates and responds to changes in society.

As fuel prices in America rose and the need to conserve energy became part of the global discussion, the firm increased its emphasis on energy savings within the buildings they designed for clients. This idea wasn't new to any of the designers or engineers at the firm – in fact, Albert's early designs incorporated low-cost efficient systems for electricity, heating, and ventilation. What was new was the mainstream understanding and desire to create efficient buildings. This manifested in both the design of the building and engineering of its systems.

In 1973, Kahn completed additions to the Washington Post Building (1963), a Kahn-designed structure in Washington, D.C. (right). In addition to modernizing and doubling its operations, the design for the Post building incorporated the latest in energy savings design ideas. Along the east side of the building tinted windows are recessed into the building, using the building's modern structure to create a shield from direct sunlight and glare, allowing the inside to maintain a constant temperature. Greenspace, with plenty of trees and flowers, was also incorporated in the design within a court on the eighth floor, reducing the heat island effect and providing a space for employees to gather.

In 1977, Kahn designed the General Motors, Detroit Diesel-Allison Division, Engineering and Test Laboratory, in Romulus, Michigan. Engineers designed a sophisticated system to capture the heat from the engine test facilities and distribute it throughout the building to conserve the amount of energy drawn from the site's powerhouse. The facility received approval to construct the first coal-fired boiler in Wayne county since World War II, to provide additional heat, power, and steam to the complex.[111] Coal was chosen over natural gas to conserve gas and oil for homes and vehicles, and unlike older coal-fired systems, this new boiler was engineered to optimize the air-to-fuel ratio increasing efficiency. Kahn engineers tested a variety of technologies for particulate pollution control, and installed an improved modular baghouse system, which is a filter used to control pollution and dust, removing particulates or gas before it is released into the air.[112]

Through innovative design, Kahn developed buildings that provided efficient, comfortable, and healthy environments for the occupants while avoiding the phenomena known as "sick building syndrome;" an unintended consequence of the energy focus of the 1970-80s. The firm focused on HVAC systems and indoor air quality, as well as the types of materials and finishes they were using to design interior spaces.

AVON SOUTHEASTERN BRANCH

ATLANTA, GEORGIA | DESIGNED 1966 OPENED 1969

A leading producer of cosmetics and beauty products, the concept of natural beauty was not lost on Avon Products, Inc., as they planned for their distribution center just outside of Atlanta. Avon envisioned a building that embraced the surrounding 72 acres of rolling countryside and pine tree forests, becoming an integrated part of the design and natural scenery for the employees.

When it was finally constructed, the combined warehouse and distribution center and corporate office space won multiple design awards. One of the most innovative aspects of the design of the structure is the implementation of a mansard roof system overhanging the large plate glass windows that envelop the facility. Composed of two long horizontal bands, one serving as the roof and the other a floor in between expansive spans of glass, the mansard roof and spandrel wall visually echo one another, creating balance and providing vital shade to the interior offices. Engineers determined that the sun's rays would reach approximately nine and a half feet from the glass of both stories. In response, the spandrel wall and roof stretch out approximately ten feet in every direction. This created a stacked tiered design that allowed employees to enjoy the view of the landscape nearby, while also blocking out some of the direct sunshine.

Kahn collaborated with a local landscape architect named Edward J. Daugherty to enhance the site and provide spaces for employees to get out and walk around the building. On either side of the lobby, pools were created and one featured a sculpture by Betty Jacob. At one end of the building, a man-made lake was created with a fountain feature, while at the other end, trees conceal the truck area.

Inside, natural elements were utilized to bridge the connection with the outside site, including a walnut veneer paneling, which is prominent throughout the design. A raised central portion of glass emerges from the mansard roof to form a clerestory, which gives additional natural light to the interior spaces. This facility in Atlanta was one of many facilities Kahn produced for Avon around the country; a relationship that has extended over 50 years.[113]

HOW WAS IT MADE? ARTISTRY IN DRAFTING

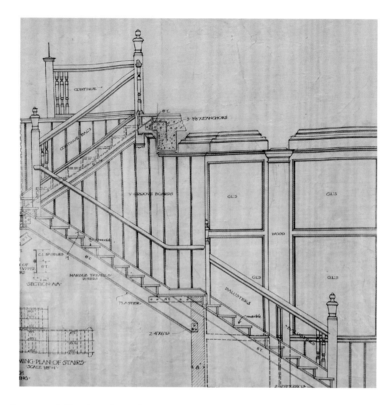

For the first 90 years of the firm, architectural and engineering drawings were done by hand. For hours entire rooms of draftsmen toiled over stationary wood drafting tables drawing, recopying, and perfecting each sheet of every discipline to create a set of drawings. Many of these early draftsmen went through an apprenticeship program and were trained in the precise methods, shapes, and linework of each discipline. Every sheet – whether it was architectural, structural, electrical, or mechanical – was a work of art.

Kahn implemented a standardized system for lettering which was used by all draftsmen. Distinctive in its slanted uppercase letters, this uniform style for architects and engineers gave the sense that each drawing was done by one person, even though many were involved. To the trained eye, however, individual styles can be discerned, in the way that lines terminate, cross, or the little extra flourish here and there inside the drawing. Renderings, too, were a work of art initially drawn in ink, and painted with gouache and watercolor on paper, and later created with colored pencils and markers on paper.

In the early years of the firm, drawings were crafted using ink on waxed linen with multiple pens used to create different line weights. While these drawings were quite beautiful works, design changes were challenging and often meant starting over.[114] Early drawings were reproduced through the blueprint or cyanotype process, eventually replaced by bluelines or whiteprints printed through a diazo process. In the office, two technicians would run drawings through the firm's diazo printer, which used an ammonia-based chemical to create multiple prints.

Before the 1960s, the firm began using pencil on tracing paper and rag vellum, which allowed for easier changes to the design, but the drawings were not durable. The industry then moved to pencil on mylar in the 1960s and Gordon V.R. Holness, former president of the firm recalls that "we had draftspersons who could do line work and lettering that looked like it was done by machine, but took a lot of time to create. There were even widespread drafting competitions."[115] In the 1970s, the firm moved to ink and plastic lead on mylar.[116] Around the same time, adjustable metal drafting desks with maple boards wrapped in a gridded paper replaced the stationary tables. These drafting desks incorporated an attached parallel bar, which offered greater precision and stability than the traditional T-square. Each night, drawings were removed from the drawing boards and stored in large fireproof flat files for protection.

A big change for the drafting practice occurred in the 1980s with the development of the pin bar drafting system. Using ink on mylar, each sheet was affixed to the drafting boards through a series of seven metal pins at the top of the board. Each discipline was developed over a base layer of the architectural plans, creating layers of detail. Sometimes "slicks," a brown flexible plastic similar to a sepia, were produced for floor plans by the architects for other disciplines to work on top of.[117]

Sets of layers were then rolled up together and sent out to an offsite company to be reproduced into a drawing that could then be used for bidding or in the field.[118] While it was a time consuming process, typically taking months to complete, it ensured consistency and accuracy. This proved inefficient on small projects, so the firm developed a multi-disciplined special projects group to handle small projects that could turn out a project in a few weeks.[119]

Drawings were meticulously reproduced, changes were erased or recopied, and paper sets were given out to bidders, owners, and others. This meant sometimes hundreds of drawing sets were needed. And, if a change occurred during the bidding process or during construction, those changes were then re-drawn and sent out to all parties. Contractors also reproduced drawings for subcontractors and other trades. This was a lot of paper and a lot of time. After the building was complete, final changes were recorded into the document set, and then stored with the thousands of other drawings in the firm's vault.

CHILDREN'S HOSPITAL OF MICHIGAN

In 1896, the children's hospital designed by Nettleton, Kahn and Trowbridge welcomed its first group of young patients (right). The hospital was originally called the Children's Free Hospital, for the treatment of children whose parents could not otherwise afford to treat them.[120] Largely financed by Hiram Walker, founder of Canadian Club Whiskey in Windsor, Walker purchased the site at St. Antoine and Farnsworth Streets, and designated $65,000 for the construction of the building.[121] Nettleton, Kahn and Trowbridge were contracted directly by Walker, a relationship that proved successful as Kahn went on to design a number of buildings for the Whiskey giant, many of which would eventually become Walkerville, in Ontario, Canada. Following a merger with the Michigan Hospital School, the hospital was renamed the Children's Hospital of Michigan in 1922. The firm continued to renovate and serve the hospital until it was demolished in the 1970s.

In the early 1960s, Albert Kahn Associates designed a new replacement hospital, located in the Detroit Medical Center (above). Designing a children's hospital isn't just about making a typical hospital more user-friendly for young and small patients. Instead, each system needs to be critically examined and altered in a way that creates a unique environment for the child. For example, even things like food delivery were altered to encourage sick children to eat while they were in the hospital: "From experience we've found that sick children don't eat well from kitchen-prepared, identical trays. They eat much better if food comes to the patient units in bulk containers and the child selects which foods, and how much of each, he wants."[122]

This facility was designed to feel more like a play place than a hospital. Medical equipment was hidden from view as much as possible, while children's quarters were brightly colored. A playroom was designed that could be easily converted to a dining room for children to eat together. Instead of private patient rooms, children were in two-bed rooms. A sliding wall could join two rooms so that groups of four children could visit and interact with one another. Between patient rooms windows allowed patients to see each other, while nurses could keep an eye on the children within several rooms at once. There were also two large color-coded drawers in the room for each child's toys and treasures; one of many unique design features to ensure that each child felt more at home.

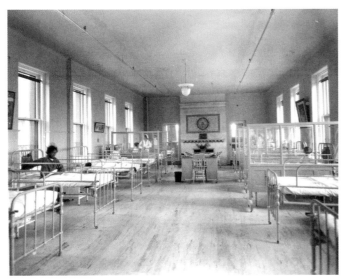

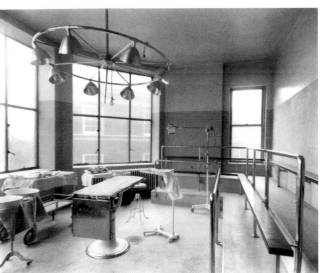

QUALITY AND COMPLEXITY

There is no honor quite like redesigning one of the firm's early projects. "It's easy to tell an Albert Kahn building in terms of quality. The building on the whole will be pretty high quality. We're not faddists. We like to use a degree of logic. We make sure something we do today won't, in five years, be seen as ludicrous or uneasy in its design."[123] While the building may no longer suit the needs of the current owner, a walk through the original structure reveals how our predecessors conceptualized space, light, and efficiency.

In 1975, Daniel Shahan became the fifth president of the firm. Shahan was the last of the firm's presidents who worked directly with Albert Kahn. As the practice continued to evolve, these leaders who worked directly with Albert ensured that the new generations of Kahn employees inherited aspects of the original culture, most importantly the devotion to clients, commitment to quality, eagerness to collaborate, and passion for innovation.

In the late 1970s, the firm had the opportunity to redesign the University of Michigan general hospital (1986) (above), which replaced the original Old Main hospital (1925). This 11-story, patient-friendly facility housed the Adult Medical Surgical ward and the Adult/Adolescent Psychiatric program. Over seven years, architects and engineers studied each system and material to ensure that the new building would serve their needs well into the future. Just like the first hospital designed by the firm on this site, the new replacement hospital emphasized proportion, natural light, and efficiency. This is one of several structures the firm has had the honor to redesign.

This period also marked changes to the firm's practice such as increased complexity in early planning and the production of drawings with the incorporation of new technology. The practice itself had become more detailed with more emphasis on initial plans and studies. Architects and engineers were more involved in value analysis and costs of development, providing a detailed analysis of prospective structures to clients early on. Industrial plants, for example, were being built closer to communities. Corporations saw the impact these plants had on the development and growth of surrounding communities, such as Smyra, Tennessee with the construction of the Nissan Assembly Plant (1983), and asked the firm to analyze locations and impacts of potential structures.

As Edgar E. Parks became the firm's sixth president, in 1985, the firm was also transitioning to Computer-Aided Design and Drafting (CADD) platform. The layers used by the pin bar drafting system influenced the development of CADD software. One of the firm's earliest uses of CADD was for Kellogg Company, a long-time client of the firm, on its Battle Creek, Michigan campus.[124] In 1985, Kahn designed and engineered Building 100,[125] the most modern food production facility on Kellogg's campus, allowing Kellogg to produce more cereal than any other plant.[126] Architects and engineers initially drew the plans and elevations for the structure by hand and then used CADD to recreate some of their two-dimensional drawings. This software allowed teams to update layers more efficiently, and drawings could easily be printed in the office using rolls of bond paper on large plot printers. However, the complaint was that drawings lost their character; they looked "mechanical" and no longer had "depth." The industry had lost some of that artistry, that individuality, in the documents.[127] Much of Kahn's architectural design was still done by hand because of that.[128] As the process of creating drawings evolved, so too did the complexity found in the drawings.

CADD linked to multiple technical software programs that covered various architectural and engineering concepts including energy code analysis, hardware selection, cost estimating, and specification editing.[129] These programs created an integrated drafting process that enabled digital collaboration with related disciplines. At this point, computer-generated finished drawings were produced for certain drawing layers such as structural framing, foundations, electrical, and building sections and elevations.[130] These programs were used to simplify the repetitive nature of drawings, making the creation of documents more efficient. What started as two computers in 1983, quickly grew to eight workstations and multiple shifts of employees to keep the production of drawings moving. Using this technology, the team could produce more design alternatives within a tighter timeframe, and achieve greater integration between design and engineering disciplines earlier on in the design process.

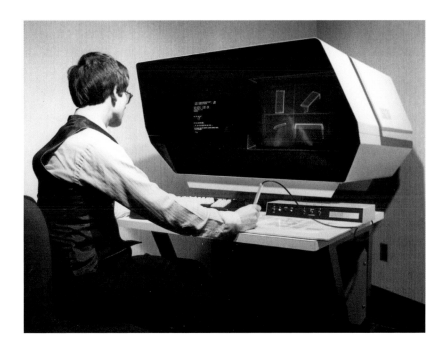

SEVENTH STREET OUTPATIENT CAMPUS

MOLINE, ILLINOIS | DESIGNED 1994 OPENED 1997

In 1994 when Kahn was hired to design a new large ambulatory care campus for Trinity Regional Health System in Moline, Illinois, it was our first opportunity to collaborate with an Affiliate of the Planetree Organization. Planetree had been founded in the mid-1970s to develop a series of demonstration projects that would increase the effectiveness of American hospitals by creating healing environments to be more effective in actually promoting the healing of sick patients. The organization considered this project an opportunity to create a prototype for future Planetree Ambulatory Care Facilities.

Through an extensive programming and development effort, this breakthrough project designed a facility that allowed every patient to have a private room during all phases of exam, treatment, and recovery. Each room was equipped for a companion or loved one to accompany the patient at all times, and finishes and furniture were selected to be home-like and not institutional in appearance. Lighting was designed to be dimmable for lower stress on patients and family members.

The facility is designed around a public "Hub" that greets people with needed services and amenities that support the physical and emotional needs of patients and their families. The Hub includes a café, a retail pharmacy, an outdoor patio, waiting areas with views of the pond and meditation gardens, and a Health Resource Center created for self or guided healthcare education for patients and their families.

The facility also included the following unique features: freestanding emergency care department, one of the first to be developed in the state of Illinois; ambulatory surgery suite with six operating rooms; 20-bed surgery recovery unit for short-stay patients expected to stay one to two days following surgery, one of two approved in Illinois; diagnostic imaging center with radiology, fluoroscopy, ultrasound, nuclear medicine, CT scan, and MRI procedure rooms; women's diagnostic imaging center with mammography and ultrasound; outpatient cancer treatment center for medical and radiation oncology; and a three-story medical office building for primary care and specialty physician practices.

When completed, the facility won a national award from the joint commission called the Ernest A. Codman Award, for illustrating that patient satisfaction in the new facility rose from the low 40th percentile to an unheard-of high 97th percentile. With the success of this first Planetree project, Kahn began to promote the advantages of designing a healing environment with all of its clients, resulting in over 20 outpatient and full new hospital facilities for Planetree Affiliates in Illinois, Wisconsin, and Brazil. And in 2009, Kahn was selected to be a founding member of the Planetree Visionary Design Network.

Author: Robert Sharrow, AIA, Former Director of Healthcare Planning, Albert Kahn Associates

DESIGN VISUALIZATION

In addition to drawings, the firm often built architectural models to scale to help clients visualize their future structure (above). With a model shop inside its offices within the Albert Kahn Building, designers led this process to construct 3-D models by hand. Equipped with a bandsaw and various small power tools, designers cut, painted, and assembled these models for clients to review and provide feedback. On projects that had a significant amount of process and mechanical work, such as the Kellogg Building 100, engineers were also recruited to assemble models of the ductwork and equipment inside the model.[131] Overall, this process was time-consuming and labor-intensive.

Architects and engineers today convey their design ideas using dimensional models through computer programs such as AutoCAD, Revit, and others. Multidisciplinary teams work on digital 3-D models of building systems simultaneously, collaborating, and updating regularly. Once each discipline's model is near completion they are then imported into a Building Information Modeling (BIM) software, which merges all of these models into one master (right). Architects and engineers can slice and create sections to pull out details from the model and print specific sections or elevations. Drawings, specifications, and 3-D models are then shared electronically with the owner, construction manager, and subcontractors.

Architects and engineers import their specific layers of the building into the program and are able to run clash detection to find areas where, for example, heating and cooling ducts might not fit within the cavity between floors as they are currently modeled. These tools allow issues to be discovered and corrected before the contractors are on site. Within these models, other types of data can also be stored, allowing designers and engineers to perform energy modeling, improving accuracy, and ensuring compliance with ever-complicated building codes.

These 3-D models can also be used on-site, allowing contractors to verify construction and installation in the field. For example, during the construction of the Polk Penguin Conservation Center (2016), the field team used the 3-D model to verify that the exterior metal panels were properly installed within the precise measurements specified. The iceberg-like structure of this project also demonstrated the further potential to create unique and irregular forms from a model. This technology will continue to drive the development of architecture and enable future fabrication directly from models in a way that wasn't previously possible from a two-dimensional drawing.

This 3-D modeling has been in use at the firm since the mid-1990s. In 1999, Kahn launched its Kahn Digital Studio group, a professional team of visualization and simulation specialists dedicated to cutting-edge visual technologies. It was part of a strategy to offer clients the ability to make enhanced design decisions resulting from the ability to build, display, and interact with computer-generated models of a physical environment.

Additionally, the firm has embraced point cloud scanning, drones, virtual reality, and other technologies to improve both their process and communication with clients. Renovations to existing structures pose a unique challenge to designers and engineers, as you need to start with reliable data on existing conditions. Point cloud scanning devices and software have been used to scan existing structures, such as the attic of the Detroit Opera Theater, to gather and input that data into a 3-D model to enable mechanical engineers in this case to design a new plan for ductwork. Similarly, drones are used to evaluate existing conditions on a site, such as upper floors, roofs, or hard to reach areas of existing structures, and gather additional data for the team to use. When collaborating with clients, virtual reality is often helpful to show clients designed solutions within a virtually recreated environment. For Mercury Marine's NVH Center (2018), for example, we created walkthroughs and a quick panoramic with virtual reality goggles to give clients a better understanding of the proposed space. Flythrough animation and 3-D printing of design elements have also been useful in communicating design phases and plans to facilitate client feedback. Together, this technology provides accuracy, clarity, and flexibility that enables decision-making to support the collaborative design process.

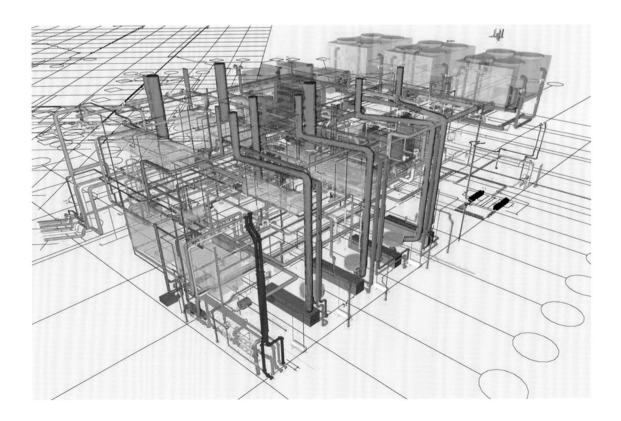

RAPID DELIVERY

A key aspect of many Kahn projects has been the speed at which projects were completed. Project Management had its beginnings in Albert Kahn's legacy of strong business orientation to professional practice. Whether it was during war-time emergencies or to help clients get to market sooner, the firm developed strategies to deliver projects faster than others.

Initially, the firm was even responsible for building and contracting on some projects.[132] Site superintendents were on staff and responsible for the day-to-day management of all subcontractors. The firm's dedication to maintaining time schedules within cost parameters in the design and construction processes gave rise to techniques and management methods that permit telescoping of the total process from the inception of design to the occupancy of the structure. This complete view of the project is critical to combat rising construction costs.

As more and more clients demanded single-point responsibility, Kahn rethought its own organization to find ways to better meet its client's desires. In 1992, Gordon V. R. Holness became the seventh president of the firm. Under his leadership, Kahn launched a new organizational structure resulting in a delivery approach that was more market-based, customer-focused, and team-oriented.

Kahn established "focused groups" geared to key market segments: Health Care Services, Research and Development Technology, Special Projects, Design/Build Services, and Program Management Services. Creating cross-departmental teams to delve deeper into our client's worlds enabled these teams to provide specialized solutions, while playing to the strengths of each team member. Those engineers who were deep thinkers, for instance, could work on process and details while others could focus on the big picture. While there was still feedback internally from other specialties, these teams were experts in their industries, speaking the same language as their clients, and engaging more deeply with trends and developments.

The firm adjusted to the market and found ways to differentiate itself as design competition grew. In 1995, Kahn created its first subsidiary corporation, the Albert Kahn Collaborative, Inc. The new entity concentrated on urban design and planning, architecture, and landscape architecture, with an emphasis on multi-family residential units, congregate care, senior housing, commercial properties, sports centers, and educational and recreational facilities.

Under the umbrella of Kahn Global Services, the firm created other subsidiary organizations to address specific concerns facing clients, including Kahn Program Management, which offered clients single-sourced administration of their projects worldwide; Kahn Manufacturing Solutions, which specialized in manufacturing and industrial engineering; Kahn Professional Resources, which specialized in contract staffing and placement of personnel for clients; and Kahn Solutions for Business, which addressed facilities, assets, business processes, technology, and people. The goal was to provide clients a one-stop-shop for everything and anything they might need concerning their facilities.

Kahn also pursued strategic partnerships to remain innovative. Partnering with IBM, the firm worked with the tech giant to deliver complete data centers to corporations across the Midwest. Data Centers are specially designed facilities that contain data processing, data storage, and communications networking equipment, a facility that has become essential. Additionally, the firm partnered with EDS Virtual Reality Center, a center based in the Albert Kahn Building, allowing architects and engineers to begin using computer-generated models, leading to more economical design decisions earlier on in the process. The center was one of the first commercial virtual reality centers in the world. All three companies were dealing with the same issue – trying to discover potential building-design and system-integration problems as close to the concept stage as possible.[133]

In 1998, the firm founded an office in São Paulo, Brazil, called Kahn do Brasil. As the largest city in South America and Brazil's main business center, São Paulo was seen by Kahn as an opportunity to develop a presence in different market segments, building upon the firm's legacy of international work and management. The firm first began working in the area as part of a team developing preliminary designs for Volkswagen's truck and bus plant to be constructed in Resende, Brazil. Kahn learned that foreign governments want local architects and engineers to do major portions of the design and engineering work, so the firm pivoted to management.[134] The first project of the newly inaugurated office was with a long-time client, Mercedes Benz, to work with a local firm to manage the design and construction of its 1.1 million sq. ft. A-Class automotive assembly plant (left and below). Like all projects, this project started with a thorough understanding of the process, the goals, and the current issues facing Mercedes. Kahn then collaborated with the local firm to produce a one-of-a-kind factory layout that solved these challenges. Kahn's strengths were its management process to efficiently run the jobs and experience designing and engineering a vast number of factories and research and testing facilities for automotive and automotive supply companies. During the office's 20 years of operation, the Brazil team's biggest market grew to be Healthcare. Kahn do Brasil was recognized as one of the country's main healthcare design companies and regarded as a leader in strategic planning.

COMMITMENT TO SUSTAINABILITY

Our imperative to build responsibly requires the implementation of intelligent planning and design practices to manage finite resources and effectively meet the needs of those that inhabit our work. We utilize a multi-disciplinary approach to create design solutions that result in healthful, productive, and efficient built environments while minimizing or eliminating wasteful and damaging design and construction practices. We not only want to build highly desirable and beneficial places for ourselves and our children, but leave a world with the same or greater resources and opportunities for future generations to enjoy.

Albert Kahn began to address sustainability and occupant well-being over 100 years ago. He is most remembered by his interest and ability to humanize miserable industrial work environments with an abundance of daylight, operable windows, and improved organizational layout. The Glass Factory (1923) at the Ford Rouge complex featured a unique building cross-section comprised of butterfly roofs and layers of operable clerestory windows to flood the factory space with daylight, introduce fresh air at the floor, and naturally eliminate the hot air at the ceiling. Albert was also quite effective in creating attractive buildings with efficient use of materials that saved construction time and material costs. Innovative truss designs, as demonstrated at the Chrysler Dodge Half-Ton Plant (1938), allowed for an efficient use of steel and glass to create expansive day lit and ventilated work areas.

We have been inspired by this legacy and are motivated to produce physical environments that allow our clients to get the most out of their investment, protect and restore the affected natural environment, and respect the culture and communities that inhabit these buildings. Design and construction practices that are energy-efficient, avoid excess waste, and preserve various components of our environment are not enough. We want our work to positively affect those that occupy the built spaces.

Over the years, we have established internal initiatives and activities to assure we remain vigilant environmental stewards for the communities that we serve. The Kahn Sustainable Design Committee has been operating for over two decades to educate, motivate and demonstrate sustainable design practices to staff, clients and the public. The committee is composed of employees from all backgrounds and expertise that meet regularly to share ideas and resources, while targeting opportunities for improvement. An avid supporter of continuing education, the firm has supported the training and certification of hundreds of LEED Accredited Professionals, ranking at one time as 21st in the nation and 1st in Michigan in the number of LEED AP's, according to *Building Design and Construction* magazine. The firm also volunteers a significant amount of time to support environmental awareness and holds leadership positions with the U. S. Green Building Council, American Institute of Architects Committee on the Environment (AIA COTE), and American Society of Heating, Refrigerating and Air-Conditioning Engineers (ASHRAE), while regularly lecturing on the topic at regional and national events.

Kahn was one of the first Architecture/Engineering firms to commit to the American Institute of Architects' 2030 Challenge toward carbon neutrality, positioning itself as an industry leader in the sustainable design movement. As part of that program, a Sustainability Action Plan has been incorporated into the firm's strategic plan, which sets quantifiable operational goals for the office and design goals for every project regardless of client requirements. In addition, we have pre-design and post-occupancy evaluation practices that are employed to measure progress and success on projects undertaken, regardless of whether a project seeks any form of certification or recognition.

Recently, we have developed a number of remarkable sustainably designed projects. Innovative energy production strategies have been employed on projects, including the reuse of landfill gas at the BMW plant in Spartanburg, South Carolina, while electricity produced from animal waste in the Anaerobic Digester at the Detroit Zoo powers site lighting and the on-campus animal hospital we designed. Renewable energy strategies have been employed on multiple projects, such as photovoltaic use at the new office building on the Volvo campus in Ridgeville, South Carolina. We have helped several clients take advantage of Brownfield development incentive programs with clean-up and remediation, currently with the Erie Downtown Development Corporation in Pennsylvania. Habitat preservation and stormwater management practices were implemented at Delta Dental headquarters in Michigan and at the Railcar Manufacturing plant in Alabama. Vegetative roofs were installed on the Vicky and Joseph Safra Pavilion at the Hospital Israelita Albert Einstein in Brazil (left). Occupant well-being strategies begin with a connection to nature, as exhibited at Chelsea Community Hospital in Chelsea, Michigan, and further developed with daylight and ventilation enhancements at the O-I headquarters in Perrysburg, Ohio.

Kahn designed the first LEED certified medical facility in Brazil at the Safra Pavilion and the first LEED certified medical facility in Michigan at Henry Ford West Bloomfield Hospital. We have designed LEED certified facilities for the Ford Motor Company, Aurora Healthcare, and Volvo Cars, amongst others. We also focus on operations and ongoing facility performance, as demonstrated in our renovation of the former Cobo Center, now TCF Center, recognized by APEX-ASTM standard E2774-11 for sustainable conferences and now certified under the LEED for existing buildings rating system. Years ago, we committed to 'greening' our standards and specifications, which resulted in energy-efficient building and system design, water use reduction, and low-emitting materials incorporation as a standard design feature implemented on all projects. Building off of our tradition of collaboration, the firm will continue to engage in multi-disciplinary, goal-oriented, and metric-driven sustainable design practices.

Author: Jeffrey T. Gaines, AIA, Former Director of Design, Planning and Sustainability, Albert Kahn Associates

TAUBMAN CENTER FOR DESIGN EDUCATION

DETROIT, MICHIGAN | DESIGNED 1928 REPURPOSED 2009

Historic Preservation and adaptive re-use of our historic structures is the highest form of sustainability. The natural resources embedded in our existing building infrastructure must not be ignored and discarded. To revitalize the former Argonaut Building, originally designed by Albert Kahn in 1928 for General Motors, the firm created a mixed-use educational facility and office complex for the College for Creative Studies (CCS) to house educational tenants and student housing. The Argonaut Building embodied the design concept of "Universal Space," which is easily converted into a variety of laboratories, design studios, classrooms, and exhibit facilities. This flexibility is found in countless Albert Kahn designs.

As an international design school and a current leader in automotive design education, CCS selected the Argonaut Building site because of its unique legacy. Significant developments undertaken in the building include the design and engineering of the "Hydra-matic" transmission and General Motors' first vehicle Design Center. The beginning of the automotive design process we know today was developed by Harley Earl in this facility, producing the first full-size clay model, and creating innovative designs like the Cadillac tail fin.[135] The engineering labs, run by Charles Kettering, were also a source of innovation with the development of the diesel-electric locomotives, Freon and automotive air conditioning, along with advances in automotive engineering.[136]

Almost 80 years later, the firm was tasked to create a 760,000 sq. ft. Center for Design and Education that provides space for a school, non-profit organizations, business accelerator, shared public spaces, student housing, and academic space for CCS design schools, while incorporating the latest technology available for the education environment. Designers were challenged to integrate each space, while at the same time, provide separation for each entity occupying the building.

The existing building influenced this revitalization project; however, the design team added a modern interpretation that results in a contrast of elements and materials. Public spaces are clad in vibrant colors mixed with neutral undertones to create stimulating and inviting environments. A previously removed circular vehicle ramp defines the unique shape for a new two-level gallery space. The classrooms were designed without walls for maximum flexibility. Custom-designed 'walls on wheels' were incorporated, and doubled as tackable surfaces for student project displays. Design and gallery spaces display a base of neutral colors and materials, allowing the student artwork and projects to define the space. And, an existing presentation area on the eleventh floor was renovated to serve as a new auditorium.

The rehabilitation project includes various structural and façade repairs, such as new windows that replicate the sightlines of the existing windows, repaired masonry that matches the existing materials, and replicated garage doors. Other notable renovations include the installation of energy-efficient systems, new insulation, and a new roof. Various safety upgrades include enhancements to the building's stairways, elevators, and comprehensive mechanical, electrical, and plumbing systems. The Argonaut Building was added to the National Register of Historic Places in 2005, and this historic rehabilitation project followed the guidelines for historic structures defined by the National Park Service.

Author: Alan Cobb, FAIA, Chairman & CEO, Albert Kahn Associates

RESILIENT

"Building of the Century." Is there a better accolade to bestow on a firm? The new millennia rang in on a high note when the American Institute of Architects named Kahn's opulent Fisher Building the "Building of the Century." This honor tops off a century of awards, including the AIA's Firm of the Year (1971), AIA Michigan's Firm of the Year (1995), and countless national design, engineering, and building awards.

Weathering the storms over the last 125 years has not been without its challenges. Change is the only constant in our fast-paced environment. To stay competitive and viable, we have adapted to changing marketplace demands. Kahn has long been balancing the markets and geographic locations that we serve, as well as the various services we offer. This has allowed us to withstand the dramatic changes in the economy locally, nationally, and internationally and remain agile in times of crisis. Agility requires a constant eye on the business climate and nimbleness in the firm structure to adjust at a moment's notice.

Kahn's internal processes have been integral to its success and its ability to be resilient. The key is never to get stuck in one process that potentially limits your team's creativity, ability to innovate, or service to a client. Kahn continuously refines internal processes to accommodate or mirror successful processes found in other markets to provide unparalleled service and speak the same language as our clients. In the late 1990s, for example, Kahn became one of the first architectural and engineering firms in the United States to achieve ISO 9001 certification, which assured clients, especially those in the automotive industry, that our processes and procedures satisfied a wide range of stringent, international quality requirements.

What worked for Kahn 10, 20, or even 30 years ago, might not be the best for our teams today. We continue to refine our processes and update the tools of our trade to become more efficient. We incorporated LEAN principles, first popular in manufacturing and then healthcare, to eliminate waste within our process. We have also implemented an Integrated Design Process and Advanced Planning Process to bring necessary teams, contractors, and community members to the table early in the design process to anticipate and resolve challenges. Once a project closes, we come back together and discuss lessons learned and make corrections on future projects. Another part of our process has consistently included the continued education of employees. "Kahn University," for instance, is an initiative that fosters a culture of continuous learning and improvement. These processes have been put to the test; Kahn continues to pivot and adjust to the constant change.

On September 11, 2001, our world stopped. The terrorist attacks on the United States shocked the market, to say the least. Many of our clients stopped what they were doing and projects were put on hold or canceled. When the initial shock and grief subsided, the firm repositioned its teams to focus on healthcare and automotive markets, which remained strong. With approximately 400 employees, the firm, now led by Stephen Whitney, needed to keep its employees working.

Building off a ten-year collaborative relationship with SRW & Associates, in 2003 Kahn and SRW opened a Birmingham, Alabama office called Kahn South. This organization provided a local node for projects across the southern states, leading numerous projects for Mercedes Benz, Toyota, and the University of Alabama Medicine (right), St. Vincent Hospital, among others. Two years later, Kahn opened an office in Juarez, Mexico, to serve American companies moving their manufacturing operations to Central America. Among the projects this team led were a three million square foot factory for Electrolux, and factories for Toyota and other automotive manufacturers.

When the U.S. stock market crashed in 2008, much of the architectural and engineering industry suffered from the economic downturn. Initially, Kahn remained largely unaffected due to a substantial backlog of healthcare work. The Hammes Company, a long-term client, approached Kahn to explore new healthcare projects in the Middle East, where their economy was booming and they desired to mirror the American healthcare system. In 2009 the firm, then led by Charles Robinson, explored potential projects in Iraq, Saudi Arabia, Kuwait, Dubai, and Qatar. Kahn joined a consortium of designers, engineers, and development partners by creating the ICON Global Architecture Engineering group.

In Iraq, for instance, the team identified a desperate need for infrastructure, housing, hospitals and other facilities that support the growth of prosperous cities and healthy communities. They completed a masterplan for Karbala, the Universities of Mosul and Fallujah, a housing study for Baghdad, and hospitals in Baghdad and Karbala. One significant project was the Oil and Gas University in Basra, Iraq. Located on 650 acres between the Tigris and Euphrates Rivers, the campus was planned to connect to city transit systems and featured an internal street system with shaded tree-lined sidewalks for pedestrians and bicyclists. Academic buildings front the campus open space, while student and faculty housing is provided within courtyard buildings along the campus's more tranquil areas. Athletics and facility operations are located along the western edge of the campus, with future expansion planned along the southern periphery. Throughout, open spaces encourage interaction between the 15,000 students and 3,000 faculty and staff. This work led to additional projects in neighboring countries.

Difficult decisions for the firm came in 2011 when the healthcare market dropped off. New commissions weren't enough, and teams quickly burned through the backlog of work. Detroit and the country were in the thick of a deep recession. During this timeframe, many firms merged with other companies or sold their businesses, but the Board refused to give over the legacy. Kahn continued through the support of long-term clients, and the patience and generosity of both employees and shareholders. During this timeframe, the firm streamlined its operations even further.

In 2013, Alan Cobb became president of the firm and led the firm through the rest of the recession. Kahn was lean and efficient with employees that remained committed to delivering excellent projects on time and within budget. The years that followed were a period of incredible growth for the firm with clients around the globe.

In 2018, the firm left the Albert Kahn Building and moved its offices across the street to the Fisher Building (right). Moving into the "Building of the Century" seemed fitting. Every day, employees walk through those hallowed halls and are inspired to keep innovating, keep collaborating, and keep serving.

Kahn built a significant backlog of projects, providing a strong base of work just in time for the firm to meet its next challenge: the 2020 COVID-19 pandemic. While the pandemic has redefined the way we all do business, the evolution of technology and the continual improvement of our processes have allowed our teams to work remotely and safely while serving clients. Delayed projects caused the firm to make difficult financial decisions to keep the business going through a period of global uncertainty. We have emerged with renewed hope and pride in our firm that continues to meet every challenge head-on. In 2021, Rick S. Dye was elected as Kahn's new president.

We are fortunate to have client relationships that stretch almost our entire history, along with the opportunity to serve new clients each year. Our mission is to be the trusted advisor for each of our clients by providing visionary leadership in the planning, design, and management of the built and natural environment. We will create sustainable environments that leave a better world for future generations. Our team will continue to adapt and pivot to new markets and new locations from our headquarters in Detroit. We will be resilient and continue to look forward. We remain committed to continuing the legacy of one of the world's most impactful architecture and engineering firms.

In the sections that follow, we have highlighted select stories of significant projects from the perspective of architectural or engineering innovations. The final chapter showcases where we expect to go next. Architects, Engineers, Designers, Project Managers, Field Representatives, and many other specialties work together on every project that enters our offices, taking each project from an initial dream through to construction. By grouping projects into two sections, The Art of Architecture and The Art of Engineering, we hope to show you what goes into "designing" and "engineering" each environment. This grouping emphasizes each discipline's strengths that, when united, create the unique portfolio that is Albert Kahn Associates.

ERIE INSURANCE

The Erie Insurance campus establishes a district within the downtown, engaging with the neighboring organizations, rather than isolating itself. Erie Insurance has been a pillar in the community since its founding in 1925. Offering the surrounding area stability and permanence, Erie Insurance remains an agent of economic revitalization and community service, investing in their city, their community, and revitalizing historic properties to preserve the city's heritage.

A relationship spanning nearly three decades, Kahn began the masterplan for the Erie Insurance campus in the late 1990s. Guiding the campus and the new office building's plan was their connection to community and commitment to service. The Kahn design team used an image analysis tool to develop the appropriate architectural and interior image. The building plan was designed around a central common area, called the "City Center," intended to facilitate communication and interaction.

The exterior design and massing reveal the balance between fixed concentrated office work areas and collaborative zones. The collaboration areas are represented by cantilevered and angular glass curtain wall panels with a random mullion pattern, embodying the unscheduled nature of open collaboration. The fixed office areas are represented by strip widows respecting the modularity of the structural system and the nature of concentrated work. These areas are marked by traditional brick patterns, glass, and stonework inspired by the existing campus architecture.

Inside, saturated colors from nature are accents on each floor. A brown earth tone is used on the lower level, green grass color on the first floor, working up to a blue sky color on the seventh floor. These accent paint colors highlight the building core and can be found in floor patterning, aiding in wayfinding throughout the building. Random floor patterns, random interior glass patterns on the conference rooms, and layered light cove ceiling elements join and unify collaboration areas. Wood tones are used in shared public spaces to add to the warmth in the building.

Sustainable design and engineering solutions were also implemented to create a building that respects the resources of the area and further links employees with nature. For instance, to reduce the heat island effect and retain stormwater, Kahn designed about 19,000 sq. ft. of sustainable vegetation over three roof areas. One of the roof gardens is also designed as an employee gathering space complete with paved spaces. Hardy sedums and tall ornamental grasses on each roof will provide color all year long, creating a strong visual character for employees on higher floors and occupants from nearby buildings.

Centered on a stacked multi-story collaborative spine, the building is divided into two primary sectors. One side of the spine terminates at a water feature wall highlighted by Pennsylvania Blue Stone and a monumental glass staircase. From there, the spine runs the building's length and opens up to a lobby and open courtyard, joining the new building with the existing Heritage Center. The Heritage Center, the original location of Erie Insurance, is now a dedicated museum occupying the northwest corner of the site. Connecting the Heritage Center and new building bridges Erie Insurance's past and future while inviting the community to engage with both.

THE ART OF ARCHITECTURE

"Architecture is the art of buildings, adding to mere structural elements distinction and beauty. Since earliest days, architecture has inspired people to express in concrete form ideals, hopes and aspirations." [137]

- Albert Kahn

Architecture is a collaborative practice that blends art and science to serve a useful purpose for clients, communities, and society. Architecture is a bridge between the built and natural environments, physical and spiritual realms, real and abstract, past and future. It is rooted in the needs, desires, and goals of a particular client or community. Architecture creates a sense of place in which we live, think, work, and restore. In this chapter, we explore a select group of significant projects throughout the firm's history, emphasizing the aesthetic, impact on the community, ability to promote well-being, and renewed purpose through the repurposing of historic buildings and sites.

Architecture both responds to and anticipates shifts in the spirit and conditions of society. As the industrial age spread throughout the Western world, cities became places of filth and degradation. Critics spoke out against the terrible living and working conditions this industrial marketplace created. As Detroit became the center of the automobile industry, Albert began his career. New forms of architecture emerged from this reality to address contemporary concerns and bring dignity and beauty to society.

The firm's early buildings show influences from the Arts and Crafts, Beaux Arts, and Art Deco movements, among others. It is in the early industrial designs for clients like Packard and Ford that Modernism's vocabulary began to fully take shape, inspiring later European architects. The "Form Follows Function" expression permeates each structure designed by the firm, demonstrating that efficiency is beautiful. As technology evolved, society's ideal of beauty has also shifted from the grandeur and crafted details to sleek, minimal, and transparent. Tracing the firm's work through various markets and periods in history, it is clear that they were working within multiple design vocabularies simultaneously.

Initially, Albert drew inspiration from his trips to Europe, bringing design elements and humanist ideals to his clients. He melded innovations and lessons learned from clients to create new solutions for each market he worked within. "Indeed, some of the best modern work follows no one particular type, but is rather a combination of various styles," explained Albert. "Good taste and common sense, not style, must govern. To meet the requirements of the present day no style of the past can be employed without sacrificing much that is characteristic thereof. The very charm of the French manor house is often the haystack, even the manure pit in the entrance court. I doubt if the most rabid stylist would care to reintroduce these…The best designers are those, who thoroughly grounded in the work of the past and familiar with the principles underlying the same, apply them to new problems, adding what they can of their own individuality and creating something characteristic of our day." [138]

Architecture is imbued with a unique ability to build, sustain, and forge communities. Greenways, parks, and open spaces allow communities to gather and recreate together – these spaces are community resources. Civic and public structures such as libraries, schools, theaters, and community centers, for example, are pillars in our communities allowing us to connect and create meaningful experiences. Built and natural environments allow users to create lasting social ties. Similarly, every environment we inhabit affects our well-being – whether mental, spiritual, or physical. Design professionals remain keenly focused on designing environments that help facilitate our desire to lead full and productive lives. When a structure or place no longer fulfills a useful purpose, architects have the opportunity to readapt and renew the structures and environments to serve and delight new generations.

Today, the firm has a team of specialists that develop unique design vocabularies that are rooted in our clients' goals while incorporating new technology to advance the design and artistically solve current challenges. In the pages that follow, you will find common design principles throughout our history, which create environments to support communities, promote productivity, foster healing, connect us to the past, and inspire users to create a better future.

FISHER BUILDING

"Detroit's Largest Art Object," the Fisher Building is the epitome of Albert Kahn's Art Deco designs. Embodying the spirit of renewed hope and economic prosperity, rich colors, lavish ornamentation, bold geometric shapes, and metallic materials such as gold, silver, and bronze are found throughout. "The design of the Fisher Building was a serious attempt to make of the skyscraper, which has seen so many varied solutions, a structure of architectural merit, and none the less practical," explained Albert, "the result may not prove as striking or modernistic as some, but the chances are it will remain good architecture longer."[139]

Kahn selected leading designers and artisans to work on the building. Géza Maróti, from Budapest, designed and supervised the ornament and color decorations in the main entrance, arcade, and banking room; Thomas Di Lorenzo, from Detroit, was responsible for the murals; Ulysses Ricci and Angelo Zari, from New York, modeled the exterior ornament next to the entrance doorway; Anthony Di Lorenzo, from New York, prepared the models for most of the bronze work; and Corrado Parducci, from Detroit, furnished models for some of the bronze and all of the plaster work.[140] "The Golden Tower," as it was called, originally had a gold-leafed tile that covered the cap of the building. Once World War II broke out, fear emerged that the shining tower would become a target for the enemy and green terracotta tile was installed over the gold leaf.

Inside, the walls, columns, and floors are wrapped in 40 varieties of marble gathered from around the world, each with rich coloring and laid out in various patterns. Warm, red marbles were incorporated from Germany, cool, green marbles from Africa, rich, brown and black marbles from Italy, and a beautiful rare rose-tinted marble from Spain, to name a few. The bronze elevator doors at the arcade level are cast into multiple square panels in the Renaissance manner with bas-relief scenes. At the upper levels, the elevator doors have an abstract intaglio floral design of blossoms shaped like cogs and gears as well as other forms of animals and nature.

Approximately 40% of the interior arcade, which stretches 44 feet high, features gold leafed details and hand-painted fresco ceilings. At the crossing of the two arcades is a shallow dome painted with nudes surrounding a patterned central medallion. The other murals consist mostly of colored and gold leaf geometric stenciling with the symbolic forms limited primarily to figures, eagles, fruits and flowers, and lunette panels depicting old adages and symbols alluding to economic concepts. Superb bronze grills, bas-relief, and wall medallions further enrich the space, lit by eight-foot frosted glass, lantern-style chandeliers designed by Edward F. Caldwell and Company.

Explorations in Africa, Latin America, and South America also impacted the Art Deco movement, demonstrated by some of the geometric and exotic imagery. In the center of the main arcade is the Fisher Theater, which was originally designed by Graven and Mayger and inspired by Mayan designs. In 1961, the interior of the old theater was demolished and rebuilt as a sleek modern theater seating about 1,600. A new brass entrance treatment was installed in the arcade at the same time.

Commissioned by the Fisher brothers, who developed a close body design for the auto manufacturers, the building's original plan included three towers: a central 60-story tower flanked by two 28-story towers. Though only one tower was built before the Great Depression hit, Kahn's design was like a city within a city. The building incorporated the Fisher Body Corporation headquarters, commercial and medical office space, a theater, retail, and restaurants on the main floor. It also included an attached eleven-hundred-car parking garage with a novel double helix ramp design. At one time, there was even a service station and waiting rooms for both patrons and chauffeurs.

The Fisher brothers had previously employed Kahn to design Fisher Body Plants in several cities including Detroit (1919), Flint (1922), Cleveland (1919), and Ontario (1920), as well as their private residences and playhouses for their children. Having demonstrated their design and engineering excellence, Kahn was given very few restraints in designing the Fisher Building. In fact, they were tasked with building the most opulent structure with the highest quality materials, and within 15 months the building was completed at the cost of $9,000,000. Immediately, the Fisher Building won several awards, including the Architectural League of New York's Silver Medal for the most beautiful commercial structure. In 1980, it was added to the National Register of Historic Places. And, in 2000, the Detroit chapter of the American Institute of Architects named this historic icon the "Building of the Century."

Albert Kahn Associates relocated its headquarters to the Fisher Building in 2018.

BURTON TOWER

The story of Burton Tower at the University of Michigan begins with Eliel Saarinen's entry in the 1922 Chicago Tribune Tower competition. It's a convoluted story. Saarinen's tower failed to win the competition, but the design inspired a number of designs that were built, among them Seattle's Northern Life Tower by Albertson, Wilson, and Richardson, and Albert Kahn's opulent Fisher Building in Detroit.

These buildings comprise an implied critique of Saarinen's design. Heresy though it is to say so, Saarinen's design begins the diminution of the massing quite low; the top, in the mind's eye, seems too tall. In Seattle's tower, and Kahn's in Detroit, the mass diminishes more satisfactorily as the eye ascends.

Saarinen came to the United States in 1923, with Kahn's enthusiastic support, and taught for a year at Michigan. He then went on to develop the school and academy on George Booth's land north of Detroit, where in the early years of the century, Kahn had built Booth's home, now called Cranbrook House. Somewhere along the way, Saarinen designed a carillon tower for the university; the design was shown on the cover of the 1927 Michiganensian yearbook.

There was a proviso in the funds that the tower was to have a practical use: it should include offices or classrooms in significant numbers. Saarinen designed the base as offices, surmounted by a more decorative upper half for the bells, which was a miniature version of the Tribune Tower.

Ensuing months brought the Great Depression, and Saarinen's design wasn't built. But the dream of a tower for the university's bell peal remained, and in 1934, Albert Kahn was asked to produce a more affordable design. He drew from Saarinen's proposal, but made major changes. He moved the point of diminishing width upward and reduced the width more subtly. And – most importantly – he made Saarinen's terribly awkward building-on-top-of-building into a coherent composition, held together, and given an aerial thrust; by the strong verticals. Kahn's design must be respected as neither a knock-off of Saarinen's proposal nor inferior to it. Kahn has produced the finer design in every way.

There is one more element to the story. Kahn and Saarinen were friends. Kahn had supported Saarinen in many ways; they dined at one another's homes, which were only a few miles apart. In a back room of Saarinen's home at Cranbrook is a rendering that is quite obviously a revision of the Tribune Tower design, in which Saarinen has moved significantly upward the point at which the mass begins to diminish. This gives the tower a much more satisfying composition, not unlike Kahn's Fisher building, and, more distantly, Burton Tower – which, inevitably, raises the question: did Saarinen revise his design before, or after, Kahn's towers?

Author: Grant Hildebrand, Author, *Designing for Industry*, and Professor Emeritus, University of Washington

CRANBROOK HOUSE

BLOOMFIELD HILLS, MICHIGAN | DESIGNED 1907 OPENED 1908

The story of Cranbrook House – and the relationship between its client and its architect – begins not in the suburbs, but in Detroit, more than three decades before the home's completion in 1920. The year is 1888. George Gough Booth and Ellen Scripps Booth are planning their first home on Trumbull Avenue, a wedding gift from Ellen's father, the influential and wealthy newspaper publisher James Scripps.[141] George Booth, a metalsmith by training and certainly of more modest means, has just sold his ornamental ironworks firm in Windsor to become a newspaperman, the business manager of the Scripps family's flagship paper, the *Detroit Evening News*.

Like Scripps's own home across the street, the Booth's "honeymoon cottage" was designed by the noted Detroit architectural firm of Mason and Rice. The commission fortuitously coincided with the period that the teenage Albert Kahn was working for George Mason as a draughtsman and receiving his first opportunities as a designer – including the Booths' brick horse barn.[142] It was the beginning of a long professional collaboration between Kahn and Booth that culminated with Kahn's design for the Detroit News Building – built after Booth succeeded his father-in-law as the publisher – and several more buildings throughout Michigan for the Booth News Service.

Booth and Kahn met with the contractor at Cranbrook on May 26, 1907, to start building Cranbrook House.[143] Booth had selected a site at the top of a hill, a neglected peach orchard on the property he was amassing in Oakland County.[144] The view looked north over a valley through which the Rouge River flowed, soon to be dammed to create a lake. To the south was Lone Pine Road, which would be completely screened by a man-made hill and a large stand of pines, part of Booth's transformation of the run-down farm into an extensive country estate. By June 1, 1908, the Booths' twenty-first wedding anniversary, the house was ready for George and Ellen and their five children to take occupancy.[145]

Booth was an Anglophile and a leading proponent of the Arts and Crafts Movement in Detroit and nationally. He wanted a house that would connect him to the sturdy Tudor architecture of the village of his ancestors: Cranbrook in Kent, England. Kahn gave him a Tudoresque home that was at once humble and grand,[146] less "ostentatious and archaeological" than the Tudor Revival home Kahn had designed for E. Chandler Walker in Windsor or the one he later designed for Edsel B. Ford in Grosse Pointe

Shores.[147] Cranbrook House is more intimate, like the architect's own home in Detroit. With its informal, almost playful massing of forms and arrangement of windows, and lively juxtaposition of materials – half-timbering, stucco, red brick, limestone, and terra cotta roof tiles – the house represents the best of Kahn's "cottage style" and is evidence of his versatile eclecticism.[148]

Although landscape gardening was important to Kahn, Booth worked with Kahn's former associate, Marcus Burrowes, to design the extensive stone-walled terraces that surround the house.[149] He returned to Kahn, however, to complete the home with two major additions: the West Wing (1918–1919) containing a spacious library for entertaining and Booth's private office suite, and the East Wing (1919–1920) containing an expanded kitchen and servants' quarters as well as the paneled Oak Room, the favored room for family gatherings.[150]

The house and grounds are replete with custom-designed furnishings and decorative arts. From entrance gates forged by Samuel Yellin to the dining room table and chairs executed by Kahn, Cranbrook House defines the American Arts and Crafts Movement. These artistic collaborations and many others – which often began with a sketch by the former metalsmith– culminate with John Kirchmayer's carved oak overmantel in the Library, a masterwork of craftsmanship that depicts the artisans who worked with George Booth on the house – with Albert Kahn at the center.

Author: Gregory Wittkopp, Director, Cranbrook Center for Collections and Research

DETROIT NEWS BUILDING

One hundred years later, Albert Kahn Associates once again began work on the iconic Detroit News Building. This time, leading the renovation and restoration of the former news headquarters to accommodate new owners and a new generation of collaborative workers.

Originally constructed for the *Detroit News*, the building housed the newspaper from its opening in 1917 until 2014. *Detroit News* founder James E. Scripps launched an evening paper that revolutionized the news industry. His paper was more affordable for the working class at just two cents a copy; more accessible to all readers, more succinct and enticing articles; and produced on smaller sheets of paper, so that they could be held easier.[151] George G. Booth, Scripps' son-in-law, was the publisher of the *Detroit News* at the time of designing its new building. Booth had previously worked with Albert Kahn to construct the Grand Rapids Evening Press Building (1904) and his residence (1908).

Once it was finished, the Detroit News Building was believed to be the largest newspaper plant in the world.[152] On the exterior, four statues of significant historical figures that revolutionized the printing industry are prominently displayed including Johannes Gutenberg, William Caxton, Christophe Plantin, and Benjamin Franklin. There are panels between the statues that serve as a reminder for all those that enter and pass by the building that the news exists for the people, "a light shining into all dark places."[153] The exterior incorporates other applied details such as crests, heraldic shields, and printers' marks.

The first floor of the building featured shipping and storage areas and housed the plant's pressroom, featuring numerous printing presses that printed, cut, folded, and counted the newspapers, all of which was visible to the public through the large windows. A mezzanine level above the press room allowed visitors to view the printing presses at work. On the floors above, hundreds of employees worked to write, set, and edit the paper each day. A library space was also on the third floor in which employees were to fact-check stories. The fifth floor originally featured a long roof monitor to let in natural light, which was later removed as a sixth floor was added. A few years later, Kahn also designed the paper storage warehouse and a mixed use parking garage that featured retail spaces on the ground floor.

As the world of media changed, the facility underwent changes to the original configuration of the building, some of which, unfortunately, hid or destroyed the building's architectural details such as the infamous dropped ceiling. This ceiling was one of the first things to go, revealing the elegant barrel vaulted ceilings throughout. Kahn brought many of the original details back to the forefront of the design. New ornamental elements were installed to replicate the original barrel vaults and period ornamentation as closely as possible. A new data center was placed where the printing presses once stood. The exterior façade was restored, and the building was brought up to modern codes. Open workspaces were designed for new tenants, and building systems were redesigned to meet the needs of current occupants and provide considerable operational savings.

DETROIT ATHLETIC CLUB

Albert filled the pages of his sketchbooks while he traveled abroad. Inspired by Renaissance palaces from a recent trip to Italy, Albert incorporated these motifs into the design of the Detroit Athletic Club. Occupying an entire city block, the eight-story building is clad in Bedford limestone with ornament, or decorative elements, applied to the façade to highlight elements of the design. Renaissance details include the rusticated quoins, or masonry blocks, on the corners of the building, the use of Corinthian columns between the fourth-floor windows, and the elaborate cornice on the top of the building, among others. The Palazzo Farnese in Rome was particularly influential in this design, providing the inspiration for the triangular and curved pediments alternating above the windows on the second floor. The structure is oriented around a large central lobby, creating a symmetrical building, both on the exterior and the interior. The main lobby also highlights the character of the Renaissance, with a marble fireplace patterned after a fifteenth century Italian mantel, and artwork, such as a marble bust of Hermes, incorporated into the design.[154]

The Detroit Athletic Club was founded in 1887 as an amateur athletics organization. It was later reborn in 1913 by a group of influential businessmen in Detroit, many of whom employed Albert Kahn to design their factories and commercial buildings. According to the *Detroit Free Press* in 1913, the building took eight months to design as it was reviewed and critiqued by club managers and experts around the country. This was expected to be the finest athletic club in America. With the committee, Kahn visited numerous successful clubs around the country and analyzed which building features attributed to the success of the organizations.

A news release from the Albert Kahn office at the time stated, "The general treatment of the interior will be that of a handsome private house rather than that customary in hotels or public buildings."[155] Inside, there are six main floors and two mezzanine levels. The main floors were divided into three main programs: social function on the first and second floor with numerous dining rooms, billiard and lounging room, a library, and barber shop; athletic activities on the third and fourth floors including a large gymnasium, pool, several indoor courts and game rooms, and a Turkish bath center, which was also to be the finest in America; sleeping quarters for members are found on the top two floors featuring 108 rooms. Below, the basement houses a bowling alley. When it opened in 1915, women had a separate dining room and a separate entrance off of Randolph street, which also served as the general carriage and automobile entrance.

HENRY FORD WEST BLOOMFIELD HOSPITAL

WEST BLOOMFIELD, MICHIGAN | DESIGNED 2007 OPENED 2009

Henry Ford Health System has advanced the delivery of healthcare construction in Michigan with the creation of the new West Bloomfield Hospital. Representing a shift from traditional institutional care, this facility delivers holistic, wellness care where the patient is the focus, and hospital services are designed around each individual.

With serene gardens, beautiful courtyards, a tranquil pond, and natural landscapes, the facility combines the warmth of a Michigan lodge with state-of-the-art care. Long before entering the facility, the patient feels as though they are checking into a tucked-away resort. Historic and iconic lodge resorts inspire the exterior design composition of fieldstone, brick, and copper-colored metal panels. Deep mullions, multiple colored glass panes, and steel channels within the curtain wall system capture a sense of the heavy timber construction. The four-story main structure creates a sense of tranquility that supports the health system's healing mission. Connecting to an existing outpatient facility at the rear, the building wraps around the site's large pond without disturbing its natural beauty.

Visitors enter an environment that emphasizes the preservation of health as much as the treatment of illness. Upon entering, they find themselves at a crossroads of streetscapes patterned after a Michigan town. Main Street gives the hospital the flavor of a small-town and an unparalleled experience for patients, visitors, and staff. A walkable neighborhood concept was brought inside with restaurants and shops focusing on nutrition, healthy cooking, acupuncture, and other ways to take care of oneself.

Michigan's geology and natural resources also inspire the interior design; natural stone is carried from the exterior and used with a natural pattern on the floor. At the same time, the ceiling features angled inset lighting inspired by glacial remnants and rock formations. Within the inpatient lodges, special attention was paid to reducing noise, glare, and other subtle touches to establish a healing atmosphere and enhance the comfort of patients, visitors, and staff. Curved walls and soft, natural colors harmonize to create a calm and soothing environment that enables patients to focus their energies on healing.

Connecting the diagnostic and treatment areas and inpatient lodges are two, three-story atriums designed to bring in daylight for the trees, plants, and landscaping featured within the atriums. There is also a grow light system that can be utilized if there are times when natural light is not plentiful. Inspiration from timber construction and industrial details influenced the design of the monumental atrium staircase. These impressive atriums create a harmonious environment for patients and visitors. One atrium is more public and features a tea kiosk with a healthy assortment of natural teas to enjoy. The other atrium is quiet and a perfect retreat for personal reflection within the natural surroundings or in the non-denominational sanctuary. Together, all of these features make the hospital of a wellness destination.

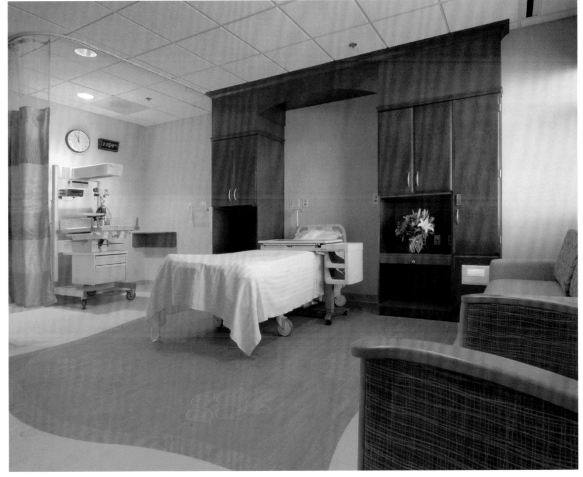

THE NATIONAL THEATER

The National Theater at 118 Monroe Street offers further evidence of the versatility of the Kahn office. Designed by Albert Kahn and Ernest Wilby, the theater is one of several performance venues that constituted Detroit's Monroe Street Entertainment District before the explosion of film theaters in the 1920s. Designed to host vaudeville acts, the National Theater's symmetrical facade featured an impressive recessed central portal flanked by domed towers articulated with perforated white and blue glazed terracotta Pewabic Pottery tile screens. The arch, with its dramatic stained-glass windows, was accented with stylized eagles, scarab beetles, and framed by rosettes. These ornamental details are evocative of the organic architectural styling of other urban designers, including luminaries like Louis Sullivan in Chicago, whose 19th century organic terracotta designs would have been very familiar to Kahn. Architectural ceramics were used frequently by Kahn's office in this period and are seen on the Grinnell Brothers Building (1908) and enhancing the facades of other Detroit landmarks. The tower domes are notable for the playful scalloped styling of their gilded roof tiles.

At the time of its construction, the National Theater was inserted into a retail streetscape where its unique form stood in clear contrast to its context. While remarkable during the day, it was the dramatic night lighting – projected from the light bulb-studded lattice-work portal arch and towers – that brought the eclectic architecture to life. Most of the design interest was on the exterior of the building. The performance space inside featured a large stage, extensive plasterwork and colorful stenciled décor, and seating for 800. The interior lobby was lined with tan Pewabic Pottery tiles.

Following the opening of the National Theater, Kahn's office took on a limited number of theater projects. They notably include the University of Michigan's Hill Auditorium (1913) and Louisville's National Theater (1913) the latter of which echoes Detroit's version in its adherence to a Beaux-Arts eclecticism. The National Theater has had many lives. Opened as a vaudeville theater, it later presented films and touring burlesque. Catering to changing entertainment tastes, the theater showcased musical performances through the 1950s including rock and roll and rhythm and blues acts. The theater was renamed the Palace Theater in the 1960s when it operated as an adult film venue before closing permanently in 1975, the year it was added to the National Register of Historic Places.[156] Since then, Kahn's National Theater has been sitting as a relic of the once vibrant Monroe Block with occasional initiatives made to restore the historic structure. Most recently, proposals have included efforts to preserve the façade's unique triumphal arch portal as the gateway to a new urban mixed-use development.

Author: Deirdre L.C. Hennebury, PhD, Associate Director, Museum Studies Program, University of Michigan

FREE PRESS BUILDING

DETROIT, MICHIGAN | DESIGNED 1922 OPENED 1925

Albert Kahn disliked the riotously novel skyscraper designs he saw rising in New York City in the 1920s. "Bedlam reigns," he said at the time, "everyone is trying something different."[157] Kahn preferred a tried-and-true concept, a stately design enriched by limestone facing with historical and artistic motifs marking the façade.

Typical of this approach was his Detroit Free Press Building built in 1925 at Washington Boulevard and Lafayette. It was not Kahn's first newspaper building; he had designed an earlier, smaller home for the Free Press in 1911, which was constructed in 1913 at 131 W. Lafayette (demolished in 2004) and he had also crafted the Detroit News Building down the street. But his new Free Press Building at 321 Lafayette proved his most memorable.

A steel-frame 13-story tower rises gracefully from the six-story wings that flank it. The limestone that faces the structure evokes a monumental feel. The deeply cut arched entryway signifies the importance of the newspaper trade and gives way to a pleasant lobby. Inside, a monumental open space on a below-grade level housed the newspaper's massive presses; a ceremonial high-ceilinged meeting room occupied much of the first floor, while newspaper staffers and commercial tenants filled the floors above.

The *Detroit Free Press* newspaper staff occupied the building for almost three-quarters of a century. Here the newspaper won multiple Pulitzer Prizes and covered the Great Depression, World War II, the Cold War, and much more. Kahn's stately design concept – a central tower rising from flanking wings – reappears in some of Kahn's other commercial skyscrapers of the era; in variations Kahn used the theme again for his Maccabees Building in Midtown Detroit and his glorious Fisher Building in Detroit's New Center district. The Free Press Building sat vacant for several years after the newspaper moved to another Kahn building in the late 1990s but has been purchased by businessman Dan Gilbert's Bedrock real estate arm, which has renovated it for retail, office, and residential use. Nearing its 100th birthday, Kahn's Detroit Free Press Building remains an elegant anchor for its downtown district.

Author: John Gallagher, Author and Former Journalist, *Detroit Free Press*

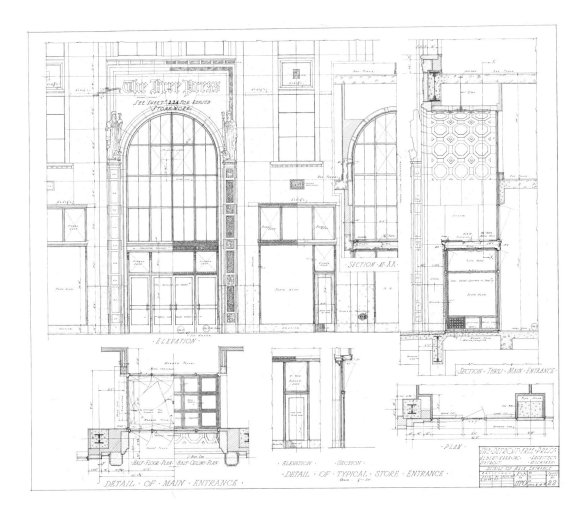

DOWNTOWN ERIE

As manufacturing has shifted or left many of our cities, a "rust belt" city like Erie has an opportunity to reinvent and reimagine its role in the community. Kahn has worked with multiple groups over the last 20 years, helping the city reinvest in the downtown, connect natural and developed amenities, and bring additional uses and vibrancy back to the city center. Most recently, the Erie Downtown Development Corporation (EDDC) has been championing this effort to revitalize the downtown area and inviting the community to help shape the future of their city. EDDC's goal is to "shock the market" with new viable and desirable uses in the downtown, not slowly over time, but all at once with something that cannot go unnoticed. Erie has no shortage of character and history – it just needed amenities and opportunities for people to visit and stay in the city.

Targeting three underutilized blocks in the downtown, EDDC and Kahn established a plan to preserve and adapt the historic structures while creating new buildings to add needed housing, dining, retail, office space, and unique experiences for residents and visitors. For instance, the flagship development of a new food hall and food market will be a culinary destination with supporting retail in the adjacent storefronts. Through the creation of smaller storefronts, this development will bring independent businesses and startups into the downtown. New and renovated residential apartments will provide desired downtown living arrangements for area students, professionals, and families that have been long awaited. With respect to the surrounding architecture, new structures will either be set back from the street to not overwhelm nearby buildings or use an individual storefront approach with changes to the façade in response to the surrounding scale.

A guiding principle throughout has been: if it is historic, save its character, but make it workable for contemporary needs. Some of these buildings are 150 years old and have a unique history worthy of preservation. The Cashier's House, for example, built in 1839, was once the private house of the CEO of the Erie branch of the Bank of the United States, previously in the adjacent building.[158] Original facades will be saved, windows will be replaced, and other details will be preserved. The team has gathered research and photographs on each building, discovering that some buildings have seen anywhere between 15-20 different storefronts. Rather than creating an exact replica, they decided to replace these storefronts with something modern that shares a similar geometry or framework of the original design. To make these structures usable, additional updates to comply with new building codes include improving accessibility, replacing mechanical systems, and adding necessary fireproofing.

This development will breathe new life and vibrancy into the downtown. Kahn and EDDC are capturing the cultural and historical significance of Erie, and a renewed interest in wanting to live, work, and play downtown; a strategy that could be adapted to other cities.

TCF CENTER

Since its doors first opened in 1960, the Cobo Center, now called the TCF Center, has been a fixture in Detroit, bringing tourists from around the globe to events like the North American International Auto Show. Fifty years later, the center required an upgrade, starting with opening the building to the Detroit River and the redeveloped riverfront. The exterior facade facing the river was demolished and replaced with a glass curtain wall, providing some of the best views of downtown, the river, and Canada. On the opposite side of the building, a state-of-the-art electronic screen system was incorporated into the facade to draw attention to the center.

Another significant feature of this renovation was the adaptive reuse of the former Arena, which once hosted sports teams and performances, into the new 40,000 sq. ft. Grand River Ballroom. The transformation involved the complete removal of the arena ceiling, ice rink, and seating areas with the structure still intact. A portion of the existing arena structure was removed and then re-supported on a new structural system to accommodate the new atrium. A new floor level was created, and the ballroom was placed on the facility's second level. With seating for 5,000, the ballroom is surrounded with an exterior glass curtain wall, and complete with a food court and supporting back-of-house spaces. The ballroom sits over a newly created meeting room space and is flanked by a new three-story atrium that visually and physically connects the inside to the riverfront.

Over five years, multiple phases of renovation and expansion occurred in collaboration with several partners including TVS Architects to make the center safer, leaner, and greener. This work immediately resulted in certification from APEX-ASTM for sustainable conferences, and more recently, it received LEED certification for existing buildings. The revitalization of this landmark facility honors its legacy and ensures its longevity. With additional improvements underway, this venue is a significant fixture in the City of Detroit's resurgence.

DETROIT RIVERFRONT

Years of neglect left the Detroit riverfront a barren landscape littered with industry, derelict land, and parking lots. Access to the water's edge from the core of the city was limited, and in many cases restricted by private land. Through a multi-phased approach over the last 24 years, Kahn reinvigorated the desolate and sporadic sites, replacing them with an accessible riverfront promenade dotted with larger plazas and park spaces. Designed for waterway and pedestrian use, ships and vessels touring Detroit now can dock and disembark in a safe and vibrant area along the river.

Starting at the Civic Center, a 3,000-foot serpentine wall winds along the promenade, creating seating both on top and built into its length. An alternating rhythm of grassy mounds offers elevated river views while buffering the promenade from heavier traffic commotion nearby. River birch trees and white pine trees frame the riverwalk, providing year-round color and texture while restoring the landscape with native plantings. Large public artworks, such as the Underground Railroad sculpture by Ed Dwight, are also seamlessly woven into the design, telling the rich history of the city. Lighting animates the pedestrian experience, creating a safe environment at night and highlighting the unique design elements. This first section of the riverfront rehabilitation was unveiled during the Detroit 300 celebration, commemorating the city's 300th birthday. As a way to involve the community, part of the design included an opportunity for the community to inscribe their names and messages on bricks and granite pavers inset into the retaining walls.

Next, Kahn designed the General Motors (GM) Riverfront Plaza, which was the first piece of the larger Ambassador Bridge to MacArthur Bridge promenade developed by the Riverfront Conservancy. Littered with unknown fill from the prior industry, the site couldn't initially support a plaza without the threat of structural damage. Kahn engineers designed a solution that called for 12' to 14' of Geofoam blocking used as a foundation below the plaza to support the heaviest manufactured military vehicle produced by GM – just in case they wanted to use the space outside of their headquarters to showcase their latest and greatest automobiles. The top of the plaza incorporates a granite world map, with GM's manufacturing facilities illuminated in the large granite sets. From the top of the plaza, a series of terrace steps led down to the promenade at the water's edge.

From the GM Riverfront Plaza, Kahn addressed additional pockets of the riverfront. Mt. Elliott Park, for instance, was disconnected from the city's core and though it was on the river's edge, it didn't make use of the riverfront. Kahn renovated the park and extended it to the water's edge through walkways and promenades, fishing piers, and interactive gathering spaces, making it a node on the Riverwalk system. A new pavilion was added to create shade without blocking the views of the water, along with a concession stand, changing rooms, and family restrooms. A custom-designed sculpture, the "Great Lakes Beached Schooner," ties in the rich shipbuilding history along the Detroit River and creates an interactive water display and high-energy splashpad for families (next page). Within the open green space hardy native plants are incorporated, and stormwater is harvested and recycled for irrigation. Together, these elements create a universally accessible park, and a unique sense of place.

Additional Kahn-designed sites include the Aretha Franklin Amphitheater Plaza Restoration, Watermark Park, Atwater Marina Extension, Gabriel Richard Park Green Parking Field, and the Uniroyal Promenade. Each phase also required close collaboration with government officials, private clients, conservancy groups, municipal review agencies, and private and public funding associations. The team navigated the unique challenges of land ownership, access, and public involvement, varying site conditions related to the hydrology of the Detroit River, and the history of civic storm drainage outfalls littered across the historic industrialized waterfront of Detroit. Stretching for miles along the Detroit River, the entire riverfront rehabilitation project creates a pedestrian-friendly destination within the Motor City.

GRAND CIRCUS PARK

Serving as both gathering spaces and anchors to the structures surrounding them, parks within a city's bounds are integral threads woven into the fabric of the community. Located in the center of Detroit's downtown, Grand Circus Park had at one time very little foot traffic and fell into decay. A restoration completed in 1998, added vital spaces for public use and restored the beauty and vibrancy to the area that serves as a front door to the downtown district.

New circulation patterns to facilitate access across the park as well as to the city parking structure below were designed. The plazas were enhanced with planters, retaining walls that doubled as seating, and turn-of-the-century style street and pedestrian lights. A variety of annuals, perennials, and ornamental grasses provide various colors and texture within the formal landscape. The park's mass plantings and radial paving patterns blend nicely under the site's mature canopy trees. This space serves as an outdoor venue for events sponsored by the city, Detroit Opera House and other nearby theaters in the area.

Two historic fountains were restored and highlighted with decorative paving and extensive landscaping. To the east is the Russell A. Alger Memorial Fountain in honor of the former Michigan governor, U.S. Senator, and Civil War Veteran. Designed by Henry Bacon and Daniel Chester French, the fountain features a 7-foot tall bronze woman carrying a sword and shield with the Michigan State Seal, often thought to be Michigan personified. To the west is the Edison Fountain, which was erected by the city in honor of the 50th anniversary of Thomas Edison's incandescent lamp. Simple in its design, the hexagon fountain features very little ornament, aside from a row of delicately carved pigeons which seem to support the top basin of the fountain. The relocated William Cotter Maybury and Hazen S. Pingree monuments were placed at the northeast and northwest corners of the park and are positioned as the gateway, greeting visitors as they travel along the Woodward promenade.

Parks like Grand Circus provide the necessary greenway within a city environment and serve as landmarks which welcome city goers to new districts within the city. "Our goal was to make the park a bold, dramatic entryway to both the downtown and theatre district," explained Ernest W. Burkeen Jr., then Director of the Recreation Department for the City of Detroit. "The historical features have been melded with new, user-friendly conveniences to make this urban park worth revisiting."[159] The once neglected jewel is again a compelling and engaging public space.

GRACE HOSPITAL FOR THE PATIENT OF MODERATE MEANS

DETROIT, MICHIGAN | DESIGNED 1929 OPENED 1932

On December 11, 1930, the cornerstone was laid for the newest building for Grace Hospital, once on the campus of the Detroit Medical Center. Grace Hospital first opened its doors to patients in 1888 as a nonprofit public hospital. The Nurses Home for Grace Hospital, completed in 1898, was Nettleton and Kahn's first project for the hospital. As the hospital continued to grow, it eventually merged with Harper Hospital and became part of the Detroit Medical Center. Albert Kahn Associates went on to perform numerous renovations and designed new facilities over the years.

Following a speech at the cornerstone ceremony by Frank Murphy, the Mayor of Detroit, Albert gave a few remarks: "No problem is of greater interest to the architect than the planning of a structure which has for its function the welfare of the community and alleviation of suffering. The building for which we are laying the cornerstone today deserved particular consideration and study, since it is to afford the full benefits of this great institution for healing to many at lowest possible cost – a cost much less than has heretofore been made available. Such problems are to our especial liking and with the close collaboration of, and attention paid to all details by Dr. Babcock, the eminent superintendent, we may confidently hope that the completed structure will prove thoroughly successful in meeting this much needed service.

The work being carried on here is the result of civic pride and interest. I am sure that all who contributed to this worthy cause must feel much satisfaction in seeing this building take form and even greater pleasure in contemplating the benefit that must result from the work carried on in the completed structure. May I extend to Grace Hospital my congratulations on this occasion and express the hope that when the keys are turned over and the building is ready for operation, our part in the undertaking may merit the fullest approval of the Board of Trustees, the superintendent, the medical staff and the nurses, and that they may find keen satisfaction in carrying on their helpful, beneficent work."[160]

According to the annual report by Grace Hospital, a number of items were hidden inside the cornerstone: "Copy of current newspapers, annual report of the hospital for 1929, booklet of the Training School for Nurses, 1930, hospital information pamphlet 1930, map of the City of Detroit, list of donors of memorials, and program of cornerstone laying. Lists of the members of the Board of Trustees, Board of Lady Managers, graduates of the Training School, and officers of the hospital. Particulars in reference to the campaign for funds that provided the building, with lists of chairmen, leaders and team workers, and a statement giving aims of project, cost of building, cost of services, and other particulars in reference to the provisions made for the patient of moderate means."[161] The budget for the building, furniture, and equipment was $850,000; the final costs came in almost $100,000 less.[162] Though much of the original Grace Hospital has been demolished, the 1898 Nettleton and Kahn Nurses Home still remains.

GRACE HOSPITAL
Albert Kahn Inc. Architect
The Otto Misch Co.
General Builders
No. 11   Oct. 2,1931

GRACE HOSPITAL
addition
Albert Kahn Inc.
Architects
The Otto Misch Co.
General Builders
No. 2   Oct. 24 30

HENRY FORD HOSPITAL PARKING STRUCTURE

DETROIT, MICHIGAN | DESIGNED 1958 OPENED 1959

Nowhere is it more apparent that utilitarian objects are an opportunity for beauty and elegance than in the case of the parking garage for Henry Ford Hospital. Using individual precast concrete panels, the exterior of the structure seems to wave as the light shifts or viewers walk by. From top to bottom, each articulated panel is aligned to form a helix shape, mimicking a strand of DNA. This was a profound departure from open deck parking structures common at the time.

Built of reinforced concrete, the structure contains approximately "1,716 hyperbolic paraboloid panels, precast from white cement, white quartz and sand aggregates."[163] The base of the garage is clad with red brick, linking the structure to the surrounding buildings on the hospital's campus. The original plans called for landscaping around the base of the structure so that it would blend with the landscaped grounds of the hospital complex.

As the hospital continued to expand, additional services such as parking were needed to support the facility. Originally, the parking structure was five stories, providing over 850 parking spots. A second structure, mirroring this design, was added at a later date. In addition to providing an interesting visual element, the precast panels also shield the view of hundreds of cars from those living, working, and playing in the surrounding neighborhood.

The parking structure won an Excellence in Design award from the Detroit chapter of the American Institute of Architects, and international recognition, "cited by the Institute of Civil Engineers of England as 'a parking structure of world-wide significance.'"[164]

S.S. KRESGE ADMINISTRATION BUILDING

DETROIT, MICHIGAN | DESIGNED 1929 OPENED 1930

"The new S. S. Kresge Administration Building is another example of the interest now taken by important corporations in housing their activities not only in a structure serving all practical needs, but one that does credit architecturally to the city. The simplest sort of building without artistic merit whatever might have served their purpose, but it is to the credit of the executives of the firm that they valued external as well as internal appearance, realizing that such not only enhanced their own investment, but that it must have a salutary effect on its employees and add prestige to its already well established reputation. Furthermore, with its large experience in building, having erected hundreds of branches throughout the country, the S. S. Kresge Co. was well aware of the fact that a well designed building need after all cost but little more than one in which design is ignored.

The exterior treatment is a straight-forward and direct one – expressive of the interior arrangement. Fluted pilasters separate the many windows and extend to the fourth floor which forms a sort of attic story, the latter crowned by a copper roof. The center pavilion is accentuated by a strong pier treatment, and its roof is carried considerably higher than the wings. Ornament is but sparingly used. The main door is of the same polished granite as the base, and a broad flight of steps leads up to the same. The entrance doorway and vestibule are of ornamental bronze. The exterior is perhaps best named of modern American type modeled somewhat upon German precedent, similar in character to that of the Fisher Building done by the same architects." [165]

S. S. Kresge, Co. opened its first five-and-dime store in 1898 and grew to become a major national retailer. Founded by Sebastian S. Kresge, Kresge contracted Albert Kahn to design his first corporate headquarters downtown in 1914 at what is now known as the Kales Building. [166] As the company grew, Kahn was again called upon to design a new headquarters, which became the face of a new corporate identity. This article from the firm in 1930 highlights the prominent role architecture played in the lives of employees and cities. Today, this building is included on the National Register of Historic Places and remains integral to the fabric of Detroit. This building is one of many that Kahn designed downtown, which dramatically shaped the growth and life of the city.

TEMPLE BETH EL

Albert Kahn was the son of German immigrants – an itinerant rabbi and a teacher. He is well-known in Detroit as the architect of several synagogue buildings – two for Temple Beth El, to which his family belonged, and one for Shaarey Zedek Synagogue. The synagogues are symbolic of Albert's art and his devotion to his religion; "he was proud to see Judaism as a mainstay of civic virtue and cultural enlightenment."[167]

Albert, newly heading his firm, was commissioned in 1902 to build Temple Beth El on Woodward Avenue, which was renovated and is used today as Wayne State University's Bonstelle Theater. At that time, American temple and synagogue architecture had few precedents on which to base a style. Albert chose as his model his favorite classical building, the Pantheon in Rome, a photo of which hung over his desk. At the age of 22, he won a $500 travel scholarship to study in Europe. It was during this period that Albert developed his love of Palladio and a wide range of architectural styles, which inspired many of his designs, including Temple Beth El. He modified his version to fit the lot size, featuring a shallow porch with only two columns in front. Behind a rectangular foyer was the main, round structure – similar to the Pantheon – that housed the congregation, the bimah or platform from which the Torah is read, and the ark that holds the sacred Torahs. One of the firm's first uses of reinforced concrete, the dome was supported by reinforced concrete trusses. The Pantheon has an oculus in its roof at the height of the dome to illuminate the space, but, in Detroit, they roofed over the entire dome.

By 1920, the congregation had outgrown its original home. Just as obvious is the Classical influence in the Temple Beth El constructed in 1922 further north on Woodward at Gladstone, currently in use as the Bethel Community Transformation Center. Once again, Albert was influenced by Roman architecture. Here the colonnade of eight impressive fluted columns topped by Ionic capitals line the edge of a shallow porch before the Roman triple entrance. Interestingly, in 1904, as a sign of its progressiveness, Temple Beth El abandoned the practice of selling and assigning seats for the high holidays, in favor of the more egalitarian free seating.

In 1927, Albert was also commissioned to design the Shaarey Zedek Synagogue at Lawton and Chicago Boulevard. For this structure, Albert designed a building in elegant buff brick accented by white stone arches. The interior space was divided by majestic marble columns into a broad 2,500-seat central hall and narrow side aisles. The large space on the first floor was designed to accommodate both men and women, following a change in 1931 that allowed mixed seating in a Conservative synagogue.[168] The completed building was dedicated in 1932. Shaarey Zedek was sold to a church when the congregation moved to suburban Southfield in 1962. The dramatic modernist synagogue was designed by Percival Goodman with Albert Kahn Associates. Goodman was responsible for the design while Albert Kahn Associates completed the working drawings and engineering for the building.

Author: Nancy Finegood, Former Director, Michigan Historic Preservation Network

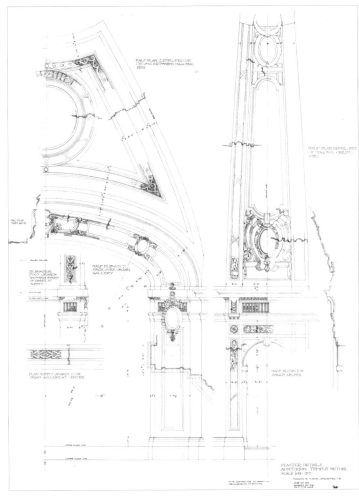

MOISE SAFRA AUDITORIUM

Located near the Hospital Israelita Albert Einstein, this modern auditorium is one piece of a broader hospital campus that commemorates the Jewish community's contributions to Brazil. The facade incorporates glass and terracotta colored aluminum, linking this building with the other new buildings on campus. Seated on an asymmetrical hill, the auditorium emerges as a uniquely canted, angled form, protruding from the existing hospital campus, and creating a dramatic focal point for visitors entering the campus. While this structure is distinctive in form, its design vocabulary is derived from adjacent buildings to ensure a cohesive campus.

Jewish symbolism is found throughout the design of the auditorium, in particular, in its orientation and reference to the architecture of synagogues. The dramatic use of natural light through irregular geometries inside the auditorium creates a contemplative and welcoming environment, similar to the use of light in synagogues. However, design elements were not conceived independently from the building's function. These windows can be closed completely for more controlled lighting when needed, and acoustic quality and external noise isolation determined the specific design density and angle of the wooden panels cladding the interior space.

This state-of-the-art auditorium and conference center is designed to accommodate a variety of events such as concerts, religious ceremonies, and presentations on cutting edge medical technologies and research across the international medical community. The auditorium has become a new focal point for the medical campus and surrounding area.

ASSARIAN CANCER CENTER

When diagnosed with cancer, patients experience an emotional upheaval. The contemporary design of this building possesses symbols that express this change, becoming a refuge for a patient's mind, body and spirit during their physical and emotional journey. This symbolism is expressed in the center's glass-enclosed, two-story atrium. Appearing as if it were sliced from the building and slightly rotated, this architectural shift exemplifies how a patient's undisturbed course in life is suddenly jolted askew after diagnosis with a life-threatening disease.

Enveloped in glass, the two-story reflection space is filled with natural light to emphasize the open area, while patients overlook a nearby pond. Color, fabric, and natural light play important roles in helping to reduce stress and inspire courage and hope. Patients and visitors are surrounded by dramatic stone sculptures, fountains, glass mosaics, metal works of art and vegetation, all working together to elicit a safe and tranquil meditation space. Concentric ripples created by a drop of water in a pond are also mimicked throughout the physical design of the center sections of the building. The main lobby, adjacent to the reflection space, has a circular floor plan and is designed with custom finishes that incorporate the concentric pattern. Dolomite stone sculptures of varying sizes, along with the dolomite stone floor, are the primary materials at floor level and serve as the inspiration for the entire color palette.

Flanked on either side of the reflection space are unique areas that support the center's holistic cancer therapy program, using a left and right brain approach. One side showcases an art therapy room and art gallery displaying the emotional artwork created by cancer patients, while the other side contains a science center featuring interactive displays and a resource center that offers treatment and care information to patients and families. These programs, in conjunction with the center's design, create a beautiful, peaceful, and reflective space for patients and their families to heal.

RACHEL UPJOHN CENTER

Depression and bipolar disorder are brain diseases that affect millions, interfering with an individual's ability to work, learn, and enjoy life. Untreated, these diseases can be fatal. In 2001, this Depression Center based at the University of Michigan, emerged due to a profound need and opportunity to unify research, patient care, education, and public policy to win the battle against depression and bipolar disorder. In 2006, the treatment center opened to detect depression and bipolar disorders earlier, treat them more effectively, and prevent recurrences and progression. The center is committed to educating and empowering patients and families afflicted by these disorders, and to diminish the stigma of depression.

As the first comprehensive depression program in the country, the center brings together researchers and clinicians from 21 different disciplines, including psychiatry, psychology, nursing, and genetics. Located on a tranquil meadow on the health system's east medical campus, this facility was designed to be the antithesis of depression. Embracing the healing power of natural light from every angle, the building uses expansive sections of glass on the exterior and a skylight-topped two-story atrium in the center. The lower level opens to surrounding woodlands and wetlands, where 1,054 trees were preserved during construction and 180 new trees were planted. This lowest level houses neuropsychoanalysis and cognitive neuroscience labs, as well as meeting rooms and ancillary support spaces. This floor also includes a high-tech 120-seat auditorium which allows researchers, clinicians, and the community to gather and broadcast new information to fight depression.

The first floor houses separate clinical areas for children, adolescents, adults, and substance-abuse patients, offering individual offices and outpatient treatment rooms where psychiatrists, psychologists, social workers, and primary care clinicians can meet with patients and families. This floor also houses a patient and visitor education and resource center, as well as two telemedicine rooms where patients can receive long-distance care.

The second floor is devoted entirely to research on depression, bipolar disorder, substance abuse, and other cognitive disorders. For the first time, researchers specializing in a broad variety of mental health and addiction specialties are all co-located in one building, creating an unprecedented synergy. Special features include a sleep-research center where clinical trial volunteers can spend the night while their sleep is monitored; an MRI simulator to help patients and research volunteers become accustomed to the experience of having an MRI scan; and observation rooms that allow researchers to witness depression's impact on families. This unique approach of locating research modules in close proximity to clinical treatment areas makes this center a truly integrated facility and a future model for the research and treatment of cognitive disorders.

ALBERT KAHN HOUSE

As we look at the impact Albert Kahn and his firm, Albert Kahn Associates, have made over the last 125 years, we are humbled to be standing in his shadow. It is with a grateful heart we highlight a special project, Albert Kahn's home. There is no better reflection of who a person is than by looking at their most personal surroundings – their home. Albert designed his home in 1906 when he was 37 years old; by this time, he had made quite a name for himself and was able to build his own home in the north end of the Brush Park district. Designed in the English Renaissance Style with brick, stone, and stucco, the house provided a stately but modest example of English architecture. Albert's fondness of the Arts and Crafts movement heavily influenced the home and furnishings, which he also designed himself. He lived in this home with his wife, Ernestine, and their four children, the oldest being only ten when they moved in. This five-bedroom home is two stories with third-floor dormers. Minor modifications were made in 1921, and a wing was added in 1928 in the Tudor style to house a gallery for their collection of Impressionist paintings, an additional bedroom, garage, den, and two bathrooms.

Two years after Albert's death, Ernestine sold the home to the Urban League of Detroit, where they have resided for over 75 years. Over that time, Albert's home has taken on another significant role in the city of Detroit, as a beacon of help and hope to the African American community. The Urban League has protected the home from the blight of many other Brush Park mansions. In 1971, the house was designated a Michigan State Historic Site; and the next year it was listed on the National Register of Historic Places.

Constructed of the best workmanship in the period, the home is very much as Albert's family left it. As the home approaches 115 years old, work needs to be done to continue to maintain and restore the home. Albert Kahn Associates is assisting the Urban League with managing the design and leading renovations to return the splendor of this significant structure. In honor of 125 years since Albert started his firm, the firm gave the gift of new landscape design around the Albert Kahn home. We chose to revive the landscape because it was one of Albert's passions. He often said that "the garden is more important than the house to me." We hope that this gift is one the entire community can enjoy. As we look forward to restoring this historic landmark, we are honored to know that it will continue to be a source of inspiration for the African American community, the city of Detroit, and the architecture and engineering community.

Author: Heidi Pfannes, Director of Business Development, Albert Kahn Associates

ALVAN MACAULEY HOUSE

735 Lake Shore was completed in 1930 for Alvan Macauley. The grand Tudor estate was one of the architectural masterpieces constructed on the shores of Lake St. Clair during the golden era of stately mansions. The Macauley residence was located on 52 acres stretching from Lake Shore to Lochmoor Country Club. At the time, it was arguably one of the largest lots found in the Grosse Pointe communities.

The mansion was similar in both construction and appearance to the Edsel and Eleanor Ford Estate, which Kahn had completed a year earlier in 1929. Prior to commissioning their new residence, the Macauley's had spent several weeks in Worcestershire, England, studying the local architecture, along with purchasing some fine English Antiques.

Meticulous attention to detail was paid to the construction of the house, which was completed under the careful supervision of a foreman from the Cotswold region of England. The exterior of the home was stone, the roof slate, and it is believed the walls were 17" thick. The interior was exquisite and filled with an abundance of wood, including intricate carvings by the Hayden Company of New York – the paneling in the grand 45' x 25' living room, which occupied an entire wing, featured a medieval linen fold motif. The second floor had five large bedrooms, four smaller bedrooms for staff, along with a 25' x 18' sitting room. In addition to the main residence, additional servants' quarters were located in the two apartments above the five-car garage.[169]

In keeping with the other grand mansions in the community, the garden received a lot of attention. Macauley hired Edward A. Eichstaedt, a landscape architect for Cranbrook Educational Community, to create a broad sweeping naturalistic landscape to reflect the characteristics of the home.

Alvan Macauley was a prominent figure in Detroit. Having grown up in Washington D.C., he graduated with a degree in engineering from Lehigh University in Pennsylvania and then earned a law degree at Columbian College (now known as George Washington University) in Washington, D.C. After moving to Detroit in 1905, he was hired by Henry Bourne Joy in 1910 as the general manager of Packard, becoming president of the company in 1916. Macauley was in charge of Packard during its golden era when the company was the leader of the luxury car market. In 1939, Macauley resigned from his position as president. However, he remained chairman of the board until 1948.

In 1952, Alvan Macauley passed. That same year his wife, Estelle, and their three children sold 735 Lake Shore. It was listed for $225,000 (around $2.1 million today), and was purchased by Alfred R. Glancy, a real estate financier and former co-owner of the Empire State Building. The Glancy's resided in the home for twenty-one years with their six children. Mr. Glancy passed in 1973; his wife, Betty, subsequently sold the property and what was left of the estate – believed to be only a third in size of what Mr. Glancy had originally purchased in 1952. The house was razed in 1973.

Author: Katie Doelle, Author of *Grand Estates of Grosse Pointe*

EDSEL AND ELEANOR FORD ESTATE

In 1926, Albert Kahn began designing the home while Jens Jensen began crafting the grounds for Edsel and Eleanor Ford's new Estate. Kahn and Jensen worked together to create a cohesive plan for the Estate. A Cotswold village inspired the design of the home, and with 60 rooms, this sprawling mansion certainly resembled a cluster of village cottages complete with lead-paned windows and a slate roof.

Inside, rich wood paneling and carved details coupled with imported fireplaces, stained-glass, and a staircase pull together the Cotswold inspiration, albeit on a much grander scale. Here, Kahn combined the couple's design taste with the latest engineering advances. Reinforced concrete for the floors and steel roof trusses were used, while the building was faced with traditional stone brought over with a team of English craftsmen.[170] In 1929, the family moved into the home, where they remained until Eleanor's death in 1976. Today, both the Kahn-designed home and the Jensen-designed grounds are a National Historic Landmark.

Over more than 90 years, the firm has completed numerous projects within the home and on the grounds of the Estate. Most recently, the team restored the swimming pool, lagoon, and surrounding landscape – an area that was treasured by generations of the Ford family. Designed as a natural swimming hole typically found in northern Michigan, the landscape created an intimate feature through its shape, topography, and overall layout. Jensen's design philosophy incorporated native plant material to provide a strong natural aesthetic and require less maintenance. Since the pool was first used, it has undergone several renovations to keep it safe and structurally sound. The lagoon and plantings have also changed significantly over time.

Kahn led the initiative to restore the spirit of Jensen's original design. The team worked with the Estate and other professionals to remove invasive species, preserve and enhance the nearby meadow, create a new pool pump house, reconstruct the limestone pool decking, improve the lagoon shoreline, and open views to visually and physically reconnect this area to the main house. The Estate once again embodies the concept Albert Kahn and Jens Jensen envisioned.

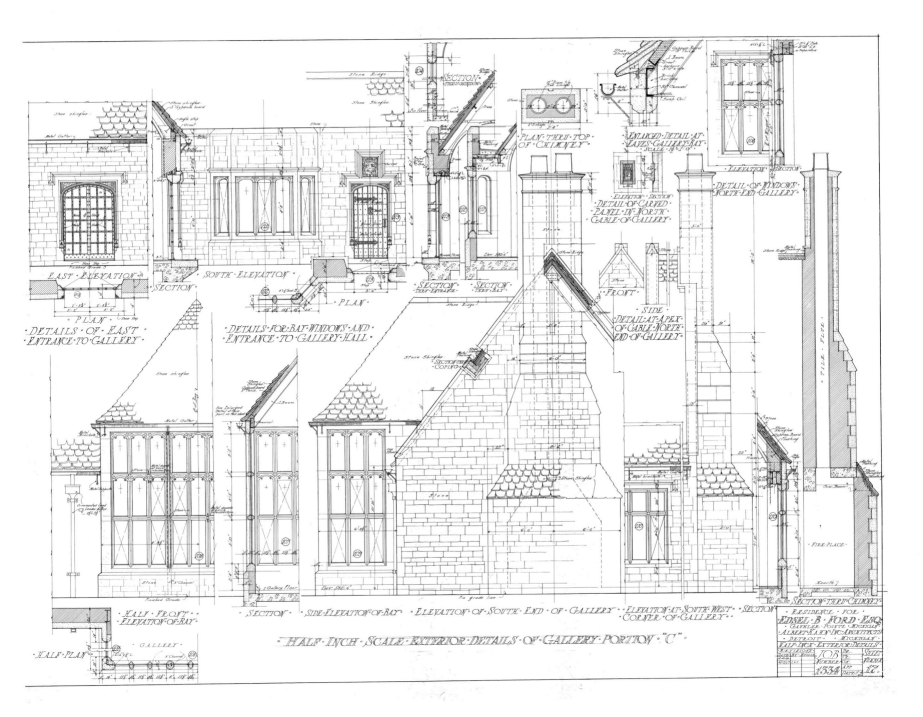

· EAST · ELEVATION · · SECTION ·

· SOUTH · ELEVATION ·

· SECTION ·

· PLAN ·

· DETAILS · OF · EAST · ENTRANCE · TO · GALLERY ·

· DETAILS · FOR · BAY · WINDOWS · AND · ENTRANCE · TO · GALLERY · HALL ·

· SECTION · THRU · WINDOW ·

· PLAN · THRU · TOP · OF · CHIMNEY ·

· ENLARGED · DETAIL · AT · EAVES · GALLERY · BAY ·

· DETAIL · OF · CARVED · PANEL · IN · NORTH · GABLE · OF · GALLERY ·

· DETAIL · OF · WINDOWS · NORTH · END · GALLERY ·

· SECTION · THRU · COPING ·

· SIDE · DETAIL · AT · APEX · OF · GABLE · NORTH · END · OF · GALLERY ·

· HALF · FRONT · ELEVATION · OF · BAY ·

· HALF · PLAN ·

· GALLERY ·

· SECTION ·

· SIDE · ELEVATION · OF · BAY ·

· ELEVATION · OF · SOUTH · END · OF · GALLERY ·

· ELEVATION · AT · SOUTH · WEST · CORNER · OF · GALLERY ·

· SECTION ·

· SECTION · THRU · CHIMNEY ·

· RESIDENCE · FOR ·
· EDSEL · B · FORD · ESQ ·
· GROSSE · POINTE · MICHIGAN ·
· ALBERT · KAHN · INC · ARCHITECTS ·
· DETROIT · MICHIGAN ·
· HALF · INCH · EXTERIOR · DETAILS ·

· HALF · INCH · SCALE · EXTERIOR · DETAILS · OF · GALLERY · PORTION · "C" ·

JOB NUMBER 1534

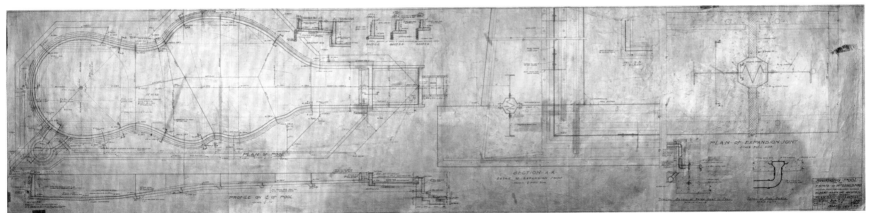

· PLAN · OF · POOL ·

· PROFILE · ON · Ç · OF · POOL ·

· SECTION · A · A ·

· PLAN · OF · EXPANSION · JOINT ·

DETROIT GOLF CLUB

DETROIT MICHIGAN | DESIGNED 1916 RENOVATED 2020

In the design of the Detroit Golf Club, Albert Kahn incorporated the aesthetic of the Arts and Crafts movement, relying more on features that evoke the natural environment than on applied ornamentation. Two striking features, which judging by his remarks were important to Albert, were the layering multi-level roof masses and the emphasis on light-filled interiors through large banks of windows. This use of light is often highlighted by Albert in his residential, commercial, and industrial buildings. Here he designed what he refers to as "a rambling structure centered around a court, or patio, giving real sunlight to the innermost parts of the building."[171] The clubhouse is oriented on the site to capture the majority of the sun as it moves around the sky throughout the day.

Founded in 1899, the Detroit Golf Club is in the north end of Detroit on what was once a large parcel of farmland. Albert Kahn was brought on to design the Club's second clubhouse, which still remains today. Donald Ross, a world-renowned course designer from Dornoch, Scotland, designed two 18-hole courses on the site.[172] Speaking of the exterior of the building, Albert noted the use of warm, red-toned shingles for the roof and bricks which were laid in an "English bond with joints of the natural color of the mortar." The vast number of windows feature white trim and mullions that add depth to the structure and contrast from the surrounding earth tones.

There are two main wings of the clubhouse. The south wing of the building contains guest quarters on the first and second floors, while the north wing contains the kitchen; and an area that was once called the servants' quarters and chauffeurs' rooms. Spaces that members use the most, for example the living room, lounge, and porch, overlook the expanse of the golf course.

The interior of the clubhouse has been renovated over the years including a recent renovation by Albert Kahn Associates. Part of this renovation included the library in which the beautiful wood paneling, ceilings, and furnishings were restored and upgraded. The firm also created a master renewal plan starting in 2015, and designed new course facilities for the Rocket Mortgage Classic PGA Golf Tour. Today, the original charm and character first designed by Albert Kahn can still be found.

CHELSEA COMMUNITY HOSPITAL

CHELSEA, MICHIGAN | DESIGNED 2010 OPENED 2012

Modern hospitals have been finding ways to bring the healing properties of nature into their design. One key aspect in the design of the new wing of Chelsea Community Hospital was the preservation of the surrounding natural site and the relationship of the building to the site. Trees, vegetation, fresh air, and sunlight are known for their physiological and psychological healing potential. Embracing the surrounding wooded features of the campus and integrating tranquil courtyards throughout, the facility gives patients an enhanced healing environment and re-energizes hospital staff with views and access to nature.

The care of the park-like campus, with its trees, wildlife, and wetlands, required extraordinary respect and attention to conserving the natural beauty while updating the fully operational hospital. One of the largest challenges of this project was the existing conditions, including the soil conditions, drainage limitations, and circulation patterns of the existing facility. The team considered each tree on the site and carefully selected those that would be removed for the new construction. Many of the mature trees on the hospital grounds had never had broad exposure and needed to be left in larger groupings for their long-term well-being, which affected the number of trees that were eventually removed. Care was also taken to provide a regenerative environment, by allowing the plant material that needed to be removed for construction to easily replenish itself over time. Therefore, large areas of pavement were avoided in favor of planting areas in-between rows of parking.

The building was woven within the constraints of the existing woodland and topography of the site. Long expanses of repetitive facades and right angle geometry were avoided in favor of following the natural movement and flow of the surrounding topography. Outdoor spaces, including the courtyard and the exterior stairs leading down to the administration suite, received as much attention as the building design. These spaces were envisioned as outdoor rooms. Building materials reference Chelsea's historic character and the existing buildings on campus, while the use of metal and glass suggest continued adaptation of future technologies. Nature was also brought inside the building with bold color and daylight. Additionally working with nature reduced the building's operational costs. Trees shaded the building in the summertime and their leafed profile encouraged breezes at the ground plane which helped to reduce cooling costs. During the wintertime, after the leaves had fallen, sunlight exposure helped to heat the building. In 2014, Kahn completed a new Cancer Center that seamlessly blended into the original building and site, offering patients and their families a tranquil healing environment.

VICKY AND JOSEPH SAFRA PAVILION

SÃO PAULO, BRAZIL | DESIGNED 2003 OPENED 2010

As patients and visitors drive around a glass cylinder and approach the pavilion, a wonderful view of the city reveals itself over the outdoor plaza. Far overhead, patients and their families can relax among rooftop gardens overlooking the city. City buses and cars enter the building, dropping off passengers before parking in the garage below. This ease of access was a necessity in a crowded city like São Paulo, and helps to minimize anxiety typically felt when entering a hospital.

The Vicky and Joseph Safra Pavilion at the Hospital Israelita Albert Einstein was the first Brazilian healthcare building to reach LEED Gold, a prestigious standard of sustainable design, construction, and operation, making it the largest healthcare facility in the world to achieve Gold certification. LEED principles, a product of the Green Building movement, allow owners, architects, engineers, and contractors to visualize a broad scope of goals through the building process, addressing global warming, dependence on nonrenewable sources of energy, and threats to human health.

These sustainable programs are challenging to implement in the hospital environment given the highly technical environment, strict safety standards, and higher demand for water and energy. Key design considerations included designing electrical and mechanical systems that lower operating costs and reduce the load on local networks, systems to conserve energy and water and reduce impact on city's stormwater drainage, reduce harmful greenhouse gas emissions, reduce waste sent to landfills, and create indoor and outdoor environments that are healthier and safer for occupants. Rainscreen clay tiles, terracotta baguette brises, and sophisticated irrigation system were some of the sustainable materials and systems incorporated. A green roof was also created, which reduces the heat island effect that would otherwise be generated and provides a unique amenity for building users.

Although outpatient facilities were relatively rare in Brazil, the hospital sought to create an independent patient-centered space to deliver specific aspects of patient care. The building has more than 200 medical offices, a complete diagnostic center, a surgery center of high technology services, and endoscopy and ophthalmology centers. On the first floor, patients and visitors are greeted by a café, indoor lounge, activity rooms, and retail shops. The design of the 16-story, 750,000 sq. ft. structure, needed to harmonize with the mixture of surrounding campus buildings, blending traditional to modern motifs. From the medical offices on the upper floors, the shape steps down to broad floor plates at the lower levels, in deference to smaller building volumes in the neighboring blocks. This enabled the large outpatient center to achieve a more human scale.

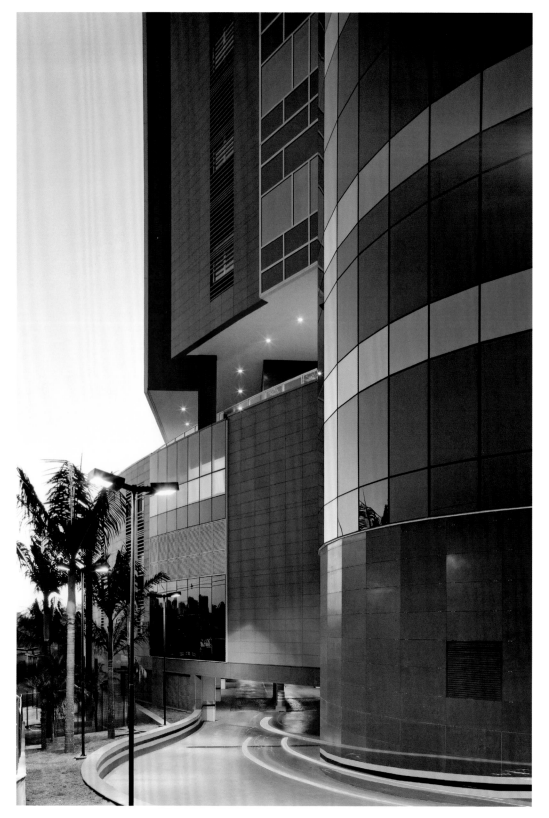

BERKSHIRE eSUPPLY

Architecture seeks a balance between built and natural environments. An early phase in most projects includes site selection and a masterplan. The team of architects, engineers, and project managers evaluate several sites for clients and make recommendations before purchase. This research analyzes each site beyond just size and location and looks at the surrounding population or potential workforce, support industries, utility infrastructure, access to roads and rail lines, and water access. This broader picture of a site considers how materials and parts, in the case of industrial facilities for example, can be delivered to the site and how the finished product will leave the site. Looking closer at the site's topography, the team will evaluate the way stormwater gathers on or leaves a site, to minimize unnecessary site development such as extensive networks of underground pipes or basins.

For Berkshire eSupply, the masterplan was pivotal in choosing the site and shaping the design of the campus, which in turn influenced the design of the buildings. Seated within a natural wetland and surrounded by dense trees, the idyllic 57-acre campus features both a headquarters building and an order distribution center in one location. With this new campus, Berkshire eSupply relocated its headquarters from Warren to Novi, Michigan, closer to the active research and product development campuses. Located near prominent highways, the site is accessible for transit of materials and products, and is near a potential skilled workforce. While access to utilities is present, a high voltage electrical transmission corridor runs through the site, putting restrictions on where the buildings could sit. Additionally, wetlands cover 12 acres of the campus. The team worked with state environmental agencies to measure and tag the area to maintain the natural wetland.

The resolution was to move the headquarters building to the edge of the property line, which also made it visible from nearby roads. A variety of materials were used on the exterior of the buildings to visually break up the structures and not overwhelm the site. Sheathed in glass and Jerusalem limestone, the façade allows employees to enjoy the scenic views of the trees and wetlands from every seat within the headquarters. A long serpentine retaining wall along the edge of the buildings manages the steep grade change near the watershed, which can be heard and seen from the windows of the offices above. Walking through an enclosed glass bridge, employees can go from the headquarters to the fulfillment center behind. Nearby, a retention pond was also created to allow the water to drain from the parking lot. Through a comprehensive masterplan, these designed and natural features work together to create a beautiful environment for employees to enjoy, while enhancing Berkshire eSupply's potential growth and inspiring a new corporate identity.

POLK PENGUIN CONSERVATION CENTER

ROYAL OAK, MICHIGAN | DESIGNED 2012 OPENED 2016

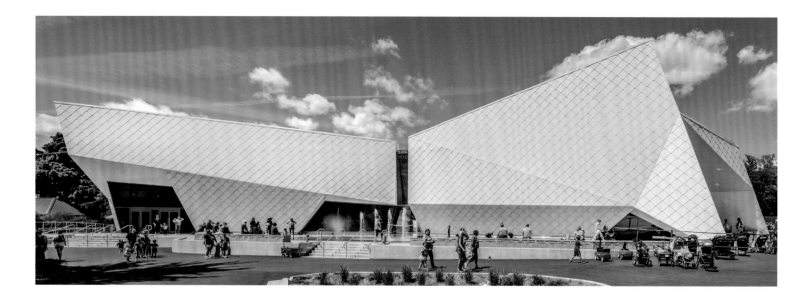

Architecture has long been inspired by the natural world, and with the evolution of manufacturing and building technologies, it can now replicate the natural world. After teams from the Detroit Zoo went to Antarctica to study the species to be housed in the new penguin conservation center, they supplied photographs and data to Kahn to design a new home fit for these incredible creatures.

As visitors approach the building, they are immediately transported to the heart of Antarctica. The irregular shape of the building is a representation of tabular or block-like icebergs near the south pole. Sections of blue glass are recessed into the structure to suggest natural ice caves and ice calving, or ice breaking apart from the glacier. The entry way is through a representation of a 25-foot-tall waterfall in a narrow crevasse made of blue glass. Through biomimicry, or design and production modeled on nature or natural systems, the exterior is clad in over 6,000 white metallic shingles that keeps the building insulated while repelling heat, a similar system found in penguin feathers.

Inside, 75 king, rockhopper, macaroni, and gentoo penguins can be found diving in and swimming through a 25-foot-deep, 326,000-gallon, aquatic area. Visitors can walk through two underwater tunnels as the penguins zoom around them. Above the waterline, penguins have an Antarctic-inspired space to nest and raise their young. The interior space was designed in collaboration with Jones & Jones Architects and Landscape Architects, and a team of museum consultants from interpretive, museum, and aquarium design, to make sure that every material selected would support the penguins' health and wellbeing. Lighting was another specially designed feature to promote the penguins' health, providing a wide spectrum of wavelengths with ultraviolet light and nighttime lighting. These lights can also be adjusted to reflect seasonal changes.

The Detroit Zoo is driven to reduce its ecological impact while educating visitors about the effects of global warming. Throughout the design of the building are references to our changing environment; for example, the "cracks" in the exterior iceberg is a result of warmer temperatures. What visitors might not see, however, are the advanced engineering systems behind the scenes to conserve, filter, and recycle water, maintain clean air and separate temperatures for public and penguin areas. A custom designed blow down system with vacuum air lines was also engineered to clean the habitat, which was inspired by the air systems designed for automotive plants.

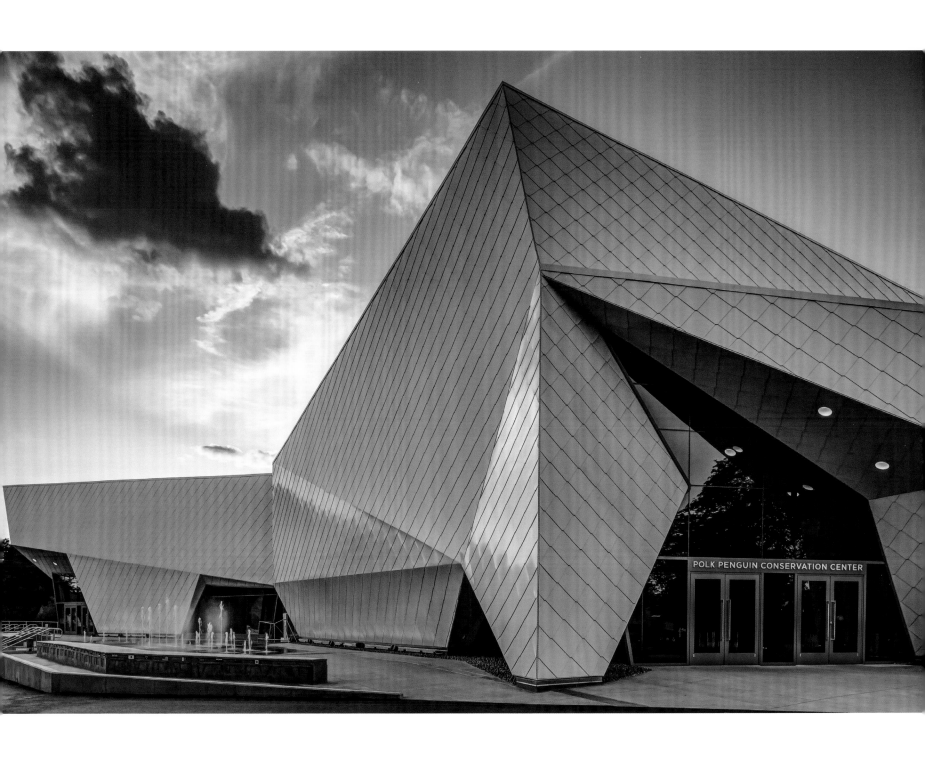

O-I HEADQUARTERS

Color, texture, opacity, and silhouette are integral to the production of glass. Naturally, as the home of a leading producer of glass bottles, the headquarters for O-I, Owens-Illinois Inc., is steeped in the same characteristics. Inspiration for this building came from both the dimension of the products and the character of the organization. O-I envisioned a headquarters that was sleek, contemporary, and, most of all, humble.

The headquarters welcomes employees and visitors to the campus, while in the distance, glass manufacturing facilities can be found. Modest and beautiful materials such as sand, concrete, and glass demonstrate the glass process's evolution with sand and concrete at the base of the building, transforming to glass on the stories above. The body of the design forms a strong silhouette of glass that rises from the surrounding green space on campus. Horizontal layers of subtle blue glass are spanned between metal mullions forming the linear pattern of the building. The entryway is pulled out from the structure with a vertical rectangle forming a frame for a Mondrian-inspired design of mullion and transparent glass.

Inside, materials and finishes feature a warm wood tone for doors and millwork, a neutral carpet for the open office areas, accented with O-I's corporate colors around the building core. Open office space was designed to promote collaboration, which reflected an intentional culture shift promoted by leadership. A free-flowing monumental staircase at the center of the building encourages employees to utilize this design feature instead of the elevator system. Above the staircase, a skylight was incorporated to create a beacon in the center of the building and provide natural light throughout the structure.

Glass is infinitely recyclable, and the O-I glass bottles have been repurposed over and over again. This sustainable concept was translated into the design of the building, which received a LEED Silver certification. Nestled into an existing hill and around a pond, the building was designed to support the surrounding site rather than overpower it. This sense of a humble connection to nature carries through in the creation of cafés located in the main atrium and lobby space on each floor, providing a tranquil environment for break areas. Terraces were also distributed around the building to encourage employees to connect with nature and offer additional opportunities for collaboration.

LTU TAUBMAN COMPLEX

SOUTHFIELD, MICHIGAN | DESIGNED 2012 OPENED 2016

Home to the schools of Engineering and Life Sciences at Lawrence Technological University (LTU), the Taubman Complex plays a central role in shaping the university's identity for advancing research in technology, biology, biomechanics and robotics, and the production of high-tech materials. The building's location reflects the physical and conceptual connection between the Engineering and the Life Science buildings. The facility bridges curricula and responds to the advancements in these fields, where the line between these disciplines is blurring and driving an integrated STEM approach.

LTU is a technologically driven institution whose history is rooted in a hands-on approach to learning and offering opportunities for learning in cutting-edge, high-quality laboratory environments. The new facility is key to the campus masterplan; its location and placement were carefully considered to improve overall campus connectivity. Designed in collaboration with Morphosis Architects, the new Taubman Complex answers the university's need for an extremely flexible, performance-driven facility that physically links formerly separated departments into new interdisciplinary learning environments. Collaborative zones, laboratories, and faculty offices are interwoven throughout the facility, supporting teaching, learning, and sharing within the multidisciplinary approach.

The Taubman Complex is designed as an expandable section with an occupiable bar that can be extended in phases to accommodate growth, while maintaining the function and design integrity of the building. At the intersection of the two wings is a four-story enclosed stairwell that takes the shape of an egg-like "orb," adding an iconic feature to the campus. Constructed out of carbon fiber, this was one of the first applications of this material in the built environment. This stairway was designed as a gathering space, transporting students and staff up through the building to additional collaborative zones.

The building's spine is formed by two floors of laboratories, which look out into an open two-story-tall flexible space that runs the length of the building. This flexible space is the heart of the Taubman Complex, providing an expansive and re-configurable hall for informal discussions, pin-up critique sessions, and lectures. The building becomes the catalyst for students and professionals to create a collaborative social environment that benefits both.

JAMES AND ANNE DUDERSTADT CENTER

ANN ARBOR, MICHIGAN | DESIGNED 1993 OPENED 1996

The University of Michigan's Duderstadt Center, formerly known as the Media Union, is a collaborative research space that bridges disciplines and the digital and active learning environments. Bringing together the resources of the schools of Architecture and Urban Planning, Art, Engineering, and Music, this facility was designed to be a catalyst for innovation across disciplines. It has become a focal point of the North Campus, a commons where students and faculty come together, and the distinction between "researching" and "doing" blur.

At four-stories tall, a pyramidal skylight radiates from the center of the building, enhancing the feeling of openness throughout the core spaces. Walking through the spacious atrium on the first floor, the expanse of glass allows natural light to filter through the building throughout the day. This floor houses a variety of makerspaces, including production spaces, practice rooms, video and music studios, as well as lab spaces for design, fabrication, and virtual reality. These studio and lab spaces are home to many specialized projects and interdisciplinary groups at the university that use technology to create, research, and innovate.

Collaboration and independent study spaces, including a teleconferencing room, are found throughout each of the floors. The second floor houses a significant library offering both electronic and traditional media, and research spaces. The third floor accommodates the integrated library and computer learning centers. Indirect lighting throughout provides a glare-free setting for study. In the basement, extensive collections of books can be found in the library stacks and rare books collection storage. There is even a robust computer and video game archive housed in the basement. Conceived with flexibility in mind, space within the center can easily adapt to the rapid changes in technology and the growing need for collaborative study spaces.

With more than 400 computers, this was the largest computer access point at the University of Michigan. When it was originally designed, the center was a pilot project for the university's library system. It changed how the university, and other universities across the country, viewed the function of a library.

DODGE HALF-TON TRUCK PLANT

WARREN, MICHIGAN | DESIGNED 1937 OPENED 1938

Starting with its earliest designs for factory buildings, the Kahn firm focused first on the function and purpose of the structure they were to design. Industrial facilities needed to house a great variety of machinery and men, with products moving from one end to the other in an efficient and elegantly designed process. The design emerged from this function, using precise measurements to accommodate every requirement within the space.

In the Export Building within the Dodge Half-Ton Truck Plant, Kahn's precise and unadorned form has received acclaim from architectural critics and historians as it exemplifies the twentieth-century technological style. The exterior building envelope consists of precise panels of glass within a grid extending virtually the entire height of the structure, providing unmatched natural light for the workers.

The Architectural Forum covered the export building in August of 1938 noting, "An outstanding feature of the Chrysler plant is the size of the interior bays, which measure 40 x 60 ft. Due to the use of cantilever roof beams no more steel is required than would be ordinarily required for a 30 x 40 ft. bay."[173] This structural configuration also provided an inclined face, with the down-turned portion sheathed in glass to provide more lighting and ventilation. On the inside of the roof, Kahn engineers used a combination of riveting and welding, depending on which was more economical.[174] Lastly, the planning of the site was done so that changes and additions to the plant could be accommodated without disrupting the original scheme of the site.

The building remains in its same use today, 83 years later. After many expansions and modifications designed by the firm, it continues to produce RAM pick-up trucks for Stellantis, formerly Fiat Chrysler Automobiles.

AURORA HEALTH CARE

What began as a humble outpatient diagnostic and treatment center in Kenosha, Wisconsin grew to become the largest health employer in Eastern Wisconsin.[175] Kahn worked with Aurora Health Care and Hammes Company from 1993 to 2013, creating health care facilities that were patient-centered, staff-focused, cost effective and efficient. With 85 facilities designed, the Kahn health care team developed a series of aesthetic elements and building blocks that afforded some of the fastest construction schedules many had ever experienced to date, with a distinctive image consistent with Aurora's patient-centered brand.

The key to this successful program was a collaborative effort to align goals and build trust between the owner, design, program management, and construction teams allowing for creativity, while still providing Aurora with facilities that met their strategic and business objectives.

Aurora Health Care adopted lean methodologies in design and operations long before "Lean Healthcare" was commonplace.[176] Similar to the configuration of a cockpit in an airplane, Aurora's intention was to create sameness in the layout of universal spaces and minimize process and procedural waste to increase staff safety and patient satisfaction. The creation of standards and prototypes was prevalent during the design process; each project utilized the best practices and universal design elements from the previous projects creating not only efficiency in the design process, but efficiency for caregiving as well.

One example of this successful endeavor was BayCare Aurora Medical Center in Green Bay, Wisconsin (right). Utilizing standardized inpatient room design, clinic pods, and typical room configurations, the teams worked collaboratively to make just-in-time decisions, allowing the contractors to continue their work. During this time, Aurora committed to becoming a member of Planetree, an international organization focused on person-centered care.[177] In the end, this facility opened with great fanfare in the community, bringing exemplary patient care and increasing employment to the community. Legend has it that at one point in time, the cafeteria was rated the "best restaurant in Green Bay," with abundant healthy and fresh food options.

Although standardization was pivotal to this program's success, each facility had signature design elements reminiscent of their respective community's character. Two Rivers, Wisconsin, located on the western shore of Lake Michigan, as an example, is a community with deep roots in fishing and boating. One of the most unique features is the nurse's station in the pediatric inpatient unit. Designed with a nautical theme, this station is complete with a boat, lighthouse and flickering lights in the ceiling, invoking the community's heritage.

Aurora Health Care's purpose is to help patients in their communities live well.[178] Integrating a holistic approach to design, demonstrated through aesthetics, operations and integrated functional elements has afforded Kahn the opportunity to be a partner in this journey to put patients first.

Author: Kimberly Montague, AIA, Former Principal, Albert Kahn Associates

ELI LILLY AND COMPANY

Eli Lilly and Company (Lilly), a leading producer of pharmaceutical and health products, selected Kahn to develop a masterplan for its Indianapolis Technology Center. This masterplan anticipated the construction of five million sq. ft. of administrative and engineering offices, employee amenities and common areas, as well as pharmaceutical research and test laboratories, process and production manufacturing, and distribution and warehouse facilities.

The site created interesting challenges for the team. It was a partial greenfield site within a pre-existing industrial park where Lilly's pharmaceutical manufacturing operations were housed. In an effort to reduce precipitation discharge from the site, throughout the parking areas stormwater was captured, stored and polished through rain gardens and bioswales. Introducing sustainable design elements such as native plant materials and prairie grasses, reduced onsite maintenance.

A critical element of design was the experience a visitor, employees, vendors, and consultants, would encounter as they approached the buildings. Kahn created a balance between public access to the building and semi-private access with more security to the manufacturing facilities. A common area in the center of the campus allowed designers to work with a clean geometry, orientation, and configuration of the new buildings, creating a hierarchy of building form.

Kahn was also presented with the challenge of redefining the brand and image of Lilly's Technology Center to accommodate the company's new culture. Kahn's design for the two and three-story administrative engineering office building and training facilities, for instance, promotes collaboration and enhances daily interaction, communication, and cooperation between staff from Lilly's various scientific, engineering, and production groups. The program for this expansive addition included office training and conference facilities, and a new central kitchen and cafeteria. The design solution confirmed that the corporate brand embodied the goals, values, culture, technology, innovation and competitiveness reflected in the building design.

Author: Alan Cobb, FAIA, Chairman & CEO, Albert Kahn Associates

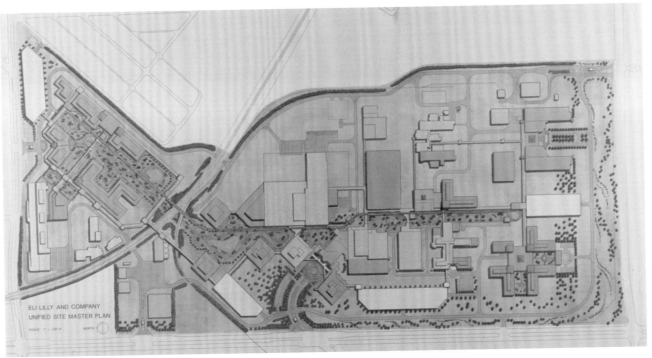

ELI LILLY AND COMPANY
UNIFIED SITE MASTER PLAN

GENERAL MOTORS BUILDING

"Designing and planning the General Motors Building offered an opportunity that come to but few architects. It was a real privilege to have been commissioned with a problem at once so large and so interesting. First of all, most office buildings are built on very costly land, with the result that it must be used with the greatest possible economy, irrespective of artistic results. The General Motors Building, located on less expensive land of ample area, made possible a plan which could not have been considered elsewhere. For here it was possible to use external courts 96 feet in each direction, while courts 30 feet wide would be considered liberal downtown.

Little Ornamentation.

The skyscraper is a distinctly American product architecturally, and many varying solutions as to design have been attempted. There are those formed of a series of buildings piled one on top of the other, using details of one type or another, and there are those which try for beauty in the simplest, most straightforward expression of the construction. It is the latter plan that was adopted in the General Motors Building. Recognizing that the mere size of the structure and its broken outline would in themselves provide distinction, it was believed wisest to depend upon these and the use of fine materials alone. More buildings suffer from over-ornamentation than from a lack of it. With this truth in mind, the General Motors Building is kept extremely simple, using detail at important points only, and there making it count.

The problem involved covering the entire ground floor space with shops to display the products of the corporation, with an office building above. This was for the main structure, fronting on the Boulevard. For the rear, there was to be a laboratory for technical research and this was to be only five stories high. To join these two structures, each with its own functions, and so different, presented a difficult problem. Both structures are frankly expressed on the exterior and it is very gratifying that the results have met with quite general approval.

Along Classic Lines.

For the Milwaukee Avenue front a design along classical lines lent itself particularly well for the interior requirements and quite a monumental front has been secured by the central portico with its Ionic columns, flanked by wings of simpler pier treatment. A note of interest has been provided by the decorative panels of the attic above the colonnade; these are symbolic of the sciences and industries.

The main office building is composed of a ground floor arcade, a plain shaft consisting of a series of piers and a uniform system of windows. Above the shaft there is an attic formed of a colonnade of a Corinthian order and this is crowned by an adequate cornice. Detail is provided in the capitals of the piers of the arcade, in the ornaments of the spandrels and by the main Boulevard entrance, where the ornamentation has been concentrated... The character of all of the ornamentation is that of early Renaissance in Italy. The models for the main doorway were prepared by a firm of sculptors in New York who excel in this particular style. Above the center arch of the main entrance is a monumental clock, flanked by two female figures, representing Chemistry and Mechanics. They are the work of a young New York sculptor, Ulysses Ricci, who was also responsible for the figure panels of the Milwaukee Avenue front.

Light A Problem.

On the interior of the building, every effort was made to provide ample light for all working space. To this end the offices were made only 20 feet deep from front to corridor line. Nothing was spared to provide every mechanical convenience and every safety appliance. In addition to all this, opportunity was afforded to provide main lobbies of a size rarely possible in buildings where space must be used economically.

The main entrance lobby is from the Boulevard and is treated in a manner corresponding to the importance of the structure... An auditorium to seat 1,500 opens off the main elevator lobby and this auditorium will have a stage, an organ and every provision for ventilation, light, etc. The shops themselves are designed with great care, and to harmonize with the rest of the building. Some of them afford open spaces without a column, 96 ft. x 96 ft... On the fourteenth floor are located the executive offices of the corporation and living quarters for visiting officials. The fifteenth floor contains staff dining and social rooms, and the infirmary. Provision has been made in the basement for swimming pools for men and for women, with the necessary dressing and locker rooms."[179]

Author: Albert Kahn

General Motors moved out of the building and in 1999, Kahn returned to complete a significant renovation and update the building's infrastructure. Today, this is one of many Kahn buildings listed on the National Register of Historic Places.

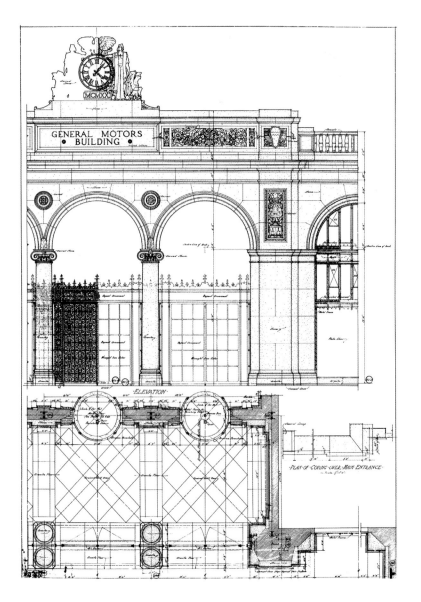

CENTURY OF PROGRESS EXPOSITION

General Motors partnered with Albert Kahn to showcase its contributions to the industrial and economic progress of America at the Century of Progress International Exposition of 1933-1934. This collaboration initiated a period of grand spectacle for General Motors that all began with a pavilion on the shore of Lake Michigan in Chicago.

Kahn's design was the largest structure erected at the Fair by a private exhibitor: 120,000 sq. ft. of concrete, glass and steel surrounded by beautifully landscaped gardens. Its striking Art Deco-style central tower rose 177 feet into the air and called to visitors from every corner of the Fair. A semi-circular fascia featured eight plate glass bays, 11 feet high and 48 feet wide, that proudly proclaimed the brands of General Motors. The exterior was painted a harmony of brilliant orange, yellow, blue, red and silver hues that were illuminated at night for dramatic effect.

The Entrance Hall's imposing columns welcomed visitors with the "beauty and dignity of a medieval cathedral."[180] This "architectural triumph"[181] was adorned with modern sculpture, intricate wood carvings and colorful murals[182] celebrating the craftsmanship of the automobile industry. Its centerpiece was a 16 foot tall figure sculpted by Carl Milles, a pupil of Rodin, that symbolized the heroic automobile worker. To either side of the Hall were vast salons showcasing contemporary and historic products of the General Motors family as well as the innovations of its Art & Colour Section and Research Laboratories.

The heart of the General Motors pavilion was a complete manufacturing and assembly line that resided in an airy, arched-roof room 420 feet long by 90 feet wide. Factory workers from Chevrolet and Fisher Body plants in nearby Janesville, Wisconsin demonstrated their quality of work by building new Chevrolet passenger cars from the ground up each day for the pleasure of thousands of spectators.

More than 10 million people visited that first season.[183] A major redesign led to similar success in 1934. The pavilion's exterior was repainted white with sea green, and trimmed in silver and touches of red. The entrance salon was transformed into a Hall of Progress featuring animated dioramas that depicted a quarter century's worth of General Motors innovations including electric headlights, four-wheel brakes, fast-drying lacquer paint that broadened the automobile's color palette, and the electric self-starter which democratized the automobile. Also new was the Frigidaire House, a demonstration of the world's first completely climate-controlled home,[184] and a Recreation Pier that reached 200 feet into Lake Michigan giving visitors an expansive view of the entire Fair.

Though the buildings and exhibits were temporary, the impression they left on visitors was everlasting. Albert Kahn helped General Motors demonstrate its vision of industrial progress to America for the very first time; and in doing so gave it a platform to share a vision of the future that is nearing realization today.

Author: Christo Datini, Manager, General Motors Design Archive & Special Collections

ELMHURST MEMORIAL HOSPITAL

ELMHURST, ILLINOIS | DESIGNED 2006 OPENED 2011

The replacement hospital for Elmhurst Memorial Healthcare was designed to create a patient-centered healing environment focused on patient experience and safety of all. Landscaped gardens, courtyards, patios, and open-air balconies on each floor provide access to fresh air and the healing qualities of nature for patients, family members, and staff. Approaching the design from the perspectives of both patients and staff, hospital processes were redesigned to consider the ideal patient day. Life-sized mock-ups of key rooms were constructed to test and refine the designs. Simultaneously, operational trials were conducted at the existing hospital to test design concepts and to refine processes.

To make the hospital user-friendly for staff as well as patients and families, the layout of the hospital is organized by function. Public spaces are located on the south side, where sun-lit corridors orient visitors to outdoor gardens and parking areas for better wayfinding. Clinical functions are to the north, with separate corridors and elevators. The building was also zoned east/west depending on the severity of patient needs; emergency and intensive care units are west while less acute areas for ambulatory care are east. Lastly, materials and service personnel circulate on the lower level and access strategically located elevators so that supplies and waste are hidden from patients and visitors.

Designed in collaboration with Pratt Design Studio, the interior design unifies the physical and emotional needs of all who enter the space, using design to evoke a restorative environment. One key design feature to improve the experience of patients was privacy starting with individual patient rooms and bathrooms in the emergency department and moving to private rooms for inpatient care. Specific materials were chosen throughout the design of these spaces to minimize noise levels and create a less stressful environment for patients and their families. Creating privacy and reducing noise humanizes the hospital experience and reduces anxiety, which allows patients to recover quicker. Staff experience was also important. Staff can retreat to small lavender respite rooms, which are comforting spaces to rest or regain composure as necessary. To add efficiency, convenient storage for 90% of supplies is located throughout the hospital within 5 seconds of the patient. Additionally, rooms are standardized to prevent errors, promote efficiency, and support safety for patients and staff.

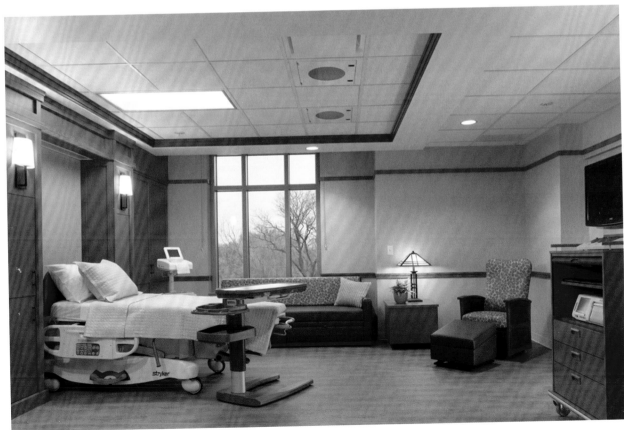

FSU GRANGER CENTER

Outdated buildings hold the potential to be transformed to fulfill a new purpose. The Granger Center at Ferris State University presented the ideal opportunity to take an existing 1960s building and adaptively reuse and expand the structure to create an active learning environment. Now, the center is a real-life textbook for students in the Mechanical Engineering and Construction Technology Management programs. All elements that make up the building's construction and services, including a wide variety of mechanical and electrical systems, building materials, and their respective assemblies, are exposed for curricular use. Everything is on display for students including the two-story mechanical room, with the ground floor for plumbing, pumps, boilers and chillers, and the second floor for air handling equipment. The toilet rooms, for example, are entered by first walking through the exposed plumbing chase, and all piping and ductwork is color-coded for easy tracing by students and faculty.

A new masterplan reshaped the North Campus to make way for the expanded building and create a new two-acre campus green by redesigning two adjacent parking lots. Anchoring this large green space, the center features a student commons, auditorium, classrooms, laboratories, and administration space. The building's central atrium is another gathering hub, which is controlled by an exposed air handling system programmed and maintained by the students. The center and surrounding green has become a university icon, defining a collaborative student place on the historic campus.

In addition, the building provides a venue to showcase this unique educational approach with corporate constituents of the program – equipment manufacturers, potential employers, benefactors, industry organizations, etc. Cultivating these relationships is critical to developing the industry ties so important for attracting recruiters to campus, advisors to their curriculum committees, and donors of equipment and funds. It makes a strong argument against those who say that current education programs are out of touch with the realities of building design and construction today.

UCM CENTER FOR CARE AND DISCOVERY

CHICAGO, ILLINOIS | DESIGNED 2014 OPENED 2018

The University of Chicago Medicine's third and fourth floors of the Center for Care and Discovery provided an opportunity to reinvent the standard hospital design to increase efficiency while delivering a therapeutic healing environment for all. Initial design planning began with four week-long "Kaizen Events," or interactive workshops to test patient room layouts, nurses' stations, and support spaces. Inspired by the Toyota Production System, often used in manufacturing, this concept organizes the interactions of individuals and supplies within the broader manufacturing, or in this case, healing process to minimize waste and cost.[185] A key tenet of this system is continual improvement and innovation. As a patient-centered facility, the University of Chicago Medicine embodies this idea, seeking to improve the quality of healthcare services, and exceed the expectations of patients, their families, and staff.

A team of approximately thirty frontline professionals were assembled, including physicians, nurses, support staff, and Kahn designers, to test designs in full-size mock-ups. Two patient units, about 35,000 sq. ft. in total, were constructed with foam boards on the vacant third floor. Every room was mocked up so the team could visualize what it would be like to work in the new units. Sixteen variations of patient rooms were then built of drywall for testing. Teams acted out various scripted regular care and emergency procedures within the spaces, and chose a unique new design layout that proved to be the most efficient and effective for both patients and their caregivers.

To improve wayfinding, color was used to delineate east and west sides of the building, carrying through corridors, nurses' stations, and elevators. A wood-slated ceiling and etched glass wall visually divide elevators from the new patient waiting rooms and link these floors to the design of the main lobby below. Evoking the natural environment, therapeutic blues, greens, and yellows, calm each patient room. Patient rooms are equipped with chairs and a sleeper sofa for families and caregivers, private bathrooms with enough space for assistance should the patient need, vital equipment to improve safety of patients and staff, and windows to bring in natural daylight.

Once the floors were open for patient care, evaluation was conducted to gather feedback from patients, their families, and staff.[186] Post-occupancy evaluation revealed that the new room design allowed patients greater privacy and reduced noise, while still promoting the feeling of safety through the inclusion of a window to the corridor. Staff could quickly see patients and vital equipment through the window. Patients and their families found the rooms to be more comfortable with fully adjustable LED lighting, sleeper sofas, and improved WiFi connectivity. They also found the floors easier to navigate with the improved layout and wayfinding. A key improvement of the floor layout was the standardization and location of medication rooms, supply and equipment rooms, and nourishment rooms, which were placed within each grouping of eight patient rooms. Staff found this layout shortened their walking distance and improved their efficiency. This feedback demonstrates that the initial planning and workshop process was integral to delivering spaces that accomplished the hospital's goals and exceeded the expectations of all who enter the space.

DETROIT OPERA HOUSE

As one of the most comprehensive interior restorations ever undertaken in the region, a crumbling theater was transformed into a world-class venue for operatic and dance productions. The 2,700-seat theater was originally designed in 1922 by C. Howard Crane, a renowned theater architect and former draftsman for Albert Kahn. Influenced by European opera houses, the theater was designed to accommodate stage shows, burlesque, and silent film. When the Michigan Opera Theatre purchased the theater in 1989, the interior was nearly beyond saving – 90% of the plasterwork was destroyed and the orchestra pit was a swimming pool. Years of neglect had reduced the once opulent entertainment venue to a leaky ruin.

Through the use of photographs and written archives, the interior of the theater was painstakingly researched and restored to ensure authenticity. The restoration of the plasterwork proved that the original acoustic design was flawless. Forensic analysis revealed an original color palette dominated by gilded ochre, browns, and blues, which were recreated through the theater. The central oculus was rebuilt and dramatic lighting was restored to the space. Sections of the original curtain were refurbished and replicated, and a fragment of the original carpet was recovered and matched. Finally, a series of distinctive wall paintings were restored with accuracy ranging from exact replication to whimsical invention, including a discrete representation of the theater's leader dressed in a Roman toga. The existing stagehouse was replaced with an addition designed to meet the needs of contemporary theater production, and the orchestra pit was expanded to accommodate larger ensembles.

Massive chandeliers in the main lobby were restored, while some lost fixtures were replaced. The Broadway lobby chandelier, for instance, once graced the original Waldorf Astoria, and is now on permanent loan from the Henry Ford Museum. Additionally, the administrative office tower was readapted to preserve certain as-found conditions that tell a poignant story about the reconstruction including exposed clay-tile ceilings, masonry walls, and raw concrete framing. Ripple art glass was salvaged from an adjacent building and re-used in the office lobby. Originally isolated from the theater, the offices were strategically integrated to accommodate administrative and educational programs.

Today, the firm remains involved with the Detroit Opera House. Recent renovations include increasing accessibility for attendees through the addition of a new elevator tower, replacement of seating in the theater, updated heating, cooling and ventilation systems, and a building wide control system to monitor and control building systems. Finally, an added terrace on the roof will be the perfect venue for outdoor events in the city.

THE ART OF ENGINEERING

"We read in buildings the history of man. We may trace therein the effects of war, religion, commerce and science. Even climatic conditions and materials available are clearly expressed."[187]

- Albert Kahn

Engineering is about finding innovative solutions to complex problems. Within the built environment, engineers develop new materials, find practical uses for the latest scientific discoveries, and design new systems to create more comfortable interior environments. Engineers also discover ways to reduce the negative impact on the natural environment and strike that perfect balance between artistry, efficiency, and economy. A design engineer must select the "right systems that best meet the needs of that client over the life of the project, and develop the detailed design engineering that will ensure that the selected systems perform and will work efficiently and reliably."[188] In the following pages, we highlight some of the significant engineering systems that advanced our clients' industries and shaped the development of the built environment. Looking at civil, structural, mechanical, electrical, and information technology, when an engineer solved a particular challenge for one client, they adapted those ideas to solve challenges in other markets. This cross-pollination marks true innovation.

Reinforced concrete was just the beginning. Upon joining his brother's firm, Julius began perfecting the revolutionary reinforced concrete system known as the "Kahn Bar." "My brother Julius quickly saw the potentialities of the new material, as well as its weak points as then employed," recalled Albert. "He promptly designed a new form of reinforcement and a scheme of construction which met immediate approval and thus gave reinforced concrete its real start in this country."[189] This engineered solution opened the doors to further innovation by the firm.

Industrial work has been a key market throughout the history of the firm. Since the beginning, industrial giants made great demands on architecture, which "literally, if unconsciously, forced revolution in design, innovations in engineering, new techniques in construction."[190] These leaders wanted a businessman instead of an artist, and they wanted their facilities completed quickly, economically, and with the flexibility to adjust to advances in production. Industrial projects require close coordination and collaboration between architects and engineers as they are inventing new spaces that can efficiently and safely manufacture, assemble, and test the most technologically advanced systems of any given time. It isn't just creating an empty box for industry to occur within; rather, it is understanding the needs, process, machines, and number and role of workers, and then proposing a facility based on those size and function requirements. Thought also needs to be given to the development of the site, ease of transport, accessibility to workforce, environmental conditions, waste disposal and impact on the environment, while accommodating the future growth of the facility.

Engineering advances in the industrial space then influenced other markets. For example, the firm introduced the single-story industrial building permitting maximum flexibility in interior spaces and ease of expansion, which became a prototype for large commercial spaces, while still serving as the standard for American industry. Modular planning began in the firm's design of industrial facilities through the development of standard sash, structural grids, movable partitions, lighting raceways, and more, which were then incorporated in other types of facilities. Advanced heating and ventilating units, such as vertical projection unit heaters, were first developed for large, open industrial spaces and became the forerunners of today's large enclosed structures with controlled environments. These are but a few examples of that cross-pollination mentioned earlier.

Yet, for Kahn engineers, there has been a necessary balance between innovation and proof of long-term impact. Just because a manufacturer develops a new building product, doesn't mean that it should be used immediately. Is there a possibility that the product could fail in extreme heat? What about a chemical reaction when you combine a waterproofing additive with mortar in a masonry wall?[191] Engineers study each and every scenario before experimenting with new products to ensure that the solution they offer will be best for the client.

Today, the firm continues to design, evaluate, develop, test, and modify engineering systems to solve a client's initial problem and create a long-term solution. Our engineers design solutions to support and propel an industry, develop flexible spaces that accommodate change, invent new products or uses to achieve greater building efficiency or reduce cost, and create healthy indoor environments for users.

BELLE ISLE AQUARIUM & HORTICULTURAL BUILDING

DETROIT, MICHIGAN | DESIGNED 1900 OPENED 1904

Detroit's Belle Isle Aquarium & Horticultural Building is an engineering marvel, melding two building types developed in the Victorian era: the botanical conservatory and the public aquarium.

In 1900, the City of Detroit held a competition among its architects to design this municipal landmark. Nettleton and Kahn won and Mason and Kahn prepared the final drawings following Nettleton's death. Kahn extended his legendary self-education further into the realm of engineering, studying recent conservatory construction and consulting aquaculture experts. The New York Aquarium was the only substantial, permanent public aquarium operating in the United States at the time, but awkward aspects of its design made it a poor model. Similarities between Kahn's aquarium and one from 1864 in Hamburg, Germany suggests that the architect also plumbed the world's best designs of the past.

Engineering and design challenges posed by this structure involved imitating the natural environment indoors. The curvilinear forms of the horticultural component approximated the dome of the atmosphere. As the sun tracks across the sky on slightly different paths from day to day, season to season, its light passes through varying glass panes at near perpendicular angles – thought to be most efficient for harnessing solar energy indoors. The orchid collection was located in the southernmost portion to best benefit from sun exposure. A pool in the adjacent tropical range was home to a South American Victoria amazonica – then considered the largest flower in the world. At the north end, the fernery floor sunk below grade to accommodate tall plants, while maintaining balanced symmetry for the exterior composition. This arrangement also allowed visitors to see the fern fronds at near eye level.

In recreating the underwater world, the aquarium's tank system required 65,000 gallons of water with 50,000 in constant circulation, day and night. Aeration was necessary to provide enough oxygen in the water to sustain the fish. In nature, this is achieved through wave action. Kahn's answer involved a raised section toward the rear of the building holding two cisterns, one for saltwater and one for fresh. Water pumped up to both fell with gravity through showerhead-type devices for natural aeration. From there the water progressed from tank to tank along each side of the aquarium, re-aerating as it went. Air pumps augmented the process while heaters and chillers regulated water temperature. As the freshwater clouded with use, it was discarded and replaced by more freshwater pumped from the nearby lake. The saltwater, brought in from the Atlantic Ocean at a great expense, was returned to a dark, underground reservoir. The absence of sunlight naturally killed off algae, purifying the water, which then recycled through the tanks. With this system, the saltwater lasted 50 years.

Now North America's oldest brick-and-mortar public aquarium, it was the third-largest in the world when it opened on August 18, 1904. The novel structure drew widespread praise from experts for its efficient design integrating complex engineering into its architecture. Its success inspired aquarium building in other cities over the next twenty-five years, often adopting variations on Kahn's design and culminating with Chicago's Shedd Aquarium.

Renovations in the 1950s stripped the Aquarium & Horticultural Building of some of its Victorian appeal, but stunning features from Kahn's original vision remain. These include the imaginative aquarium entrance and the unique ceiling of variegated, green glass tile, evoking a sense of underwater wonder for visitors. Strolling through the conservatory, enclosed by some 25,000 sq. ft. of glass, one has little trouble grasping that its architect would soon garner fame as the designer of daylight factories.

Author: Chris Meister, Author of a forthcoming book on Albert Kahn

NISSAN TECHNICAL CENTER

FARMINGTON HILLS, MICHIGAN | DESIGNED 2002 OPENED 2006

The renovation and expansion of Nissan's Technical Center established a more significant presence for the car manufacturer in the Detroit metropolitan region. A key part of this campus renovation was the expansion of the 27,900 sq. ft. Design and Styling Studio, completed in collaboration with Luce et Studio Architects in San Diego, California. Serving as the sister studio to the San Diego design studio, where the majority of Nissan vehicles are designed, this studio was created to link this process with research and pre-production efforts already happening onsite in metro Detroit.

Departing from the original studio space that was hidden in the back of the Technical Center, the new Design and Styling Studio was brought front and center as a way to celebrate the vehicle design process. The studio provides unique daylighting opportunities through the introduction of interior courtyards and viewing courts, while maintaining strict product confidentiality. Housed in the studio is a private conference room containing an 8' x 20' powerwall screen that facilitates the sharing of design concepts worldwide. It also features clay modeling bedplates that allow designers to work on five full-sized vehicle models at a time while viewing the models under 585 color-corrected lights that simulate a variety of daylight options. Another noteworthy addition to the Design and Styling Studio was an increase in the number of thermal storage ice tanks from 24 to 60 tanks. These ice tanks allowed Nissan to take advantage of off-peak energy rates at night, making the facility more energy efficient and decreasing their energy costs considerably. During the daytime, they use the ice to cool the facility, and create more ice during the nighttime.

An iconic feature of this space is the viewing courtyard affectionately referred to as "the egg." The elliptical structure is designed in a funnel shape and clad in perforated metal to prevent passersby from viewing prototype vehicles on display within the courtyard. From within the courtyard, designers and engineers are able to view the prototypes from all angles and in natural light conditions. Given the shape of the structure, each metal panel needed to be precisely cut, resulting in each panel being slightly different from the next and requiring meticulous attention to detail during construction. Together, each of these features created a collaborative, efficient, and state-of-the-art Design and Styling Studio that brought design teams closer to their research and pre-production colleagues.

AMERICAN ARITHMOMETER PLANT

One might think daylighting is a relatively new building requirement. Most sustainable design certification programs today include criteria for natural daylight and proper ventilation in indoor environments. Daylighting is not new to Albert Kahn-designed buildings – we have been incorporating daylight for more than a century. An early example is the American Arithmometer Company Plant, built at Second Avenue and Amsterdam Street in Detroit, which became the Burroughs Adding Machine Company.

The plant was constructed of non-combustible materials when heavy timber-framed construction was common. Walls were brick to the exterior and white enameled brick on the interior. Roof and floor construction used the Kahn System of hollow clay tile and reinforced concrete, completed by the Trussed Concrete Steel Company. The machine room was constructed of 16'9" bays with column spacing at 20'10" on center. Overhead large electric lights were installed, and each machine had an incandescent work light.

The machine shop was flooded with natural daylight from the sawtooth shaped roof with a seven-foot-tall sash. Every other sash in the sawtooth was arranged to swing on center pivots, operated by a geared ventilating apparatus. Gutters were placed between the sloped sawtooth roofs, and rain was collected in copper scuppers and conveyed to interior cast-iron columns. The windowsills were 16 inches above the high point of the gutters to accommodate heavy rains and snowfall. Constructed below the sawtooth sash was an interior copper gutter for collecting condensation. Hot water heating pipe coils were located at the base of the sawtooth sash to assist in keeping the gutters from freezing in the winter.[192] Though the building has since been demolished, the designs reveal that natural daylighting and ventilation were just as important in 1905 as it is today, over 100 years later.

Author: Donald Bauman, AIA, Former Director of Architecture and Historic Preservation, Albert Kahn Associates

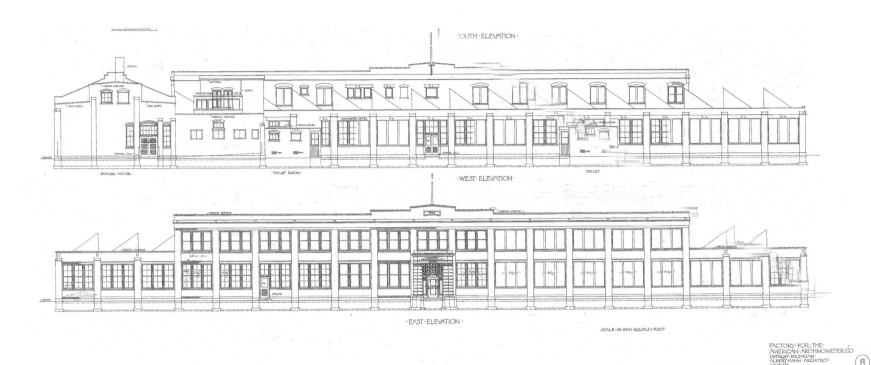

·SOUTH·ELEVATION·

·WEST·ELEVATION·

·EAST·ELEVATION·

·SCALE·1/8·INCH·EQUALS·1·FOOT·

FACTORY·FOR·THE·
AMERICAN·ARITHMOMETER·CO·
DETROIT·MICHIGAN·
ALBERT·KAHN·ARCHITECT·

AUG-16-04

NAC RAILCAR MANUFACTURING FACILITY

CHEROKEE, ALABAMA | DESIGNED 2007 OPENED 2009

Built in the Shoals region of northwest Alabama, the Railcar Manufacturing Facility of National Alabama Corporation is the single largest railcar manufacturing plant in North America and a marvel of modern industrial architecture. The fusion of function, form and sustainable design in this facility has successfully created a flexible production environment with a reduced carbon footprint that will endure for decades. Spanning 3/4 of a mile in length and covering 2.1 million sq. ft. of heavy industrial space, sustainability was integrated from the start.

The facility is relatively narrow across the middle and only slightly wider at its ends, where paint and fabrication facilities are housed. Its slender frame was critical in meeting the most formidable challenge: devising an economical ventilation system capable of producing a comfortable working environment without air conditioning.

By modernizing a design innovation first implemented by Albert Kahn himself more than 100 years ago, Kahn engineered a 2,000-foot long clerestory section over the construction area. The clerestory functions as an enormous glass skylight and ventilates the building by using the buoyancy of the heated air in the summer to create a natural draft that pulls in cooler air from the outside. Motorized relief dampers located in the clerestory 65 feet above the floor and inlet dampers located along the building perimeter at 10 feet above the floor are automatically opened when the interior temperature exceeds 75 degrees Fahrenheit. As the temperature increases within the building, exhaust fans located in the clerestory space operate to increase airflow into the building. During the heating season when the dampers are closed, the building's make-up air units provide heat and ventilation to the process spaces.

Additionally, each building space is equipped with carbon dioxide sensors that are used to determine the indoor air quality of the space. When the carbon dioxide sensors sense that additional outside air is needed, the central building management system will open up the clerestory and perimeter dampers to increase the amount of outside air into the building. The building operator can also command the dampers to open to purge the building space or to close the dampers in case of inclement weather. Additionally, the system can monitor and control all the mechanical equipment and building lighting systems. Electrical distribution and process gases are individually metered, allowing National Alabama Corporation to monitor energy and utility usage for each production line. Together, these systems create a more efficient and sustainable plant.

UM ENGINEERING BUILDING

Originally the home to the schools of Engineering, Architecture, and Naval Architecture, the Engineering Building at the University of Michigan inaugurated one of the longest relationships in the firm's history – over 100 years of projects including more than 30 new buildings and thousands of additions and renovations. In 1900, Albert rejoined George Mason to form Mason and Kahn. The New Engineering Building, was one of several iconic structures that emerged from this brief partnership.

Mason and Kahn, and Julius as the structural engineer, designed a portion of the structure using steel-reinforced concrete with an exterior façade of brick and stone. Unique for the time, the structural concept creates a foundation and first floor of reinforced concrete. In the lower level space, the Naval Architecture Program housed a water tank used for designing ship hulls (above). The second and third floors, which featured extensive lab areas, were designed with a riveted steel frame, and the roof structure was heavy timber and wood.

Work on the building began in 1901, and when the 94,318 sq. ft. building was completed in 1904, the final construction cost was $275,000.00. As the college grew, so too did the need for space. In 1909, Kahn returned to the site with his then partner Ernest Wilby to design a significant 63,000 sq. ft. addition to the north end of the building. A second engineering building was constructed in 1923, and the New Engineering Building was renamed West Engineering Building.[193] When the School of Engineering moved to the North Campus in 1996, the building was renamed West Hall, which it is still called today.

In 1999, the firm returned to West Hall to renovate the existing spaces to accommodate new academic departments while respecting the historical significance and original design intent. Major aspects of this work focused on upgrading the entire building's infrastructure, including the mechanical and electrical equipment, as well as making the building more accessible and ADA compliant.

To this day, this building creates the quintessential campus experience. Virtually every new student or visitor that comes to the central campus takes that scenic walk under the arch that serves as a gateway to the central gathering space, the "Diag." This L-shaped structure wraps the southeast corner of the campus green and is engrained in the campus experience.

FORD HIGHLAND PARK PLANT

Henry Ford approached Albert Kahn in 1908 to build a manufacturing plant for his Model T automobile on a new 180-acre site in Highland Park. The Piquette Avenue Plant, where the first Model T's were built, had become obsolete. This began a long-term partnership between two geniuses and two organizations. For more than 100 years, Kahn has completed thousands of projects for the Ford Motor Company.

Ford envisioned key changes in his assembly process and wanted an assembly building that could support his vision of the assembly line – initially an orderly manual flow of components and vehicles which eventually led to a gravity-fed system that moved components through the building as the vehicle was assembled. Components were manufactured in the nearby machine shop, then fed vertically by four elevators to each floor of the assembly building, where Model T's were initially built using stationary assembly practices. The moving assembly line evolved between 1910 and 1913, one sub-assembly at a time. A single elevator on the north side of the building then moved assembled vehicles to the shipping platforms.

Kahn and Ford collaborated to design a building that could support this assembly process and was adaptable enough to accommodate Ford's evolving vision. Later additions resulted in a building where raw materials and subassemblies entered the building on rail cars in the center of the building. These materials were then delivered by cranes to landings at different levels so the materials were at optimal locations along the assembly line. As the vehicles moved along, workers had access to what they needed when they needed it – an early version of what is now referred to as the "just-in-time" assembly process.

The use of concrete construction in the original four-story Highland Park Plant assembly building provided greater spans, less vibration, and larger wall openings. The structure opened great expanses of wall to air and light, creating superior workspaces where production efficiency was improved, better craftsmanship was possible, and the safety of the worker was enhanced. This building was also the first to use the steel window sashes imported from England, allowing maximum light to flood the space, giving it the nickname "Crystal Palace."[194] Later expansions joined two separate structures enclosed with a vast skylight that flooded interior workspaces with natural light and allowed the movable cranes to transfer materials.

The Highland Park complex brought factory construction from utilitarian construction into the realm of architecture. In its stunning simplicity, its innovative use of steel, brick, and glass, and its aesthetic principle of form following function, the "Crystal Palace" is thought to have inspired the work of Walter Gropius in his 1911 Fagus-Werk[195] and influenced the development of European Modernism.

FULLER SHOWROOM AND SERVICE BUILDING

BOSTON, MASSACHUSETTS | DESIGNED 1909 OPENED 1910

Kahn designed countless showrooms around the world for automobile manufacturers such as Hudson Motor Car Company, Ford Motor Company, General Motors Company, and Packard Motor Car Company, among others. One of the most interesting is the Fuller Showroom and Service Building in Boston, which was commissioned by Alvan T. Fuller, a dealer for both Packard and Cadillac Motor Company. Fuller was touted as "the most successful automobile dealer in the country" having built up a retail business of $3,000,000 a year in 1910.[196] This was one of New England's first combined auto sales rooms and service stations, featuring assembly, storage, and repair facilities.[197] Understanding that some customers might want to purchase used cars, Fuller began selling cars that were repaired in his shop with his quality guarantee.

At over 120,000 sq. ft., and four stories tall, this showroom and service depot rivaled many automobile factories at the time with the ability to work on 300 cars at once.[198] It was complete with a full service station to make all mechanical and cosmetic repairs, and a stock room that contained parts for virtually every model of Packard and Cadillac automobiles. Newspaper coverage at the time noted that this stock room was designed after the Packard stock room in the Detroit factory.[199]

Constructed of mostly reinforced concrete, the engineering of the structure allowed for great spans between columns and large windows to let in vast amounts of natural light. On the top floor, steel trusses carried weight from the roof to allow for large column-free areas along an entire side of the building. This flexible workspace allowed Fuller to work on a variety of special automobiles including limousines. Freight elevators and ramps moved the cars between levels of the building depending on the repair needed. Dumb-waiters and speaking tubes allowed employees to easily communicate between floors of the shop space. Among the various repair specialties throughout the building, there was also a finishing room, for cars that came in direct from the factory, and a paint shop which required concentrated heating to cure the paint and varnish. Once all the work was complete, cars were then washed in the basement and ready to go home.

On the first floor, in the front of the building, was the showroom designed as if it were a luxurious exhibition space with attendants close by to "give any information that may be wished for regarding new cars or cost of repairs or adjustments that individual owners may desire."[200] Surrounded by large windows, the high-ceilinged showroom was flooded with natural light. Fluted columns, high-quality decorative fixtures, and two grand electroliers, or chandeliers, created a glamorous space similar to a hotel lobby. Nearby, Fuller also incorporated office space for employees as well as a full employee dining room and restaurant. Within this building, Fuller created a one-stop shop and forever changed the car buying experience.

MACK TRUCK PLANT

One of the largest producers of heavy-duty trucks in America, Mack Trucks Inc., needed a new plant to advance their production. They decided to take this opportunity to expand their operations outside of Allentown, Pennsylvania. Kahn and a team from Mack studied twelve sites across the southeast United States before arriving in Winnsboro, South Carolina. The 150-acre site was a prime location for transportation to and from the plant and offered a strong labor base. The location of the plant positively impacted the community; shortly after the project began, several Mack suppliers set up satellite operations to support the new plant. Not only did this new plant and related suppliers create jobs, but it also led to additional housing, schools, and higher education institutions, along with a variety of related businesses.

The Mack Truck Plant was the first heavy-truck plant in the world to employ a modular assembly process. With ten different types of advanced conveyors moving materials and products, this plant bridged historically separate phases of production and combined them simultaneously. Using both the ground level and mezzanine levels, teams completed major sections of the truck before they are joined to the chassis in final assembly. These subassemblies are joined both "off-line" and "on-line," rather than a single continuous assembly line. This modular design increased efficiency and productivity by removing constraints of a traditional process, and required less floor space.

Designed to produce 70 trucks per day, the plant housed frame fabrication, chassis assembly, subassembly, paint shop, cab grooming and final assembly operations, quality control activities, and a maintenance shop. In addition, warehouse space for up to 9,112 component storage units was provided in a high cube storage facility with an automatic storage and retrieval system.[201] The entire process was driven by computers and statistical process control, enabling quality checks during the production process instead of only at the end. Data from this plant was then shared across Mack's network of plants and its headquarters in Allentown. From top to bottom, this plant created a state-of-the-art manufacturing operation.

MERCEDES BENZ ASSEMBLY PLANT

This project represents the first passenger vehicle assembly plant ever built in the United States for a prominent German manufacturer. The one million-sq. ft. plant, situated on 966 acres in Tuscaloosa County, Alabama, is the site of a former tree farm. The rolling terrain was master planned for future growth, with the initial facility occupying approximately 200 acres, while preserving as much of the existing tree cover as possible.

Initially designed to produce 70,000 sport utility vehicles per year, the plant included a body shop, paint shop, assembly shop, energy center, and centralized administration and employee facilities. The preferred planning concept arranged the three major production shops (Body, Paint, and Assembly) along a two-story central spine. Central to the design was the co-location of production offices adjacent to the manufacturing process on the second level of the plant. The physical proximity of the three major production shops promoted communication and cooperation to foster a closer working relationship between different functions within the manufacturing process, allowing staff to address and solve problems face-to-face quickly and efficiently.

Entering through the triangular "prow," natural light fills the atrium from north-facing sawtooth roof monitors. The glass wall at the south end of the atrium frames a scene of painted vehicle bodies on their way to the final trim assembly line. Incorporating the assembly line as a design feature reinforced the integration of the manufacturing process with office administration within the complex.

The exterior is clad in white and silver vertical metal panels, which were selected to express the machine technology of the interior processes. Energy conservation was also important in the systems design. Glazing on the north wall formed a continuous curtain wall, while the east and west elevations have punched windows to minimize solar heat gain, while providing a generous amount of natural light. Reflecting pools and porcelain tile paving accent the cafeteria and entry. A single-ply membrane roof, utilizing shed and gable type slopes, allows storm water to be collected at the perimeter walls. This technique reduces the number of roof openings over production areas and minimizes interferences with process pits and trenches due to under-slab piping. Since opening, Kahn has continued to work with Mercedes Benz to upgrade and expand facilities and systems as needed.

VOLVO MANUFACTURING PLANT

RIDGEVILLE, SOUTH CAROLINA | DESIGNED 2015 OPENED 2018

Volvo Cars' first North American manufacturing facility brings the automaker's production direct to an expanding group of consumers. The design was unique for Volvo capturing the brand identity for their North American production campus and capturing the inherent simplicity and functionality of the Scandinavian design. Simplicity was ruled by elegant proportions as an economical approach to creating visual interest in the buildings. While the functionality of the campus was captured in the clarity of the design, driven by program and purpose.

Designed to be walkable, the campus is oriented along the concept of front and back of house. Main buildings, such as the three-story office building and guardhouses, are in front of the campus, greeting employees and visitors. An internal street system for employees connects these buildings to the manufacturing facilities, including paint, assembly, body shop, and vehicle processing center for imports/exports in the back of the campus. Manufacturing buildings are connected by enclosed overhead bridges conveying parts, body panels, and vehicles. Flexibility was key in the design of the campus. Each building is designed to easily accommodate production changes that occur with each new model year. Even campus systems such as electrical and IT were installed underground throughout the site to allow for building expansion, to track inventory as it moves through the site, and to enable employees to track trucks and supplies from shipping yards.

Located just outside of Charleston, the site is strategically located near key ports and a direct distribution network through multiple transportation options. However, this ideal location also put the campus within a hurricane, earthquake, and flooding zone. Each building was engineered with seismic reinforcement including concrete beams placed diagonally in floor slabs, and steel bracing throughout the buildings and foundations. Taking the winds and size of buildings into account, 14-inch expansion joints were run along the walls and roofline, allowing each building to move independently in a storm. All of this additional bracing needed to fit within each building without disrupting the flow of production or interfering with office layouts.

Sustainability was also a big factor in the design and engineering of the campus. In fact, Volvo's campus is on its way to becoming a LEED certified campus, with main buildings expected to achieve LEED Gold certification. The campus has designated land protected from future development, restoring the natural habitat as an outdoor amenity and mitigating the heat island effect from impervious surfaces. Reducing light pollution and minimizing impact on nocturnal wildlife were also concerns for the campus. Generated light is strategically localized within site boundaries and is Dark Skies compliant. Bioswales and permeable landscapes collect and filter stormwater and limit overloading of the storm sewer system, while all irrigation is drawn from rainwater collected on-site. Vehicle charging stations were incorporated to support alternative fuel vehicles and bicycle storage combined with showers and lockers are provided for employees and visitors.

Within the buildings, low emitting materials, including paints, adhesives, flooring, and formaldehyde-free wood were installed, helping to avoid sick building syndrome. Approximately 30% of building materials incorporated recycled content, and over 25% of materials were sourced locally. Water-efficient plumbing fixtures reduce potable water use by over 35% in all buildings. 90% of all construction waste was diverted from the landfill or incinerator and put to use elsewhere. Finally, thermally efficient building envelopes, efficient mechanical and electrical systems, and advanced building control systems enable these buildings to operate more efficiently than required by ASHRAE standards.

Author: Rick S. Dye, PE, President, Albert Kahn Associates

FORD RIVER ROUGE COMPLEX

DEARBORN, MICHIGAN | DESIGNED 1917 RENOVATED 2020

Ford Motor Company's River Rouge Complex has been a source of continuous innovation. The story of the site predates our official start date of 1917, and begins with the work of Henry Ford and Albert Kahn at the Highland Park Plant (1910). Yet, Ford envisioned a far grander full-scale production facility where raw materials enter at one end and finished automobiles exit at the other, producing cars more quickly and more affordably. The process operation was a monument to vertical integration; it has been said the only part of the vehicle not manufactured on site were the tires only because rubber trees didn't grow in Detroit! Ford contracted Kahn to build the world's largest and most ambitious factory on 2,000 acres along the banks of the Rouge River, strategically located near major rail lines and connected to the Great Lakes.

Kahn designed the first building in 1917, which is part of the Dearborn Assembly plant today. The design called for a single-story factory with a sawtooth roof, similar to the factory Kahn produced years earlier for the George N. Pierce Company in Buffalo, New York.[202] The new building was originally designed to replace Model T assembly at the Highland Park plant.[203] However, shortly after construction began, the building was modified to accommodate assembly of the Eagle Submarine Chaser for the U.S. Navy toward the end of World War I.[204] Kahn and the team of architects, engineers, and contractors needed to quickly redesign and construct the factory in a few short months. Though production of the boats was short lived due to the end of the war, the plant then transitioned to produce the Fordson tractor, which greatly revolutionized the work of farmers.

At 1,700-feet-long by 350-feet-wide, or about 13 acres, the single-story factory building encompassed a complete manufacturing process, rather than simply the assembly of finished parts. Using the sawtooth roof design further improved the environment for workers by providing an abundance of natural lighting and allowing the windows to open to ventilate the hot air coming off of the various machines. A single floor plant allowed for flexibility in the layout of the production process, and operational logistics were improved as all components were kept at one level from where they entered the building to where the vehicle left upon completion.

Steel, sawtooth roofs, and glass and steel sash cladding became the hallmarks of Kahn's industrial work. While concrete was preferred for multi-storied factories to reduce vibration from equipment and reduce the threat of fire, structural steel could provide greater freedom and flexibility in single-story factories.[205] Steel buildings were able to be constructed quickly, and the design allowed the plant to be continuously extended and modified without disrupting production. Machines and conveyors could be supported on grade of a single-story structure, reducing the load on the structure of the building.

Kahn went on to design and engineer numerous buildings on the Rouge site including the iconic Glass Plant (1923) (below), with its unique roofline that specifically responds to the needs of the glass manufacturing process. The highest point of the Glass Plant is directly above the furnaces that continuously burn at 2,500 degrees Fahrenheit. Clerestory windows on either side of this point allow for ventilation and naturally eliminate the hot air at the ceiling, utilizing the Venturi effect through window placement and volume proportions. As the molten glass moves from the furnace and cools over the lehrs, the heat is pulled up to the next highest points of the roof and directed through the open windows. Between these larger points in the roofline, smaller skylights were included to provide additional natural light.

Following Albert's death, the firm remained active on the site, retooling and renovating the original structures and designing new modern facilities to accommodate the advances in production. The complex quickly became world-renowned both for its scale of production and as the pinnacle of American Industrial Architecture. In 1978, the Ford River Rouge Complex became a National Historic Landmark. Today, Ford manufactures and assembles the Ford F-150 truck on the Rouge site. Hundreds of thousands of visitors also come to the iconic complex every year, where they can see inside an active assembly plant.

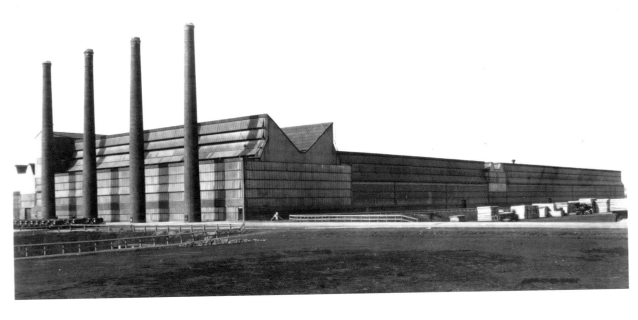

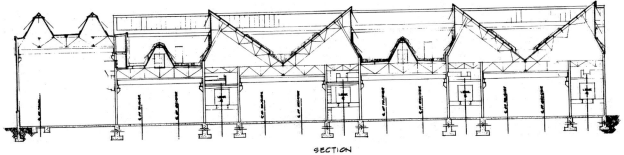

SECTION

FORD DEARBORN STAMPING PLANT

DEARBORN, MICHIGAN | DESIGNED 1936 RENOVATED 2016

Kahn has designed many automotive stamping plants throughout its history. Perhaps the most fascinating of these is Ford Motor Company's Dearborn Stamping Plant – it is historical, unique, and state-of-the-art. Dearborn Stamping is located in the famous Rouge complex where Kahn designed hundreds of projects over the past century. The heart of the operations, the stamping of metal automotive parts, is in the original stamping building designed in 1936 (right). Metal enters the building as coils and travels through a series of press operations depending on the size of the final stamped part to be produced.

A typical stamping plant is a one-story building with a basement or pits under the press areas. Press operations are at the ground floor level with press foundations, support machinery, and metal scrap collection in basement areas. At the Rouge complex, poor soil conditions forced press foundations to be supported by piles driven to solid rock, typically about 110 feet below grade. This created a unique building configuration with the ground floor level serving as a full basement area and the operations level elevated as a second floor. This rare building configuration resulted in several unique design features. The elevated operations level on the second floor allowed for the four-lane Rouge access road to pass beneath the building at grade level. The second-floor operations level featured a remarkable array of mezzanines, ramps, and bridges to convey stamped parts and subassemblies, which today are transported via automatic guided vehicles traveling on elevated "highways." Stamped parts are stored, distributed and then joined together in "subassembly" operations located in adjacent buildings, most originally designed by Kahn in the 1920s.

While upgrades to the plant have occurred continuously over decades of operation, significant modernization of the plant started in the 1990s with the installation of two transfer press lines in the primary stamping bay. The most transformative modernization program began in 2011 (above), when Ford made the decision to stamp body panels for their F-150 trucks out of aluminum instead of steel. As part of that program, four new tandem press lines, two blanking lines, a shear line, a tryout press and other equipment were added to manage the special requirements necessary for the production of stamped aluminum parts.

Radical building modifications that were required to accommodate the new press lines included the conversion of eight 60-foot-wide bays to four 120-foot-wide bays and the roof level elevated in portions of these bays to install new presses and support traveling bridge crane operations. Additional upgrades included the demolition and reconstruction of the second-floor operations level in the new press line areas and the adoption of a new technology for metal scrap removal. Highly valuable scrap aluminum is recycled by first shredding the metal into small pieces and then conveying the scrap to exterior cyclone separators via pneumatic tubes. The successful conversion to aluminum stamping generated the latest improvement, when a fifth new tandem press line was added in 2016 within an adjacent Kahn-designed structure from 1925. This improvement included an elevated parts storage and conveyance facility constructed over an existing parking lot.

Today this state-of-the-art and historic stamping facility boasts over three million sq. ft. of floor area, producing and conveying stamped parts and subassemblies to the adjacent assembly plant or for shipment to other facilities.

Authors: Hank Ritter, PE, Principal, Engineering, Albert Kahn Associates
Peter G. Lynde, PE, Senior VP & Director of Research and Technology, Albert Kahn Associates

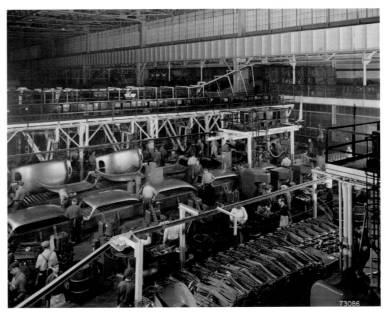

GUARDIAN FLOAT GLASS PLANTS

In partnership with The Lathrop Company, a Toledo, Ohio-based contractor, Kahn designed two float glass plants for Guardian Industries, a leading producer of exterior and interior glass for commercial, residential, and automotive applications. Both facilities have a building footprint of approximately 850,000 sq. ft., which include a batch house, furnace, tin bath, lehr, forced air coolers, coating lines, and warehouse space. Both facilities have rail access so that hopper cars filled with sand, limestone, and soda ash can be unloaded. These materials are mixed with cullet and tinting additives in the batch house and fed into the furnace.

Float glass derives its name from the use of a molten tin bath that floats a continuous river of molten glass, creating a ribbon of even thickness with a smooth surface. Once placed in operation, the furnace operates continuously for 15 years to produce molten glass at a temperature of approximately 2,500 degrees Fahrenheit to feed the molten tin bath. The process generates a lot of heat. Roof-mounted gravity ventilators with grade mounted intake louvers were used to remove heat from the building areas that contained the furnace, tin bath, and lehr.

Once the glass exits the tin bath at approximately 1,100 degrees Fahrenheit, it enters the air-cooled lehr, which anneals the glass to reduce strain. Exiting the lehr after passing through forced air coolers at close to ambient temperature, the glass is inspected. Glass that fails inspection is cut, then dropped onto a conveyor that returns it to the batch house as cullet for reuse. The glass is then cut into specified segments. Coatings are then added to reduce solar glare and solar heat gain. The finished product is packaged for transport to fabricators that produce the finished framed glass for installation. Glass manufactured at the Geneva Plant was used at the Erie Insurance New Office Building (2021) in Erie, Pennsylvania.

The weight of the process and materials required extensive foundations to support the furnace, furnace stack, batch house, tin bath, and lehr. At both facilities, a 29-foot-deep basement was provided with a four-foot-thick concrete mat to support the furnace. Although both buildings are very similar aboveground, the foundation system used for each site is vastly different. In DeWitt, the geotechnical conditions required the use of concrete-filled drilled piers of up to 70 feet in depth to reach solid rock to achieve a bearing pressure of up to 90,000 pounds per square foot. Steel beam piles were driven to support the furnace stack. The Geneva facility was built on glacial moraine, which required about 900 steel pipe piles to be driven up to 100 feet in depth. The steel pipe piles were filled with concrete to achieve loading capacities of 60 tons or 100 tons depending on the diameter of the steel pipe.

Author: John Cole, PE, Principal, Mechanical Engineering, Albert Kahn Associates

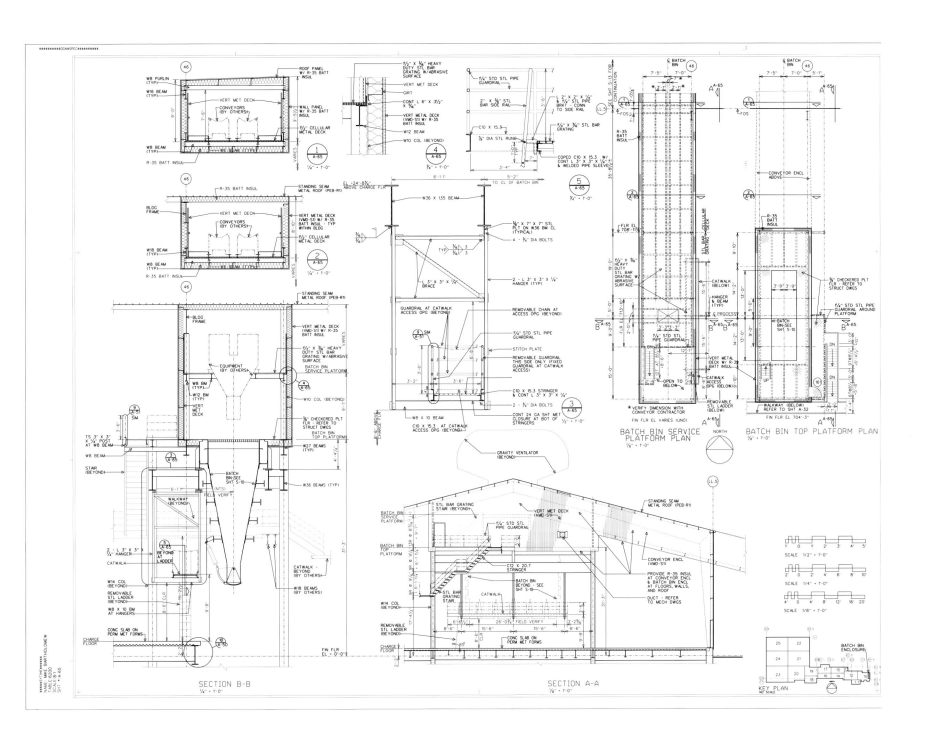

SECTION B-B
¼" • 1'-0"

SECTION A-A
⅛" • 1'-0"

BATCH BIN SERVICE
PLATFORM PLAN
⅛" • 1'-0"

BATCH BIN TOP PLATFORM PLAN
⅛" • 1'-0"

KEY PLAN
NO SCALE

SCALE ½" • 1'-0"

SCALE ¼" • 1'-0"

SCALE ⅛" • 1'-0"

BOOK DEPOSITORY BUILDING

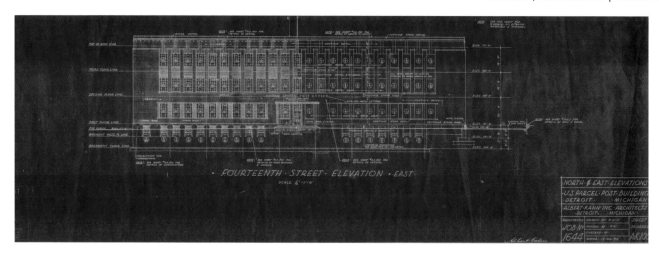

Originally designed as Detroit's main post office in the early 20th century, the expansive three-story building collected and sorted mail delivered by trains from all over the country. The mail was shuttled from the adjacent Michigan Central Station to the post office by a tunnel connecting the structures. Albert Kahn was commissioned to design the new federal postal building after launching a vigorous lobbying campaign, about the time he was designing industrial complexes for the Soviet Union. Construction began in 1934 and the building opened the following year. The Art Deco building featured an unusual architectural element: a curtain wall. The light gray and brown brick exterior covering was non-structural, unlike other buildings historically.

In classic Kahn style, another element of the 277,000 sq. ft. building was its forest of mushroom columns. These large, flared support structures, extending into a disc-like capital have a unique load-bearing design that allowed for maximum support with minimal space utilization. The columns used reinforced concrete – which was a revolutionary new design in the early 1900s – and allowed for a fireproof structure.

The post office eventually sold the building to Detroit Public Schools, which used the facility as a warehouse for books and supplies. The building became known as the Roosevelt Warehouse or the Book Depository building. In 1987, a fire erupted quickly in the vacant building, still stocked with books and school supplies. Kahn's design – thick concrete floors, walls, and columns – spared the Book Depository from ruin, leaving the building structurally intact for renovation. Remaining abandoned for more than 30 years, the Book Depository was purchased by Ford Motor Company, as part of the automaker's plans to create a new mobility innovation district in Corktown. Michigan Central Station, which Ford also acquired in 2018, is being restored to its original grandeur as the centerpiece of the district. Entrepreneurs, start-ups, and companies that will join Ford to develop and test future mobility solutions are expected to use the newly renovated, open spaces of the Book Depository for maker, office and technology areas.

With 20-foot ceilings and large windows along each floor of the building, the possibilities for the space are endless. The Book Depository's "modern style" became a visual trademark for the Kahn firm in the mid-to-late 1930s and echoes of the design can be seen in the Ford Rotunda and the small power plant at The Henry Ford Museum.

Little of the Book Depository's former life as a post office was salvageable, though a 10-foot section of a metal catwalk that hung from the ceiling will be saved as an historical artifact. Postal police used the catwalks to secretly spy on workers through small, sliding windows. A large open space through each floor in the building's center, mostly likely used for some sort of machinery, will remain intact, accenting the open floor plans and improving lighting. The renovated Book Depository is expected to open in 2022.

Author: Greg Tasker, Writer for Ford Land

FIRST NATIONAL BUILDING

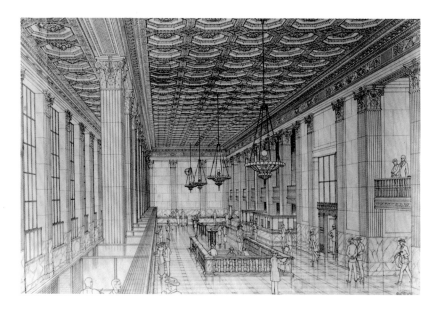

Formerly known as the First and Old Detroit National Bank, this building was originally designed to be built on the existing foundation of the soon-to-be demolished Hotel Pontchartrain. According to an article published in *The American Architect* in 1921, the downtown site historically presented a number of challenges for construction including the proximity of surrounding structures, location on a main thoroughfare, and the soft clay conditions.[206] In 1906, when the original foundation for the hotel was underway, excavation caused settlements in adjacent streets which then caused cracks in nearby buildings. Lawsuits ensued. After many tests, and borings down to 75 feet below the surface, engineers had to design a different type of foundation. Wood piles were sunk every two feet to carry a reinforced concrete mat which would then distribute the weight of the hotel.

Kahn's early designs called for the bank building to be clad in terracotta and columns to be spaced strategically throughout to carry the load of the building on the current concrete pad and wood piles. Engineers determined that the weight of the building was going to be less than the original hotel. "Then the changes which every architect knows are inevitable, came, and the whole scheme was changed."[207] The scope of the building increased; new floors and a new wing were added, so the prior foundation could no longer support the new building. Crews began to remove sections of the concrete mat.

In collaboration with a foundation consultant from Chicago, Kahn engineers developed a new system to support the building.[208] They decided to use what was called a "Chicago Caisson," a column of concrete often with a bell shaped-end, many of which were modified with three small bells along the column to stabilize the deep foundation. Typically, caissons would extend to bedrock to reduce the likelihood of settling. This was the approach taken years earlier during construction of the Ford Building nearby. As crews sunk the caissons, they encountered a water bearing stratum which rapidly rose through the caisson shaft and into the basement of the structure. Worst of all, a noxious gas was carried up with the water and asphyxiated two workmen in the basement.[209] To prevent a similar calamity, Kahn engineers calculated that the bell shape could rest on soil without the risk of going down further to bedrock.

Working a few feet at a time, buckets of earth were brought up to the surface by a cable connected to an engine, and wooden planks held by iron rings lined the holes to prevent collapse. Once crews reached 85 feet down, concrete was poured to form the caisson. Only those original wood piles that got in the way of the new caissons were cut up and removed in sections; the others remain. The original basement and sub-basement of the Hotel Pontchartrain became part of the new building. For a short time, the First National Building was the tallest in the city – defining the new era of Detroit.

HUMMER H2 PLANT

Manufacturing plants typically take several years to establish a program, design, and construct. Kahn, however, has an extensive history of fast-tracking projects to meet aggressive deadlines that others would believe impossible. The Hummer H2 plant was one such project – within 22 months the first batch of new Hummer H2's drove off the site. This program was the fastest vehicle development from concept to market in the automotive industry at the time.

Located on a 96-acre site near South Bend, AM General's new 630,000 sq. ft. facility was engineered to deliver the Hummer H2, a new sport utility vehicle to market. For over 150 years, AM General has been producing legendary military, commercial, and consumer vehicles. The H2 facility is located just east of the existing plant and part of the complex that produces both the Humvee military vehicle and the commercial version, the Hummer H1.

Using its rich history as Master Architect, Kahn provided overall management and single-source responsibility for the new facility, serving as the owner's primary representative. This was in addition to the complete design and engineering responsibilities of the plant. Kahn also partnered with a Detroit automotive engineering firm, Chiyoda AES, to develop the manufacturing process that would be integrated into the plant. Small manufacturing plants in that area were typically around one million sq. ft. in size. Kahn had to design a major plant within a relatively small footprint, which resulted in one long continuous building without separation between the shops, creating an efficient process. Once operating at full production, the new plant could produce approximately 40,000 vehicles per year and employ around 1,500 people.

FORD WILLOW RUN BOMBER PLANT

YPSILANTI, MICHIGAN | DESIGNED 1941 OPENED 1941

In April 1941, as World War II was intensifying, Ford Motor Company broke ground on a 1,875-acre farm plot near Ypsilanti, Michigan at the behest of the United States government. The Willow Run Bomber Plant, designed by Albert Kahn, was named for a small tributary of the Huron River that ran along the property. Construction of the plant took place in sections and was completed later that same year, allowing bomber parts production to begin by November. Willow Run was, at the time, the largest factory in the world under a single roof.

Comprised of thirty-eight thousand tons of structural steel and five million bricks, the L-shaped building, which would eventually contain over seven million sq. ft. of factory space, was laid out to facilitate the flow of raw materials from the receiving dock, to parts cribs, and onto final assembly. Designed with the aid of a 1:98 scale model, the two parallel assembly lines within the plant were over a mile long. Ford separated production of the B-24 Bombers into three subassemblies to increase efficiency: tail, center section, and nose.[210] These three sections moved down the line to two large turntables allowing the bombers' fuselage to be rotated 90-degrees for final assembly. Because of the nature of the defense work happening within the plant, it was a windowless building lit with artificial lights, instead of the natural daylight employed by Kahn in other Ford factories.

Between July 1942 and June 1945, Willow Run would produce 8,685 B-24 Bombers. At its peak in 1944, the assembly plant housed upwards of 40,000 employees, 35% of which were women, and produced an average of one bomber per hour. The Rosie the Riveter character was born at Willow Run, where each B-24 contained over 300,000 rivets of more than 500 sizes. Many women and minorities were hired at the plant to fill jobs vacated by men who were fighting at the front lines of the war.

The Willow Run Bomber Plant would be the last of many buildings Albert Kahn, who died in 1942, designed for Ford Motor Company. Owned by the United States government, the plant was leased to Kaiser-Fraser for jeep, automobile, and cargo plane production after World War II ended, and was sold to General Motors in 1953 for powertrain and automobile assembly. The majority of the plant was later demolished, with the exception of one original building, which is currently home to the Yankee Air Museum.[211]

Author: Leslie Armbruster, Manager, Ford Motor Company Archives

CHEVROLET GEAR AND AXLE PLANT

DETROIT, MICHIGAN | DESIGNED 1926 RENOVATED 1979

Halting production to repair automotive production facilities is often not an option. Instead, Kahn engineers along with Chevrolet's in-house engineers developed a solution to renovate and replace the roof of the 60-year-old Kahn-designed Detroit Gear and Axle plant without ever shutting down the plant's operations. The new roof was constructed over the old roof, and once finished, the old roof was removed in sections from the inside of the plant.

The new roof system raised the ceiling height from 14 feet to 34 feet to accommodate the latest production equipment and processes. Existing columns and footings could be used to support the load of both roof structures, while larger I-beam sections were added to extend the length of the columns and support the new roof on top of the old. Then, by using the extended columns for basic support and the old roof as a floor, the new roof structure was completed without interrupting plant operations – a real accomplishment that involved nearly 10 acres of steel, insulation, and asphalt.

Due to the size of the plant and the constricted access to the site, a new construction technique was implemented as well. Roof-mounted cranes were used to build the new roof one bay at a time, building their own runway for support as they went.

Additionally, modernized mechanical and electrical systems were added to improve the interior environment which had become too hot and lacked proper lighting for employees. An innovative stratified ventilation system was employed where mechanically cooled air was pushed to the lower level into the employee occupied zone to maintain a comfortable environment. Warm air was then ventilated through the new roof, removing heat from the production process, lighting, and thermal solar gain.

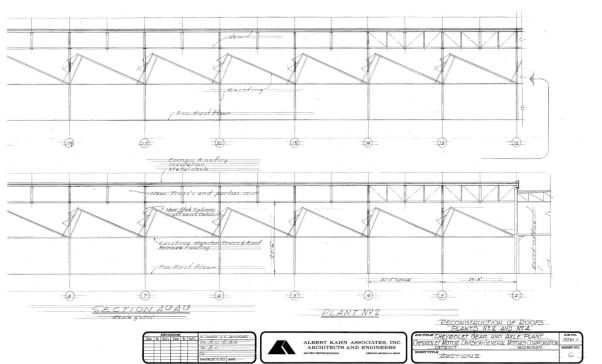

SECTION A³-A³
Scale ⅛"=1'0"

PLANT N°2

RECONSTRUCTION OF ROOFS
PLANTS N°2 AND N°4

ALBERT KAHN ASSOCIATES, INC.
ARCHITECTS AND ENGINEERS
940 NEW CENTER BUILDING   DETROIT, MICHIGAN 48202

JOB TITLE CHEVROLET GEAR AND AXLE PLANT	JOB NO.
CHEVROLET MOTOR DIVISION-GENERAL MOTORS CORPORATION	1336-X
DETROIT MICHIGAN	SHEET NO.
SHEET TITLE SECTIONS	6

235

CHRYSLER JEFFERSON NORTH

DETROIT, MICHIGAN | DESIGNED 1986 OPENED 1991

Chassis assembling

Detroit's newest and most advanced plant was erected across the street from one of its oldest. On the other side of Jefferson Avenue, originally sat the Chalmers Motor Car Factory, designed by Albert Kahn in 1907, becoming part of Chrysler in 1925.[212] The historic plant closed in 1990, 80 years later, and was replaced by the Jefferson North plant to produce the iconic Jeep Grand Cherokee.

Jefferson North included a body shop, paint shop, trim, chassis, and final assembly building, and a building for centralized services such as offices and the energy center. This was the first Chrysler assembly plant in the U.S. to be air conditioned for worker comfort and utilized a pre-cooled air ventilation system, where conditioned air was delivered at low levels along the assembly line to maintain a maximum of 80 degrees Fahrenheit in the summer.[213]

From its sourcing of materials, with a goal of 85-95% just-in-time production by suppliers located around the plant,[214] to value engineering efforts to study and reevaluate each building system, manufacturing process, and technology, Kahn and Chrysler's goal was to design the most efficient and cost-effective plant. These measures take into account not only initial costs, but also long term maintenance costs. In the process, the team spoke with industry leaders and suppliers around the world, which resulted in electrical motor driven systems instead of hydraulic power systems, electric robots in the paint shop, and automation in labor intensive or ergonomically difficult operations.

These studies extended to seemingly low-tech elements of the building such as the shop floors, and resulted in the novel use of steel fiber reinforced concrete slabs.[215] Within manufacturing, the quality of the floor is extremely important as it supports millions of dollars' worth of heavy equipment, requiring flat, uniform, and stable floors. Typically, industrial concrete slabs rely on steel reinforcements and contraction joints to control cracking due to shrinkage. Increasing the number of reinforcements minimizes the size but can increase the number of cracks. By strategically locating contraction joints, the team can determine where cracks will occur for both aesthetic and performance purposes. However, on an industrial floor, each joint must be saw cut, cleaned, and filled with an epoxy resin, which not only increases time and cost, but also requires maintenance in the future.[216] Kahn, Chrysler, and a group of contractors formed a floor slab committee early on in the design process to research and debate alternatives to control cracking and reduce maintenance costs.

At the time, reinforcing concrete with steel fibers was fairly new in the United States. Jefferson North became the largest application of steel fiber reinforced concrete slabs for industrial floors in the United States, incorporating more than 500 tons of steel fibers.[217] The steel fibers are added to the cement mixture in the truck, and evenly distributed in the slurry. This even distribution allows the fibers to better control shrinkage cracking throughout the entire slab. These fibers also allowed for greater distances between contraction joints, meaning fewer joints for the owner to maintain in the long run. This was just one of many initiatives the team evaluated and enacted to construct a longstanding and efficient plant Chrysler could count on for another 80 years.

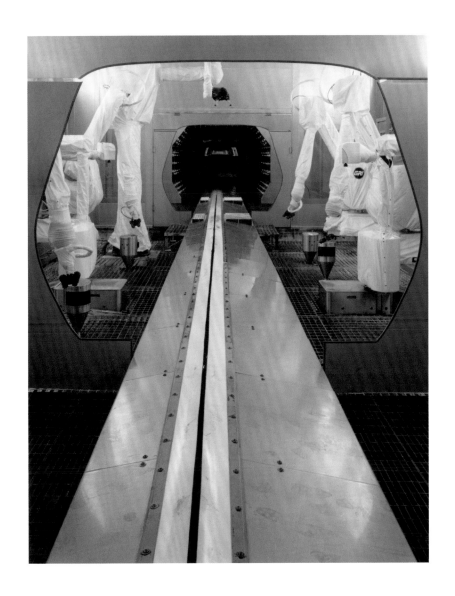

GM GREY IRON FOUNDRY

In 1919, General Motors began casting the original grey iron castings for Chevrolet, Cadillac, Buick, Oakland, and Oldsmobile.[218] Production quickly grew from over 88,000 tons of grey iron in the first year to over 600 tons a day, just a few years later.[219] In 1928, Kahn began working on this site, performing a number of renovations to existing office and factory buildings and adding new production facilities.[220]

In the 1960s, the firm completed a new foundry, referred to as the "experimental foundry" in Kahn company records, and the iconic administration building located nearby. This "experimental foundry" coincides with the plant's exploration into a new nodular iron, which was more flexible, stronger, and fares better under impact than grey iron.[221] Later, in 1976, the firm designed a heat recovery system from the iron ore cupolas to provide energy for heating and ventilating the Administration Building.[222]

This innovation happening at the foundry spurred the Kahn team to experiment with a new exterior treatment on the structure of the office building. This one-story office building housed administrative and engineering offices for the foundry complex. Exterior columns are spaced along the perimeter with large panes of glass wrapping the entire structure. Press releases and articles at the time highlight these exterior steel columns that were engineered to "paint itself" within approximately two years, depending on the atmosphere conditions. 315 tons of exterior steel were coated to rust, as a way to minimize maintenance costs; "The 'weathering' process involves formation of a dense, tightly adherent oxide film which will not flake off or crack. As this 'skin' seals off the base metal, it will retard further atmospheric conditions, preserve the building's structural integrity, and eliminate the need for painting."[223]

At the top of these exposed columns, the roof extends out in all directions protecting the building's interior from direct sunlight, keeping the climate consistent within the office and preventing solar glare. To conserve space on the site, the building was elevated, creating covered parking below the structure for employees and visitors. The intent was also to elevate the building above grade so it was at level with the nearby highway.[224] Large berms were also created to shield the view of the parked cars below. Certainly innovative at the time, this building won multiple design and engineering awards.[225]

FORD ENGINEERING LABORATORY

"Distinctive design will mark advance step in modern industrial architecture."[226] That was how the *Ford News* described the Engineering Laboratory when ground was broken on March 16, 1923. Ford Motor Company was at the peak of production and sales leadership. The company had developed the moving assembly line, stunned the world with its five dollars a day, and opened the Rouge complex nearby.

Henry Ford was looking to build a laboratory where he and his engineers could develop and experiment with many different aspects of Ford products. As a child, Henry was said to have played on the site and witnessed a steam engine powering machines that pressed bricks from materials dug from that very ground. That digging left three ponds on the property that added to the beauty of the future building.

The building exterior is faced with white Bedford limestone. It is a single-story structure 800 feet long by 200 feet deep, with a two-story center along the front of the building, highlighted by limestone columns and etched names of individuals who contributed to the advancement of mankind in fields of art and science. The 21 names were debated by Ford President Edsel Ford and representatives of Kahn until they decided on names like: Charles Darwin, Leonardo Da Vinci, Eli Whitney, Marie Curie and, Henry's idol and friend, Thomas Edison.

"Mankind passes from the old to the new on a human bridge formed by those who labor in the three principle arts – Agriculture, Manufacture, Transportation."[227] As visitors enter through the main entrance, this quote is etched just above the door. They continue on to a large reception area that leads to the executive offices, including Henry's and Edsel's, and a grand staircase to the second floor. All the offices, hallways, and the second-floor reference library are paneled in walnut. The library and Henry's office have fireplaces faced with Alp's Green marble, and the restrooms and drinking fountains are made with marble as well.

The main laboratory is one large room designed to be flexible, with pillars that divide the space into forty-foot by fifty-foot bays. These pillars also house all electrical, plumbing, and air ducts from the basement to the main floor. At the time, it was unheard of to have all the building systems hidden in the structure in that way. The most dramatic feature is the three overhead bays of A-frame windows that run nearly the entire length of the building. Between these bays of windows and the windows on the exterior walls of the building, there is a total glass area of 64,000 sq. ft., the equivalent of 40% of the floor area, which gave an abundance of natural light. This feature was central to several Kahn and Ford buildings of the time.

While the Laboratory changed over the years, including large additions, the loss of two of the ponds for parking, and "modernizing" with drop ceilings and carpet, the building still retains its traditional beauty and significance. A historical highlight that intrigues visitors to this day is from 1938, when Ford executives marked their heights on a pillar in the central area of the building, including Henry and Edsel. It's also the only building left where Henry Ford had an office. While it pays homage to those that advanced the fields of science, arts, and modern industrial architecture, it seems the perfect link to take Ford's research and engineering practices into the future.[228]

Author: Jamie Myler, Research Archivist, Ford Motor Company Archives

DETROIT SCHOOL OF ARTS

The Detroit School of Arts is a public high school specializing in artistic endeavors ranging from orchestra and dance productions, to theatrical and vocal performances, and even TV and radio studios. This is in addition to classroom, lab, and workshop spaces typically found in high schools. Kahn partnered with Hamilton-Anderson Architects on this unique and highly technical school. Due to the mixed-use nature of the school, a variety of advanced engineering systems were incorporated. The scenery workshop, for example, was designed with welding arms, dust collection, a paint spray booth, and corresponding exhaust and make-up air systems. As a center for performing arts, acoustics also played an important role in the design and construction of the entire building and its systems. As such, strict acoustic design criteria and guidelines were followed to isolate vibration from sound sensitive spaces and prevent sound transmission between spaces.

A carbon dioxide (CO_2) monitoring system was also designed for the facility, monitoring general CO_2 levels through the return duct. The system provides feedback on space ventilation performance, and warns the building's operators if readings rise to dangerous levels. To ensure proper mechanical systems design and acceptable indoor air quality, the team contacted a local air quality monitoring station from the US EPA to obtain outdoor contaminant concentrations for sulfur dioxide (SO_2), nitrogen dioxide (NO_2), ozone (O_3), carbon monoxide (CO), lead (Pb), and particulate matter. The information was analyzed to determine compliance with the minimum outdoor air quality standards and the possible need for outdoor air treatment.

Another space within the building that posed a significant engineering challenge was the auditorium lobby atrium. In the case of a fire, code dictates that the maximum velocity for air travel into the atrium is 200 feet per minute. The team had to develop a method for providing the large quantity of make-up air required for the atrium's smoke evacuation system. They discovered an innovative solution using operable windows around the curtain wall of the auditorium lobby. Each window is equipped with a small, low voltage motor which drives a chain arm to open the window. The device is triggered when the fire alarm signals the smoke exhaust fan to activate. This solution was recognized by the curtain wall and motor manufacturers as a unique and innovative solution for use of their products. In fact, these companies have gone on to share the team's solution with other architects in the Detroit area and nationally.

GM CLIMATIC WIND TUNNEL

The Climatic Wind Tunnel on the General Motors (GM) Warren Technical Center campus was designed to vastly improve and shorten the development process of their vehicles. Prior to wind tunnels such as this, automotive manufacturers shipped their vehicles to various sites to test temperature extremes. Shipping a car to the desert of Arizona in July and the plains of Minnesota in January means that testing has to occur within a specific time and at a specific site, adding both time and expense to the vehicle development phase. Climatic Wind Tunnels allow for four season testing within a highly controlled environment. Engineers can test the heating, ventilation, air conditioning systems, powertrain cooling, drivability, and thermal effects on vehicles and components. The facility houses three separate tunnels which can replicate temperatures from -40 degrees Fahrenheit to 140 degrees Fahrenheit.

Commissioned by GM under a "turnkey" contract, Kahn partnered with the contractor and an engineering firm that specializes in wind tunnel designto design and engineer the facility. The three tunnels, rated in terms of the size of the wind tunnel nozzle, are sized at 50, 100 and 150 sq. ft. The largest tunnel was a renovation of an existing horizontal concrete tunnel, whereas the 50 and 100 sq. ft. tunnels are new vertical steel tunnels. Chief among the many special systems developed for this facility is the ammonia refrigeration system used to chill a synthetic fluid for use in wind tunnel cooling coils. Ammonia, one of the oldest and most efficient refrigerants, was selected because its efficiency allowed for significant reduction in the physical size and capital costs of the refrigeration machines. Equipment rooms housing ammonia systems were carefully engineered to satisfy relevant building codes and GM standards for safety.

PRATT WHITNEY X218 HIGH ALTITUDE TEST FACILITY

EAST HARTFORD, CONNECTICUT | DESIGNED 1978 OPENED 1980

How do you replicate high altitude conditions of 47,000 feet and -20 degrees Fahrenheit, while a state-of-the-art 100,000 pound thrust passenger jet engine sucks in a quarter of a million cubic feet of air per minute? And, do that without freezing up the cooling coils or collapsing the entire structure.

One of the key factors was the building enclosure itself. The major issues were structural integrity to withstand 106 pounds per square foot differential pressure and a thermal transmission value of 0.038 British Thermal Units. After reviewing a wide range of options, we ended up selecting a pressure bonded sandwich panel construction having an expanded polystyrene core, exterior grade plywood structural skin, faced with stainless steel on the inside and embossed aluminum on the outside. Joints were tongued and grooved with silicone sealing. Panels were through-bolted to avoid use of sheet metal screws, which could vibrate loose during testing and damage the engine. Not only did these structural materials address the differential pressure and required thermal concerns, but they also provided moisture and air tightness and corrosion resistance.

To replicate the intense cold environment for the engines a two-stage refrigeration system was chosen. The primary system uses 40% ethylene glycol refrigerant for primary cooling from 95 degrees Fahrenheit to 36 degrees Fahrenheit with double stacked six row coils for maximum moisture removal. The primary system is served by two 2,200-ton chillers. The secondary cooling uses trichlorethylene refrigerant fed from two 1,450-ton chillers, cooling the refrigerant down to -23 degrees Fahrenheit and using double stacked eight row coils. To prevent frost, the coil face is sprayed with 1,200 gallons per minute of 50% ethylene glycol to continuously de-ice the coils.

While the frost removal system was itself pretty innovative, recovering the 1,200 gallons per minute of ethylene glycol was critical for efficient, cost-effective operation. At the time, ethylene glycol cost $3.00 per gallon, or about $3,600 per minute of testing. Placing a heat recovery coil on the back side of the jet engine allowed the heat to be captured and be used to boil the glycol solution. The glycol was then distilled and able to be reused.

While these major elements themselves were enough to offer significant engineering challenges, every facet of the design required close attention to detail as we addressed air intake louvres and air filtration, piping and coil materials, blow-in doors for emergency pressure relief, and the specialized engine exhaust system. Oh, and about those high atmospheric conditions – we developed an engine inlet Venturi system with stacked 24" butterfly valves that could be sequenced and regulated in response to the test simulation engine load and altitude.[229]

Author: Gordon V.R. Holness, PE, Chairman Emeritus, Albert Kahn Associates

CHRYSLER POWERTRAIN TEST CENTER

AUBURN HILLS, MICHIGAN | DESIGNED 1995 OPENED 1999

The Chrysler Technology Center is a sprawling complex of offices, labs and test facilities. One of the most significant aspects of this center is the Powertrain Test Center, which included four test cell wings housing a total of 80 engine test cells providing 113 testing sites. This facility enabled engineers to test a whole host of conditions and scenarios within a controlled lab environment, with greater accuracy, faster product development schedules, and improved driver experience.

What previously required long lead times and the expense of shipping cars to various points around the world for environmental and road condition testing, now happened within one complex. The test cells allowed for performance, endurance, and emissions testing of engines, transmissions, and transaxles; thermal conditioning of air and fluids; control of powertrain speeds and loads; in-cell maintenance; small parts storage; and operator safety and egress. Located near the test cells were the Powertrain Support Labs which featured labs and equipment required to support the Powertrain Test Center such as vehicle garages, machine shops, engine build-up and teardown, storage as well as office space for technical engineers.

Perhaps the greatest construction complexity of the expansion project involved the test cells. Each test cell is served by a multitude of mechanical and electrical utilities, all confined to a space not much larger than a single car garage. In addition, each engine durability test cell required a thermal oxidizer engine exhaust abatement system to satisfy regional limits on air pollution. Each oxidizer served four test cells and connected to a common manifold, allowing for redundancy in the event of failure or equipment maintenance.

A great deal of consideration was given to the safety of the test technicians operating the engines in the test cells. Fire protection and toxic gas detection systems constantly monitored each test area, and set points were in place to automatically shut down operations in an emergency. Each test cell was also equipped with explosion relief panels, which are designed to vent excessive pressures to the exterior of the building. Similarly, the interior walls and roof of each cell were designed to contain explosive forces, up to a pressure of 100 pounds per square foot. Careful consideration was given to the location of the fuel lines and their point of entry into each test cell as the test cell fuel supply represented the greatest potential for causing explosions. The team decided to route the fuel lines within a conditioned enclosure hung off the exterior wall above the explosion relief panels and around the entire perimeter of the test cell wings. The finished fuel piping enclosure blends seamlessly into the exterior facade of the test cell wings, and was designed to prevent possible leaks from contaminating the surrounding area.

This Powertrain Test Center vastly improved Chrysler's ability to accurately test and develop new vehicle systems within a lab environment that dynamically simulated real-world conditions.[230]

ETHYL RESEARCH CENTER

RICHMOND, VIRGINIA | DESIGNED 1990 OPENED 1994

As one of the world's top four suppliers of fuel and lubricant additives, the Ethyl Corporation works with major oil companies to improve the performance of automotive fluids. Located nearby their corporate headquarters, the Research Center was constructed on the site of a former state prison constructed in 1800. The new research campus brought a new life to the site and the surrounding area.

The state-of-the-art research complex featured a six-story office and laboratory building tower and an adjacent low-rise mechanical laboratory building. The office and laboratory building tower housed chemical research in five floors of chemical laboratories, and the adjacent low-rise mechanical building consisted of test cells and support facilities. Both buildings incorporated a number of advanced safety features to protect researchers and staff from the risks of chemical leaks, including hydrocarbon, carbon monoxide, and nitrogen dioxide detection systems.

Below the structure were 33 underground tanks with a total capacity of 160,000 gallons. Fuels were pumped from the underground storage area into a patch panel where the researcher can choose which type of fuel is pumped into the blend tank. A second patch panel is used to send the blended fuel to the specific test cell where the fuel is required. Fuels blended in this area are fed to the test cells with multiple line configurations. The mixed fuels can be delivered to and from any one of 90 locations. The fuel is transported by air pumps, which eliminates the risk of an electrical spark that might ignite fuel vapors.

As part of their environmentally conscious initiatives, the office and laboratory tower building incorporated the latest in exhaust emission-control. All engine exhausts, which are a bi-product of testing in the facility, are collected and treated by a catalytic incineration system to reduce pollutants released into the atmosphere. A pollution-control room was developed to house this specialized equipment. The room is a six-story shaft that houses the Econ-Nox unit, catalyst bed, quench unit, wet scrubber, mist eliminator, and all the various components that serve the main pieces of equipment. Engines used for testing in the facility exhaust into a central system that pulls fumes through a hydrocarbon burner, a catalytic converter, and finally, a scrubber which removes impurities. The stack gasses are continuously monitored to guarantee pollution control and automatically adjust the system to optimize performance. Additionally, should Ethyl want to expand their testing capabilities in the future, the pollution-control equipment is sized for additional capacity.

FORD ADVANCED ENGINEERING CENTER

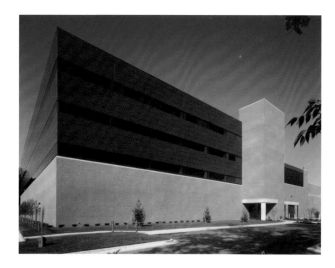

Ford's Advanced Engineering Center was once the largest automotive Noise, Vibration, and Harshness (NVH) facility in the United States. As competition between domestic and international automobile manufacturers continued to build, American manufacturers realized it was no longer enough to build a quiet vehicle. The NVH characteristics of a vehicle must be designed to match the customer expectations of the product. For example, the sports car buyer may wish to hear the roar of the engine or the growl of a tuned exhaust system. The facility includes a Sound Quality/Human Factors Lab which translates subjective customer preferences into measurable engineering terms, and relates those measurable terms to NVH and other vehicle test/analysis results.

Numerous test chambers were included, each replicating specific conditions to test one or several systems on the vehicle. The hemi-anechoic chamber simulates the ideal vehicle environment on an open highway where noise radiated vertically and to the sides is lost to the environment. To achieve this simulated condition, the test chamber walls and ceiling are acoustically absorbent.

This facility presented an opportunity to research and test new solutions to the traditional fiberglass and foam wedges frequently used to line the walls of these chambers. Although they were popular for more than 60 years, both fiberglass and foam present a number of issues including fiberglass' inability to withstand physical abuse and potential to release glass fibers into the chamber environment, and foam's quick burn rate and the release of noxious chemicals when exposed to fire. Additionally, both products are subject to discoloration over time.[231] Kahn, Ford, and an acoustic product manufacturer collaborated to develop and test a metal wedge. The exterior of the new wedge, now called a Metadyne Anechoic Wedge, featured perforated sheet metal and multiple density fiberglass batts inside. Not only did the Metadyne Wedge solve many of the inherent issues of the fiberglass and foam wedges, but the test results also revealed that the metal wedges performed better than these materials at low frequency and matched their performance at high frequency.

One challenge when designing the center was making sure the building and test chambers were protected from noise and vibration from sources both outside and inside the building. Vibrations from the surrounding soils, nearby machinery and other equipment, heating, ventilation, and air conditioning systems, etc., can all change the effectiveness of the NVH room and its test results. The acoustic chambers were completely supported by steel springs which supported the floor, walls and ceiling. They were constructed as a box within a box. The outer box was made of 12" thick masonry walls and 12" thick concrete ceiling. The interior box was a heavy gauge metal stud system which supported the metal wedge panels. Independently supporting a 250,000 lb. room on vibration isolators, or acoustically isolating the noise of a 300 HP dynamometer from an adjacent test chamber represent engineering accomplishments on this project that, when taken individually, are noteworthy in their own right. Taken collectively, and integrated under one roof with multiple similar engineering functions, marks the truest measure of overall design quality.

MERCURY MARINE NVH CENTER

Mercury Marine has been at the forefront in Noise, Vibration, and Harshness (NVH) testing and the development of marine products for decades. They consistently lead the industry in the production of outboard and sterndrive motors, and additional test capacity allowed them to exceed product development goals. Two highly flexible fully capable test chambers were designed specifically for testing a variety of marine products and higher horsepower engines.

Hemi-anechoic test facilities are nothing new within the NVH testing community. However, supporting test rooms on a steel coil vibration isolation system above a 66,000 gallon water reservoir was a one-of-a-kind installation. The test rooms are a room-within-a-room, self-supporting, and only contact the spring-isolated floor slab, maintaining the highest degree of vibration isolation possible. Vibration isolating mounts are placed between the foundation walls and piers and the underside of the test room floor to isolate the test room floor and acoustic room structure from any remaining unwanted ground-borne vibration.

Marine product testing must replicate the open water environment to best simulate real world NVH characteristics. Each NVH test room is placed over a basement water reservoir, but just a simple water tank is not enough. Replication of the flow characteristics realized in open water conditions was critical to accurately simulate the real-world environment. Mercury engineers used computational fluid dynamics (CFD) analysis to optimize the depth and shape of the reservoir to mitigate unwanted turbulence and wake formation. This analysis aided in confirming placement of floor support piers, ideal radius of reservoir corners, and configuration of underwater baffle plates. The mat foundation is 24-inch-thick steel-reinforced concrete bearing on compacted native soils. It supports poured concrete walls and piers that bear the load of the test room concrete slab. The perimeter foundation walls average 36 inches thick to resist the lateral forces associated with water on one side and earth on the other, as well as the unique geometry required for the vibration isolation systems.

Hemi-anechoic test rooms are generally sized to allow sound pressure level measurements in the free field of the test source. The test source for this facility was established by Mercury to allow the majority testing of the Brunswick family product line. This required an unprecedented level of flexibility to be designed into the test room infrastructure to accommodate a very wide range of acoustic test sources, both in physical size and sound level signature. Internal room dimensions (wedge tip-to-tip) were optimized at the minimum desired room cutoff frequency of 60 Hz.

The inherent complexity of NVH facilities demands open and frequent communication between the owner, architects, engineers, and contractors. Mercury Marine's NVH technical center has established an industry benchmark for excellence.[232] It stands as a testament to the high achievement possible with successful collaboration amongst the entire team.

Author: Peter G. Lynde, PE, Senior VP & Director of Research and Technology, Albert Kahn Associates

HILL AUDITORIUM

The unique parabolic shape, exceptional acoustics, and large size of the Hill Auditorium created one of the most significant concert halls in America. Designed by Albert Kahn with noted acoustic scientist Hugh Tallant, the auditorium was dedicated on June 25, 1913, and immediately became a centerpiece of the University of Michigan campus.[233] Albert's son Edgar recalled, "About all A.K. knew about acoustics was that when a pin was dropped on the stage of the Mormon Temple in Salt Lake City, it could be heard in the most remote part of the hall. A series of articles had just been written on acoustics by Hugh Tallant, a New York engineer. The problem was put to him by A.K."[234]

In creating both an architectural gem and an engineering feat, Kahn and Tallant were able to accommodate a record number of seats strategically placed so that the slightest sound from the stage could be heard by every audience member within fractions of a second. "When Hill Auditorium was almost completed in 1913," Edgar continued, "I drove with my father to Ann Arbor. We climbed to the highest seat in the second gallery of the auditorium. I then went down onto the stage carrying a pin we had with great foresight brought with us, dropped it, and father heard it."[235]

The building's design featured decorative terracotta, tapestry brickwork, massive stone masonry, ornamental plaster, and a rich polychromatic decorative finish. In the late 1940s, the original seating was replaced and the original Arts and Crafts interior and rich auditorium lighting were eliminated. Great performances and literary presentations continued, even as the Hall became technically more outdated with each new decade. The building was placed in the National Register of Historic Places in the late 1970s.

After almost 90 years, a complete renewal of all building and theatrical systems was imperative. Plans to renew and thoughtfully upgrade the auditorium to a state-of-the-art performance venue emerged in 1998. Collaborating with Quinn Evans Architects, Kahn restored the exterior of the historic structure including the monumental limestone and tapestry brick façade. The large stone and brick front terrace was also reconstructed. Inside, the auditorium has been returned to the original Arts and Crafts interior, with the unique 2,000 sq. ft. interior skylight and special bands of ornamental lighting that gave the original hall such a special quality. The acoustic characteristics were preserved and the 1949 seats were replaced with historically appropriate fixed seating. Elevators, restrooms, and new lobbies have been carefully inserted into the restored building. A west addition was completed to allow barrier-free access to the stage and orchestra level of the auditorium. Now a new grand staircase extends below the historic grand stairs to the new lower lobby and concessions area, which also displays the School of Music's Historic Stearns Collection of Musical Instruments. Behind the walls, a comprehensive building system upgrade was performed including the replacement of all plumbing, heating, ventilating systems, and air-conditioning was introduced. With this massive restoration complete, the Hill Auditorium will continue to serve the University and the greater Michigan public well into the 21st century.

GE APPLIANCE PARK

LOUISVILLE, KENTUCKY AND COLUMBIA, MARYLAND | DESIGNED 1951 AND 1968

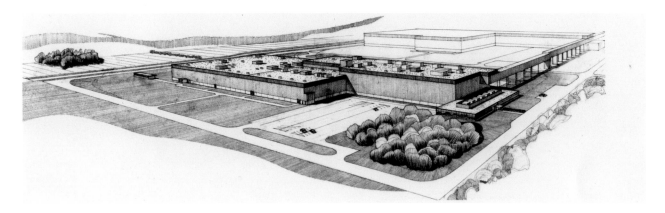

Remnants of the "War Room" on the 11th floor of the Albert Kahn Building were still in use well into the 1960s. This time, instead of top-secret work for the military, aerospace, or automotive industries, a sequestered team at Kahn developed two new manufacturing complexes for General Electric (GE), first in Kentucky and later in Maryland.[236]

After World War II, GE planned to consolidate its operations to meet an increased appliance demand from American households. The company set its sights on Louisville for its new headquarters as the city had a large labor base, centralized location, and access to natural resources and distribution chains. As a leading producer of home appliances, GE has a long history of product innovation, including the first residential refrigerator, automatic washing machine, heat pump climate control system, among many others,[237] which necessitated the top-secret status of the projects. GE's innovations spread to the process of mass production as well as, "it was an early adopter of plastic molding technologies, computers and (eventually) robotics."[238] In 1954, GE bought one of the first commercial computer systems UNIVAC I, a 30-ton multi-piece machine with a processor that filled a 25 x 50 foot room, to manage inventory, budget, and payroll.[239] Kahn collaborated with GE to incorporate these new manufacturing ideas and technologies, designing entire campuses that facilitate these processes, while creating a safe and productive environment for workers.

With manufacturing comes new jobs and new residents, which translates to more housing, public infrastructure, and a boost for the local economy. However, producing a monumental manufacturing complex that stretches over 1,000 acres, such as at Appliance Park East, Maryland, poses certain risks to the surrounding area – specifically, the potential for blighted areas to emerge amidst the facilities and on the outskirts of the complex. To mitigate that risk, Kahn developed a comprehensive masterplan that didn't strip the site of its natural beauty, but instead merged the natural landscape and the manufacturing process. In 1970, former Kahn President Sol King spoke of the recent completion of Appliance Park East, noting that the industrial park "respects and preserves the natural environment and, above all else, it respects the people working in the plant for whom it provides a physical environment conducive to human satisfaction, as well as to productivity and efficiency."[240]

To take advantage of the wooded areas within the park, the office buildings are located on the opposite side of the manufacturing buildings, allowing employees to enjoy the views of nature as well as outdoor space. An 85-million-gallon water retention pond was also created to gather stormwater from the roofs and pavements of the park, adding another tranquil design feature and releasing the stormwater at a slower rate to prevent downstream flooding.[241] To address the park's connection with the surrounding area, a natural buffer of native vegetation was created along the periphery of the site, broken only by rail or vehicle entrances to the park.

Both Appliance Park campuses allowed GE to consolidate and expand their operations to employ over 10,000 people, and further push their product innovations to rank number one in major household appliances.[242]

LEAR HEADQUARTERS

As a global vehicle systems provider, Lear was in search of a distinguished yet progressive solution for its new headquarters. The seemingly weightless cantilevering structure is wrapped in a translucent glass curtain-wall. Within, an open office floor plan provided flexible department layout and collaboration with easy access to technology. The first floor housed a reception lobby and product display area, a 300-seat auditorium and conference center, coffee shop, kitchen, cafeteria, and other core service elements. The second and third floors are designed as flexible, open office and private office space. The use of nimble, butt-jointed glass allows borrowed light from the exterior offices to filter into the conference rooms and common spaces. Using structural steel girders cantilevered beyond support columns, the structure of the building is stepped outwards, giving the illusion that the glass offices float in mid-air. The cantilevered structure allows the floor areas on the upper floors of the building to increase; lateral stiffness for the structure was achieved through the use of braced frames hidden in the cores.

However, before the structure could take shape, this 24-acre brownfield site needed to be remediated. The project's masterplan and site redevelopment efforts called for the creation of an expansive green inner-core capable of supporting 500,000 sq. ft. of office space. Once dotted by tool, die, wood and machine shops that routinely dumped chemicals – including asbestos, PCB's, petroleum, and heavy metals – into the ground adjacent to their plants, the team needed to remediate the hazardous soils that permeated the project site. This meant that contaminated groundwater and over 5,000 tons of soil were safely removed and hauled to a hazardous waste landfill, and buried chemical storage vessels were located and removed from the site. Following this incredible cleanup effort, an array of indigenous vegetation and over 470 trees were planted. Below-grade retention and infiltration galleries along with an innovative rain garden and CULTEC system were installed on the site to filter and clean the stormwater before it reached the nearby river. Upon completion, the site was returned to the environmentally safe, pristine setting of years past.

Lear is a company that develops and exercises environmentally friendly manufacturing practices. As such, remediation and sensitive use of the site were key priorities throughout this project, and is just one sustainable aspect of this LEED Gold building. Lear also wanted to readapt a building that remained on the site. Kahn repurposed an old tool and die shop to become Lear's collaborative design studio. In the end, the team created unity between the ethereal form of the building and the renewed natural environment of the site.

NISSAN MANUFACTURING FACILITY

The country was in the midst of a recession, and foreign automakers were in a race to expand their operations in America. Nissan won that race, and built an immense plant employing around 3,000 people, generating more than $3 million in local and state taxes, and bringing more than $30 million in new industrial projects to the small town of Smyrna.[243]

Originally designed at over three million sq. ft., Nissan's industrial plant and corporate headquarters was designed to increase the company's production and ease of distribution while being flexible to accommodate future growth. Oriented along one central spine are the corporate headquarters on one side and the three major production facilities – body, frame, and stamping, paint, and trim and chassis – on the other. Woven between these buildings were large outdoor areas that provide space for employees as well as room for future expansion. In addition to these four main buildings, onsite ancillary facilities were also created, including an outdoor test track, emissions testing facility, storage warehouse, employee training facility, power house, and waste treatment center.

This plant was one of the most advanced automotive plants constructed at the time, where computer systems monitored and controlled the manufacturing process, security, maintenance, and energy use across the campus. Additionally, over 200 robots performed welding and painting tasks as part of the assembly process.[244] Part of the challenge when working with any foreign automaker is melding their ideas, expectations, and processes, with industrial building codes and practices in the United States. For example, in Japan, many of the industrial facilities are not heated or air conditioned. Kahn engineers worked with Nissan's American team to implement a HVAC system that delivered warm or conditioned air 10 feet from the shop floor.[245] Instead of paying to heat or cool the entire structure, the system focused on the worker occupied zone to provide a more comfortable and productive environment for them to work in.

With the incredible teamwork and coordination between the owner, construction manager, and architect-engineer, automotive production began two months ahead of schedule.[246] Within Kahn, the project was led by three lead architects, each with their own buildings, collaborating to quickly design and engineer the vast campus.[247] Not only was this project significant in size, technology, and impact, but it was also significant for the firm, carrying us through the recession and offering a long term client.

By 1991, additions to the site made the Nissan plant the largest automotive assembly plant in the world at five million sq. ft. under one roof.[248] Kahn returned to the site many times, including the 2013 addition of a Lithium Ion Battery Plant, Storage, and Lab facility. To produce batteries for electric and hybrid vehicles, Kahn designed a highly regulated environment with controlled electrical supply and advanced systems to limit electrical fluctuations and testing interference. The battery plant features clean, dry, anti-static rooms using desiccant dehumidification, vapor sealing, and electrostatic discharge coating on the floors. Today, the plant continues to increase its production and advance its technology, and has grown to more that six million sq. ft.

DELTA DENTAL

Located on 57 acres of pastoral farm land, Delta Dental desired a campus that could sensibly accommodate their current and future growth. This translates to the physical spaces, employee wellbeing, as well as the functional support needs of the company. Existing buildings were renovated to provide additional office space, gathering space, and collaboration spaces. A new three-story curved glass lobby, clad in a highly efficient low-E coated glass curtain wall, enhanced the building entrance. Constructing this curved glass wall required the entire team of designers, contractors, and suppliers to work collaboratively in phases and calibrate their software to ensure accurate geometries for each component and system involved in the construction, avoiding the potential for gaps between the curtain wall and the curved concrete floors.

The new construction on the site was designed with sustainability in mind, while complementing the existing buildings on the site. The orientation of each building was carefully studied to properly maintain heat gain and loss and capitalize on daylighting options that reduce artificial lighting during the day, all resulting in improved energy consumption and occupant comfort. Building materials and systems selected improve the health of occupants by utilizing resources that reduce indoor air pollution, providing a working environment that is both healthy and stimulating for occupants. An existing pond was expanded to properly drain and filter stormwater run-off while offering an attractive amenity.

Another aspect of the renovation and expansion of Delta Dental's corporate campus was the relocation of the data center from the lower level of an existing structure into a separate building. Nestled into the back of the site, this partially recessed semi-bunker style structure employed the same palette of materials as the other campus buildings. Data centers are highly secure buildings with advanced building systems to handle the heat generated by the large servers. Four 1,000 kVA diesel back-up generators were provided to ensure that the data center has a redundant source of power. Within the electrical system, a second set of paralleling switchgears provide clean power from the generator output before it reaches the servers. This center will remain active regardless of power-failure or natural disasters. The building featured one entrance and no windows or glass, to ensure security. It also contained double-reinforced alternate corridors where air can be directed in the unlikely event of a fire or other emergency. Constructed of reinforced concrete walls and roof, this hardened structure is designed to withstand all manner of weather, including an F2 tornado.

For the data center to operate as an effective disaster recovery unit, all operations must, among other things, maintain an "N + one redundancy" configuration, which meant that backup systems are in place should one system or component fail. The data center is a certified "Tier III" facility by the Uptime Institute, making it one of a few data centers to achieve this certification worldwide.

UM UNIVERSITY HOSPITAL

The University Hospital is one of three main hospitals and numerous medical facilities on the University of Michigan's medical center campus. Starting in 1978, Albert Kahn Associates designed this hospital to replace what was affectionately known as "Old Main," the adult general and teaching hospital on campus. Old Main was also designed by Kahn beginning in 1917 and completed in 1925; construction was delayed due to World War I. Similar to Kahn's industrial and commercial designs at the time, this early public hospital was engineered to provide an optimal amount of natural light and air through a double Y shape of the building, used reinforced concrete for its fireproof qualities, and was designed along a modular block plan to create optimal efficiency for both patients and staff.[249] This hospital featured "more than two miles of main corridors, 10 acres of floor space, 2,799 windows, and 280,000 sq. ft. of floor space," and approximately 700 patient beds.[250] In front of Old Main, Kahn designed the hospital's administration building with an iconic entrance arch. When Old Main was demolished following the completion of the new hospital, the entrance arch was saved and placed in storage where it remains today for future display.[251]

The state-of-the-art replacement University Hospital contained a vast array of adult medical and surgical services, including specialty operating suites for neurosurgery, cardiac care, and organ transplant within over one million sq. ft. Kahn engineers spent seven years researching systems and products that would meet the needs of the hospital and ran detailed tests and calculations to make sure that the selected systems performed as intended. In the end, they were able to design one of the most energy efficient hospitals in the country.[252]

Starting from the outside, the building envelope is thermally insulated to reduce heat gains/losses, allowing for the use of a centralized air heating and cooling system rather than radiators along the perimeter. Primary heating and cooling was provided by a central refrigeration plant equipped with electric drive centrifugal heat pump chillers. A pathological waste incinerator equipped with heat recovery technology, generated additional heat to support the central campus steam supply for heating, humidification, and sterilization.[253]

Underground, a thermal chilled water basin was filled with two million gallons of water. Water was cooled at nighttime by three 1,000-ton chillers and stored in the thermal basin. The chilled water was then used during the day to cool the hospital. This storage basin was connected to variable air volume air-conditioning units that both filter and condition the air for the entire hospital. Refrigerating the water at nighttime, when the energy costs are lower, resulted in a significant annual energy cost savings. The size of the water storage tank was determined by calculating how much cooling would be needed for 12 hours of continuous use. In addition to energy savings, this type of storage basin was reliable and able to maintain cooling in case of a chiller failure or power outage for up to 12 hours. Energy use was centralized and controlled from one operating system with customized control algorithms to optimize use. When it opened in 1986, all of these systems allowed the hospital to operate at approximately 20 percent below the national average energy use for similar facilities.[254]

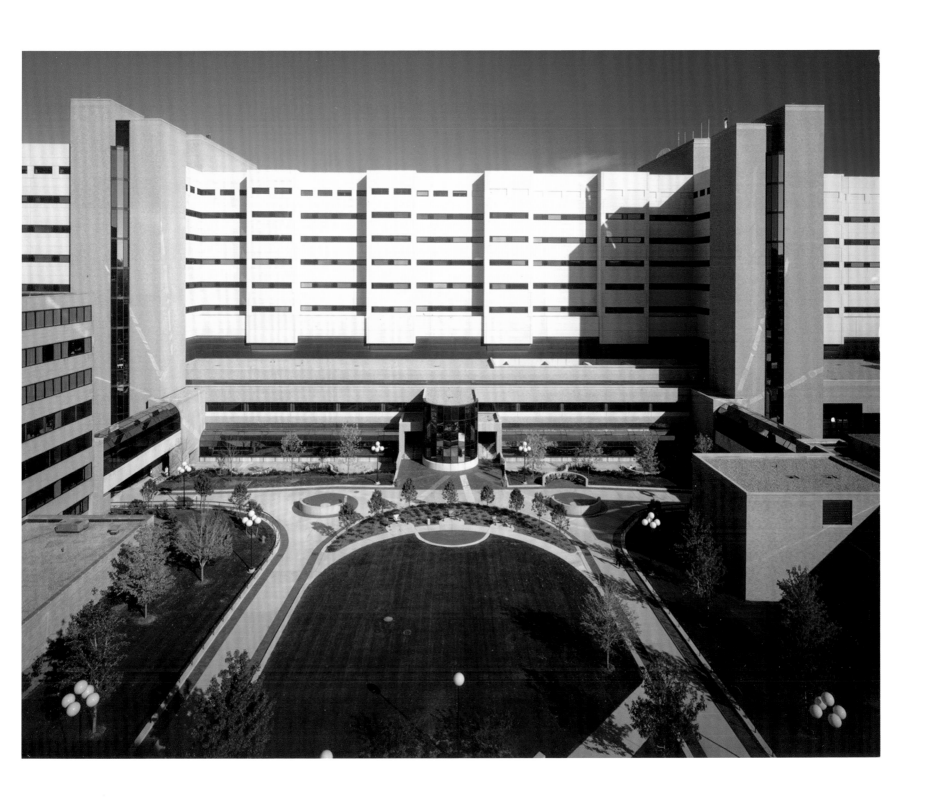

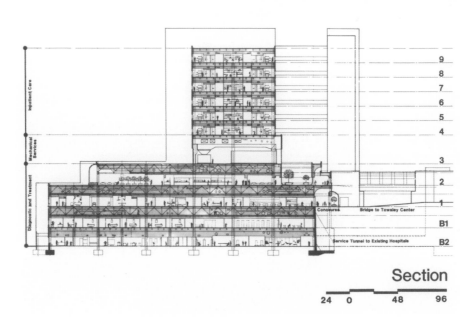

Section

24   0   48   96

MSU COLLEGE OF ENGINEERING

The College of Engineering Building at Michigan State University presented an accessibility challenge for students and staff. Before the American Disabilities Act of 1990 went into effect, accessibility in public buildings became a priority for architects and their clients.[255] These spaces needed to accommodate people of all abilities. Kahn began working with the university on programming for a complete renovation of the building and a new addition in 1976. In 1979, they began designing a significant addition that increased the space for classrooms and facilities, and addressed these accessibility concerns.

Part of the accessibility challenge became clear during off-hours when the rest of the building was closed. Students or staff wishing to access the second and third-floor computer labs during off-hours could only reach these spaces from a nearby staircase. To encourage access to these spaces whenever schedules permitted, an underutilized freight elevator was converted to an accessible passenger elevator. In addition, a new entryway was constructed and designated parking spaces were created near the new entrance. The sidewalk was also extended to permit easier access to the building for wheelchair users. For users who relied on the university buses, university officials worked with the intercampus bus system to create a stop at this location.

Taking a step beyond the building codes at the time, the university was concerned about access during the winter months when the area receives several inches of snow and frequent ice. These conditions can be especially difficult for students and faculty using a wheelchair, crutch, or other mobility devices. A solution was to design a snow melting system at this entrance that is automatically activated once the outdoor temperature drops below a set point. Below the surface of the entryway and sidewalk, heat exchangers warm an ethylene glycol and water solution using steam from the central campus heating system. The snow melting pumps circulate the solution through an extensive piping grid system embedded in the concrete slab. Through careful spacing of these pipes, the snow melting system provides consistent heating over thousands of sq. ft. of driveway and walkway, eliminating ice and snow to make it safer for students and staff to get into the building.

BMW MANUFACTURING PLANT

SPARTANBURG, SOUTH CAROLINA | DESIGNED 1992 EXPANDED 2008

The first automotive manufacturing plant in the United States for BMW sits on more than one thousand acres and was originally designed to build 300 vehicles per day. The campus featured numerous facilities including the Main Assembly Building, Parts Distribution, Paint Mix and Storage Building, De-wax Building for imported vehicles, Product Distribution Center, Analysis Center, Test Track, Chemical and Waste Storage Building, Process Fluid Tank Farm, Energy Center, and a Visitor Center and Museum.

Shaped like an "L," the main assembly building housed all manufacturing operations under one roof. Project designers created a layout that would eventually be expanded to include three body shops, two paint shops and two assembly lines immediately adjacent to one another, and connected with a shared, center court. This new building layout replaced the commonly used "E-plan" or spine-like configuration for automotive plant design where the body, paint and assembly functions are interconnected but independent buildings. This design also allowed the plant to more than double in size by 2008 and increase its output over threefold.

The BMW plant is able to generate a portion of its own electrical power and thermal energy through gas-fired turbines by a process called Cogeneration. While a common practice in Europe where energy costs are historically high, this was the first auto plant in the United States to take this approach. To reduce the peak electrical demand for the assembly plant, BMW purchased and refurbished four little-used natural gas-fired electrical turbines. In 2008, the original four natural gas turbines were replaced with two new 5.5 MW gas turbine generators that use landfill gas as a source of fuel. The generators produce electricity and the exhaust from the generators is then routed to heat exchangers to heat water. The hot water boilers, that use the waste heat from the turbine exhaust gases, provide a portion of the hot water to building air handling units in the winter. Two absorption refrigeration machines generate up to 2,600 tons of cooling, which supplemented 7,000 tons of cooling generated by the original electrically driven chillers. The chilled water plant operates at a constant output, which allows excess chilled water to be generated overnight and then stored in two 1.2 million gallon combination chilled water and fire protection water storage tanks for use during peak cooling periods. The Energy Center has been expanded several times so that by 2008, the chilled water system was capable of supplying a peak load of 20,000 tons of cooling.

The system was engineered to meet year-round process heating requirements. Each of the original gas turbine generators was capable of producing 4.4 MW of thermal energy and 1.2 MW of electrical energy, which means the system is able to provide approximately 30% of the plant's overall energy needs. With the increase of generator capacity and building size, the landfill gas turbine generators continue to produce approximately 30% of the plant's overall energy needs. This cogeneration system gives the plant the flexibility to shift energy usage, and to generate chilled water to meet building and process needs, while optimizing the operation of the hot water heating system.

ANAEROBIC DIGESTER

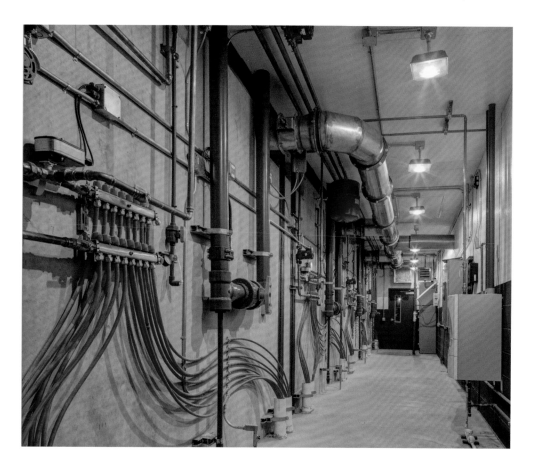

Green energy comes in many forms. The Detroit Zoological Society is home to the first biodigester in North America that uses the animal waste of zoo animals to generate electrical power for the zoo. Detroit Zoo animals produce approximately 400 tons of manure annually, which traditionally has resulted in high costs for disposal to offsite locations. Now, the facility uses an anaerobic digestion process to sustainably dispose of the waste and convert it into energy that can be used to support the operations of other buildings within the zoo.

The digester has four distinct bays and a complex engineering system that captures all of the gasses created. Animal waste is collected and placed into the digester chambers where it is heated to 100 degrees Fahrenheit. Micro-organisms digest the waste in an anaerobic or oxygen-free environment and produce biogas, renewable energy comprised of methane and carbon dioxide gases. The biogas is then combusted to generate heat and electricity, used to power a generator that powers the Animal Health Complex at the Zoo. The leftover waste from the process can then be used as fertilizer on campus and given to the surrounding community.

The firm worked closely with Michigan State University's Anaerobic Digestion Research and Education Center to implement the digester requirements. Kahn previously helped the zoo, a leader in sustainable zoo campus design, to design a master plan for their alternative energy and electrical power resources and has designed and engineered numerous centers including the Polk Penguin Conservation Center (2016) and the Animal Hospital (2004). Though the biodigestor is small at just over 1,200 sq. ft., it has the potential of leaving a negative carbon footprint, saving the zoo approximately $120,000 annually, and impacting future green energy initiatives.

FORD DRIVING DYNAMICS LAB

Located trackside at Ford Motor Company's Dearborn Development Center, the Driving Dynamics Lab (DDL) is a multifunctional building that embodies Ford's research-driven culture and anchors their campus redevelopment. DDL remedies the workflow and efficiency challenge Ford experienced when related departments, such as those that test vehicle performance, durability, and acoustics, are scattered across a vast campus. Now, DDL houses trackside operations and engineering functions within one building, creating unity and cohesion between product engineers and test technicians.

Natural daylight pours inside the large garage space where technicians and engineers test and swap out parts on prototype vehicles before they go out on the test track. Nearby, acoustic testing laboratories, mechanical testing laboratories, engineering offices, and fabrication spaces can be found. Meanwhile on floors above, employees have a variety of spaces for collaborative work, a large cafe, and terraces that overlook the track. Designed to achieve LEED Gold, this facility reduces its impact on the surrounding area and supports the wellbeing of employees.

Looking forward to the future of automobile design and technology, DDL also incorporates advanced testing spaces like the Driver Autonomous Technology laboratory and the most advanced vehicle Noise, Vibration, Harshness testing facility Ford has constructed to date. This includes a Hybrid Acoustic Test Chamber that accommodates a large range of test vehicles, is capable of environmental temperature testing ranging from -40° degrees Farhenheit to 140° degrees Farhenheit, and has an all-wheel drive chassis roll dynamometer. A sound transmission loss suite, incorporating a spring-isolated anechoic chamber and reverberation chamber carefully isolated from structure-borne noise, allows for accurate prediction of acoustic performance.

The design of DDL also recalls the rich history of the site. For well over 100 years, Kahn has been designing and engineering new facilities alongside Ford's team of engineers and project managers. This legacy is especially apparent on sites such as the Dearborn Development Center, formerly called the Dearborn Proving Ground, where Kahn has designed unique structures linked to the evolving functions of the site. In 1924, Henry Ford opened the Ford Airport on this site, which remained in use until October 21, 1947.[256] Albert Kahn designed several airport buildings including an airplane factory, where the famous Ford Tri-Motor Airplane was created, as well as an airplane hangar. After the airport closed, the site transformed into a hub for testing vehicle performance.

Salvaged historic items feature prominently in the design, reminding users of the site's prior role as Ford's airport. A nose cone and blades from the original wind tunnel, as well as windows, doors, and wooden roof planks from the site's former passenger terminal, hold places of honor within the new facility. As the center for vehicle testing and innovation, the design of this facility is driven by its function as a world-class engineering center, the future of mobility, and the legacy of Ford Motor Company.

THE FUTURE

"Each new problem must, of necessity, develop standards of beauty entirely its own."[257]

- Albert Kahn

More than 125 years of designing and engineering environments across six continents is indisputably a marker of success; but, to us, the true marker of success is our relationships. We have an unyielding passion to design structures that inspire and improve our communities, with the engineering expertise to solve any challenge, allowing our clients to thrive. With relationships stretching 20, 50, or more than 100 years, our clients inspire us to innovate and succeed. It is our responsibility to contribute to our client's success.

This longevity extends to our employees as well. One of the unique characteristics of Kahn is the devotion of those who have worked at the firm – it is common to meet individuals who have called Kahn home for 30, 40, or even 50 years. The legacy, the clients, and the culture all play a role in why so many people stay with Kahn. Throughout our history and far into our future, it has and will be these continued relationships by which we measure our success.

Our founder was humble: "Without the teamwork of my associates, I would be nothing." Albert knew that architects and engineers can accomplish much more as a team than alone. This lesson has been passed on from generation to generation at Kahn. Our founder set up a company based on the idea of collaboration, a multi-disciplinary approach to design. For this, he was a true pioneer. This practice is integral to who we are today and has been the catalyst for continued innovation.

Individuals introduced to the culture at Kahn find themselves practicing in an office where all disciplines and all individuals have a voice. Our process incorporates thoughts, ideas, and solutions from the entire team. The synergy in a collaborative environment can be truly inspiring. Even when individuals leave Kahn, they take these ideas and processes with them. Many practitioners in the industry have worked and been mentored at the firm. We see the impact their time at Kahn has on their respective firms where they find themselves practicing today. These former employees never really leave though, they simply become "Ex-Kahns," rarely severing their connection to our legendary firm.

While we cannot predict the precise challenges we will face in the future, we know exactly how to remain flexible and agile to change. Our history reminds us of the necessity of working across multiple markets at a time. Shifting market strategy depending on the economy, enabled us to weather over a century of economic ups and downs.

The Kahn office is able to learn from different industries and apply innovative designs and engineered solutions from one building type to another to solve unique sets of challenges for our clients. In the pages that follow our teams have identified 10 ideas and predictions of what they believe will impact the built environment in the future. As society continues to evolve and adapt, so must the environments we design and engineer. Looking forward, Kahn will find multidisciplinary solutions to the greatest challenges facing all of us – from the place that started it all, Detroit.

ROLE OF ARCHITECTS AND ENGINEERS

Our future role will be to find innovative ways to improve every aspect of our human experience in a more complex and technology-driven world. Architects and engineers will adapt to become more like Environment Experience Facilitators. We will need to be scientists, psychologists, and technical experts with advanced education in psychology, biology, and technology. Architects will need to identify the range of adjustments necessary to serve the needs of the projected environmental users. Engineers will need to expand their knowledge in environment affect engineering to include all of the senses and emotional needs of the users. Advanced design tools will enable architects and engineers to explore new geometries to create one-of-a-kind environments, with building materials that can be custom printed or manufactured and assembled with the help of robotic assistants onsite. As artificial intelligence continues to develop, this will result in greater use of immersive environments for learning, collaborating, and entertainment.

We expect that the environment we deliver in the future will be constructed more quickly, cost-effectively, and with new materials and techniques that improve their overall quality and user experience. Prefabricated, technologically-advanced environment modules will continue to evolve. Constructed in factories and assembled on-site, contractors may become more assemblers and technology specialists. With continuous advances to 3-D modeling and immersive technologies, the 3-D building model could evolve to a live hologram model used by the entire team of designers, engineers, and contractors on the job site. Assembly methods and design details would then be experienced in real-time, either through the hologram or augmented reality goggles, reducing ambiguity and errors in the field. Once construction is complete, these models and tools would then be shared with owners, allowing their teams to better monitor and maintain their facility. Architects and engineers will still collaboratively design and engineer environments that anticipate the full range of human needs and desires – physical, emotional, and spiritual – but with the tools and ability to address novel challenges facing our world.

OVERLAP OF VIRTUAL AND REAL SPACES

Movable Partitions

Transparent Active Screen

Flexible Seating

Headset View

Humans seek a sense of community; this longing will not go away in a virtual or semi-virtual world where so much of our daily lives are conducted online. How we relate to one another in the future will be considered through the design of physical and digital environments that seamlessly integrate. This idea is already being explored through the way retail corporations make use of virtual, augmented, and mixed reality to allow users to "try on" virtual products. Applying this technology to the environments that we design, we will need to consider how remote workers, for example, will participate in physical spaces such as conference rooms. Most employees crave the social interaction that comes along with collaboration, and the efficiency of group problem solving over individual work. These technologically-advanced spaces might incorporate modular furniture assembled around devices that can virtually project remote colleagues in a real-time multidimensional format. On-site and remote workers will be able to collaborate simultaneously, where the nuances of human behavior will be more perceptible, and will allow for a more genuine experience.

While the virtual environment will support and enhance the physical experience, it will not supplant the real environment. Consider education. The steady rise in online learning programs has led prospective students away from the central campus; instead, they are able to learn from the location of their choice. While the majority of learning may be done virtually, there are disciplines that will continue to require the use of physical spaces housing the tools, technology, and equipment that support hands-on learning. We will design lab spaces that can quickly morph into alternative configurations, accommodating a wide variety of equipment to support multiple programs and disciplines. Students can access and check out the lab space on their schedule, and be able to consult instructors either in person or virtually. These real spaces will support online learning and could lead education providers to develop multiple community-based satellite facilities for students to drop in. Or perhaps, multiple providers might partner to share these spaces, allowing for more labs to be closer to where students are located.

ENVIRONMENTS THAT ADAPT TO THE INDIVIDUAL

The future will bring advanced materials with which we can construct new environments for groups and individuals. Prefabrication and modular construction, when materials and units are produced in a factory and assembled on-site, are often showcased as the way of the future. Though these ideas and terms have been around for decades, they continue to be thought of as innovative because they address a number of benefits, including the ability to improve quality and consistency, reduce construction time while increasing worker safety, and can be customized throughout the manufacturing process. It is the architect and the engineer's job to take these manufactured elements and combine them in unique ways to create one-of-a-kind environments for users. For example, in the workspace, modular furniture can be customized for particular work styles, or modular designs allow individual workspaces with movable walls and sound control to be incorporated within a collaborative floor plan. Architects and engineers will consider the needs of many to create an inclusive environment in which each person will construct their own sense of place.

Within those spaces, further consideration can then be given to personalized experiences, adding another layer to the design. The ability to overlap virtual and real spaces will allow for this personalization. Smart devices currently monitor biological indicators and gather data on our behaviors. In the future, this data will be essential to our experience of the physical environment. The environment will constantly monitor inhabitants and adapt to each user's evolving cognitive, emotional, and physical needs through virtual experience technology. Virtual reality, augmented reality, mixed reality, and extended reality will continue to advance how we learn, shop, work, and interact. These technologies are progressing – smell, touch, and taste are now overlapped with audiovisual elements. Upon entering a physical location, the emotional measures will set the beginning feeling or mood of the individual. Sensing what is needed to improve mental and physical health, the environment will create sound, smell, and visual elements on the premanufactured building blocks to create an appropriate environment for healing, thinking, or just relaxing.

RENEWED SENSE OF WELLBEING

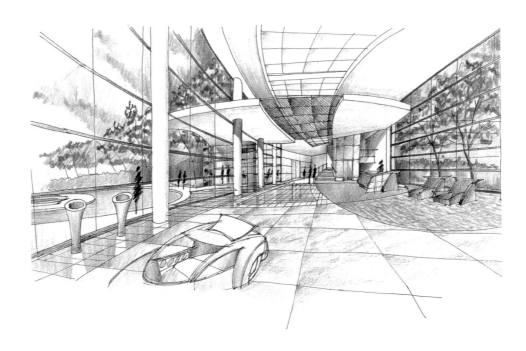

Our health and wellbeing are at risk in a rapidly changing world. Wearable technology allows us to take more responsibility for maintaining our own health, communicating health warning signs, and connecting wirelessly with healthcare professionals. These devices reduce the need for physician visits, minimize acute episodes requiring emergency treatment, and enable home-based care services for many individuals and seniors. However, among the many factors threatening our wellbeing is an increased reliance on technology that pulls our attention to devices over people or activities, increasing our stress and often leading to a sedentary lifestyle. Architects and engineers will find ways to incorporate technology that improves our overall wellbeing without adding distractions or becoming the focal point of our lives. In the future, environments will need to reduce the noise and stress caused by the constant string of beeps and notifications emanating from our devices, and from surrounding noise pollution as well. Technology will be a tool that helps all of us live a more fruitful life through its thoughtful integration to facilitate collaboration, and improve mood, concentration, and wellbeing.

Architects and engineers will design restorative environments that reconnect us to elements that are integral to a healthy lifestyle. For example, we know the benefits of natural daylight inside an environment, and it will continue to play a vital role in designs. Natural daylight will be supplemented by lighting fixtures equipped to shift color temperature through the day, reinforcing our natural circadian rhythms. Access to nature will continue to be essential for reducing stress, and its integration in the spaces we design will be paramount. Vertical gardens, indoor courtyards, and green spaces with native plantings will provide seasonal color and enjoyment. Their growth willl be supported by smart engineering systems that sense when the plants need water or more light, or even added nutrients. Nature will be brought to the user and incorporated in the physical environments they desire to visit. To combat the health risks of our sedentary lifestyle, physical activity will be encouraged through the design of internal and external environments, with an increased emphasis on the journey users take from one place to the next. Cities, for instance, will continue to move toward more walkable and bikeable designs, encouraging easy access to physical activity and interaction.

HEALTHY ENVIRONMENTS

The COVID-19 pandemic has brought indoor air quality back to the mainstream consciousness. There is an increased focus on innovations in the development of materials that support a healthy environment, including glass, fabrics, natural and composite materials. In the future, each element that goes into an environment will support users' health and combat the spread of contaminants. Mechanical systems will also play a large part in minimizing the spread of airborne infections. Relative humidity will be augmented to reach 40% to 60% health levels, air filtration will be improved, and more spaces will be designed for increased air changes and 100% exhaust, across all types of facilities. We will continue to emphasize the importance of creating healthy indoor environments that promote the wellbeing, productivity, and creativity of occupants in every facility.

Currently, only about 1% of hospital rooms nation-wide have been designed for infectious isolation. In the future, there will be a revolution in the design of emergency departments, intensive care units, and infectious isolation rooms to completely isolate patients with potential airborne infections. This will affect the ventilation and gowning facilities for individual rooms and entire departments. And, there will be a host of new equipment developed to isolate caregivers from infectious patients. For the entire hospital, advanced technology will monitor building inhabitants and adjust the lighting, climate, and other elements that affect all the senses in order to help the healing process.

COMMUNITIES OF SERVICES

With freedom and control in how we conduct our own lives through advanced technology, our services will adopt a community approach. Services, such as healthcare, will be strategically located throughout the communities in which we operate, whether urban, suburban, or rural. As in-home monitoring, telemedicine, and interconnected care will ultimately reduce the need to visit a healthcare professional or facility, healthcare systems are developing a more decentralized structure to better serve patients. Medical centers will be smaller hubs focused on high acuity and medically complex patients, while smaller integrated clinic spaces will be created within communities for lower acuity, outpatient diagnostic, and treatment services. In more dense urban centers, a healthy living corridor will be created where healthcare facilities are intermixed within a physical and daily activity zone. These facilities will become part of the everyday experience, providing convenience, improving access, and encouraging regular patient participation.

In the future, communities will need robust data systems so that all residents have access to technology. Rather than each home purchasing its own system provider, communities will invest in a centralized system to accommodate the expanding role of technology. Increasing the use and number of devices connected to the internet and the seamless transition between work or learning locations, will require advancements in high-speed wireless networks, power, and IT infrastructure to accommodate the enormous data load. With all of this data and interconnected devices that will drive our future, the question of security emerges. Whether data is stored on the cloud or onsite servers, extra layers of protection need to be put in place to ensure that personal and proprietary data is protected. One potential solution to improve data security includes adding up to three authentication stages, including facial recognition and biometrics such as retinal scans or fingerprint technology on devices, software, and networks. While technology will continue to provide endless opportunities and benefits, individuals, companies, and service providers must move cautiously to make certain that necessary protections and safeguards are in place to protect each entity.

REINVENTING URBAN CENTERS

Urban centers will need to revisit their purpose and find new ways to incorporate a unique experience for residents and visitors. A challenge facing many cities is moving visitors and residents through and around the various districts and amenities, which have often been separated by large motorways or, in some cases, vacant and underutilized development. Architects and engineers can adapt roadways and traffic patterns and program new uses for vacant land to create more human-centric cities with less congestion. Increasing walkability and accommodating multimodal transportation options, along with creating central gathering spaces such as parks and town squares, are strategies that will only grow in the future. Interaction and access to amenities will continue to draw people to urban centers, but the types of amenities might change. As more consumers choose to shop online than in-store, more retail will move exclusively online. Brick and mortar shops could become more like incubators or maker-spaces that emphasize artisan collaboration and introduce new local businesses to consumers.

The beauty of urban centers is that they are unique. We travel around the world to experience cities and the cultures that they encompass. Cities of the future will need to retain their particular sense of place to preserve their cultural identities while still growing and changing to accommodate new uses, new purposes, and new groups of people. Kahn's recent work in Erie, Pennsylvania, demonstrates how design and engineering can embrace the past through readapting historic structures and propel cities forward through the creation of new environments and new uses that attract more diverse communities. As cities in the future become more "smart" – embracing technology to become safer, more sustainable, and healthier – architects and engineers will design inclusive environments that maintain a city's identity and promote the wellbeing of every community within.

REGENERATIVE DESIGN

The buildings we design will strive to make a positive impact and maintain or restore our natural environment. In the future, net-zero energy building designs will become a requirement, and embodied carbon and overall carbon footprint values will be as familiar to the public as one's clothing size. The world population is expected to hit 9 billion around 2035, a three-fold increase from 1960. This rapid increase in the population will continue to strain natural resources, including access to land and water. It will require innovative solutions to produce food, such as sustainable greenhouses that can use less to produce more. Built and designed environments of the future must find ways to better their surrounding communities. For example, buildings will be designed to generate more power than they consume, providing extra power to the community. Centralized cooling systems in towns and cities could be created with an extensive network of underground piping, reducing the need for independent facilities and dramatically reducing the amount of carbon dioxide produced.

Increasing the amount of green space and vegetation within every type of project will continue to be a priority. There will be a greater reliance on self-sufficient building designs that can operate off the grid with renewable energy solutions, on-site water collection, and waste treatment to help accommodate a growing population with infrastructure limitations. Alternative energy sources will be further developed, such as generating electricity by converting composted food waste and landfill methane gas to cogeneration power production. More products will continue to be developed to allow the built environment to become smarter and more efficient. Architects and engineers will benefit from technology and software that is able to more accurately and quickly gather information on building performance to inform the design process and make smart decisions that will positively impact the site.

ADAPTABILITY AND FLEXIBILITY

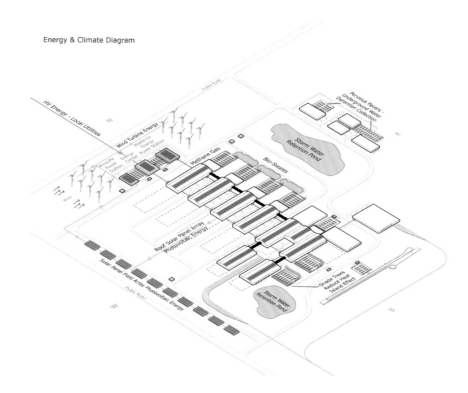

Energy & Climate Diagram

Adapting buildings for new uses will become increasingly prominent in the future. As the world continues to reflect on our ecological impact, the dialogue will shift from "replace" to "reuse." Most buildings were designed for longevity, and their programming can be reimagined to suit any future use. There are numerous Kahn-designed buildings, for instance, approaching 100 years old that have been readapted to serve a new purpose, and will likely be readapted again to solve a future need. Whether the new use is for manufacturing or retail, education or corporate, healthcare or residential, or a combination of them all, repurposing older facilities is a sustainable practice and will bring new life to communities and cities, where other uses once thrived. For new construction that does occur, innovative materials and technology will allow these buildings to have a longer lifespan and be easier to adapt and change with new uses.

Flexibility for change has been a consistent design strategy throughout our history and will continue well into the future. Manufacturing facilities, in particular, will continue to be designed with flexible floor plans to optimize process operations and easily allow for equipment upgrades and evolving technology. Consumer demand for updated and customized products will require flexible and customizable manufacturing operations, with on-demand ability to change and alter processes to suit the specific need. A digital twin of the building will be created and used by clients to model their processes virtually, shortening product changeover cycles and reducing the need for physical improvements. Digital twins can be used along with building management systems to provide a basis for managing, optimizing, and modifying building systems remotely in real-time. When improvements are needed, architects and engineers will use immersive reality and digital tools to test alterations to facilities, allowing us to test a new process quickly, while ensuring that the health and safety of building occupants are maintained.

DESIGN AND BUILD IN NEW EXTREMES

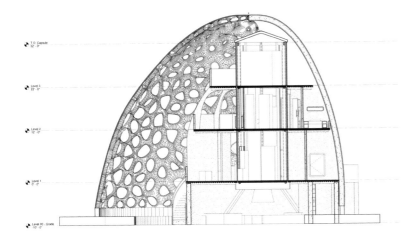

In the future, we will design for new extremes on Earth and beyond. Kahn designed a self-printing habitat for deep space exploration to Mars as part of a NASA challenge. Designed to hold four astronauts for one year, the Kahn team developed a habitat that would travel through space for eight or nine months. Once it landed on the planet's surface, it would self-print the remaining necessary components of the habitat. To prevent failures from occurring in transit, redundant and resilient design concepts were employed to ensure a backup option was quickly available if needed.

Incorporating a mixture of aesthetics and functionality, the design features a dome-shaped habitat with an organic pattern of translucency and opacity that temper the sunlight. The cellular-like Voronoi pattern used on the facade incorporates light openings of various sizes, allowing more light in shared use areas, such as lab spaces and gardens, and less in private spaces. Components that weren't 3-D printed were designed to be constructed using naturally occurring elements found on Mars, such as the use of sulfur-based concrete. NASA's multi-phased challenge was designed to advance construction technology, which could be applied to new environments in harsh conditions in the arctic, at the bottom of the ocean, or in the most inhospitable desert.

Whatever challenges and opportunities lie ahead, Albert Kahn Associates is ready and looks forward to continuing the legacy of innovative architecture and engineering.

While the firm continues to look forward and innovate, the Albert Kahn Legacy Foundation will be there to honor and preserve the legacy of the world-renowned architect and the firm he started. A reporter for the *Detroit News* once commented, "Like the old British Empire, the sun never sets on the thousands of buildings designed by Albert Kahn Associated Architects and Engineers." [257]

Established on May 14, 2020, the Albert Kahn Legacy Foundation creates a central repository to link researchers with the breadth of Kahn archives and provides educational opportunities and experiences that will inspire our community. Interested in learning more? Visit AlbertKahnLegacy.org and find us on social media.

CREDITS

The projects in this book are the work of many individuals from initial design through construction and on to final occupancy. While it is not possible to list all names involved in each project, we would like to thank everyone who worked tirelessly to bring a shared vision to life.

Similarly, a book such as this requires the work of many. Thank you to everyone that contributed, assisted with research, read drafts of copy, and provided images to help tell our story.

Every effort has been made to identify the photographers whose images appear in this book. In addition to the names and institutions below, we would like to thank our clients for providing images of their facilities.

Albert Kahn Associates, Inc.
Balthazar Korab, Ltd.
Beth Singer
Bentley Historical Library, University of Michigan
Bryan-Young
Charles Babbage Institute Archives, University of Minnesota Libraries, Minneapolis
Charles R. Messinger
Clayton Studio
Damora
Daniel Bartush
Daniel Ducci
Detroit Free Press
Detroit News
Detroit Publishing Co., Library of Congress
Eric Oxendorf
FCA Group
Ford Motor Company
General Motors
Glen Calvin Moon
Glenn L. Martin Company
Haas Studios
Hance
Hedrich Blessing Photographers
Heidi Pfannes

Henry A. Leung
Henry Ford Hospital
Hillis-McGregor
Jeffrey White Studio
James Haefner Photography
John Wallace Gillies
Maconochie Photography
Manning Brothers
Meadows & Co.
Michael G. Smith
Museum Windsor
Lark & Associates
Laszlo Regos Photography
O. R. Forster Co.
Paul Bednarski
Pratt & Whitney
Timothy Hursley
The Henry Ford
Thomas Ellison
TVS Design
University of Michigan
Walt Hinchman
Walter P. Reuther Library, Archives of Labor and Urban Affairs, Wayne State University
W. D. Benham Co.

CONTRIBUTORS

Caitlin Wunderlich is the Corporate Historian and Communications Specialist for Albert Kahn Associates. With research degrees from the University of Michigan and the University of Glasgow in Scotland, Caitlin has published articles on art and artifact collections and Detroit architecture. She is a board member of the Albert Kahn Legacy Foundation.

Leslie Armbruster is manager of the Ford Motor Company Archives, where she has worked in various roles for over 20 years. She earned her Master of Library and Information Science and Graduate Certificate in Archival Administration from Wayne State University, and her Bachelor of Arts in English Literature from Oakland University.

Donald Bauman, AIA, is the former Director of Architectural Development and Historic Preservation, Corporate Historian and Archivist at Albert Kahn Associates. During his 39-year career at Kahn, he has worked on almost every project that entered the office, resulting in an unparalleled knowledge of the firm.

Alan Cobb, FAIA, is the Chairman and CEO of Albert Kahn Associates. Alan joined Kahn in 1976 and has since delivered award-winning sustainable environments that exceed each client's expectations. In 2006 he was inducted into the AIA College of Fellows and in 2015 received "Gold Medals" from AIA Detroit and AIA Michigan.

John Cole, PE, is an engineer and former Director of Mechanical Engineering at Albert Kahn Associates. For 42 years, John has worked on large industrial and research and development projects for Kahn. He has served as the Detroit Chapter President of ASHRAE and is currently a board member of the Albert Kahn Legacy Foundation.

Christo Datini is Manager of Archive & Special Collections for General Motors. A professional archivist by trade, he has been a leader in GM's efforts to document, preserve and promote its global heritage for more than 20 years.

Katie Doelle is a freelance writer and graphic designer. Originally from England, she moved to Grosse Pointe in 2012, and became fascinated by local architecture. Since 2014, she has written a weekly architecture blog for realtor Higbie Maxon Agney. Her first book, *Grand Estates of Grosse Pointe*, was published in 2020.

Rick S. Dye, PE, is the President of Albert Kahn Associates. Rick joined Kahn in 1997 as a project manager, shortly becoming the Director of Project Management. He has led project management, A/E design, and specialized process consultants for complex industrial projects in both national and international markets.

Nancy Finegood was the executive director of the Michigan Historic Preservation Network for 17 years. She created the MHPN Tax Credit partnership program that has been instrumental in partnering on major Detroit projects. Nancy is a board member of the Albert Kahn Legacy Foundation and the National Preservation Partners Network.

Jeffrey T. Gaines, AIA, is the former Director of Design, Planning and Sustainability at Albert Kahn Associates. For 20 years at Kahn, Jeffrey has led sustainable design programs for clients across all markets and has championed training and mentorship within the firm and the community.

John Gallagher is a veteran journalist who spent 32 years with the *Detroit Free Press*. He has published several books including *Reimagining Detroit: Opportunities for Redefining an American City, Yamasaki in Detroit: A Search for Serenity, and Revolution Detroit: Strategies for Urban Reinvention*. He is a board member of the Albert Kahn Legacy Foundation.

Deirdre L.C. Hennebury, Ph.D., is the Associate Director of the Museum Studies Program at the University of Michigan and the co-chair of the Albert Kahn Research Coalition. A historian, designer, and dedicated educator, Deirdre holds degrees from Princeton University, Harvard University, and the University of Michigan.

Grant Hildebrand obtained an M.Arch from the University of Michigan. After practice with Albert Kahn Associates and Minoru Yamasaki, he taught at the University of Washington. He has authored several articles on Kahn, and ten books on architecture including *Designing for Industry: The Architecture of Albert Kahn* (MIT, 1974).

Michael H. Hodges is the former fine arts reporter for the *Detroit News* and author of *Building the Modern World: Albert Kahn in Detroit*. Both the Kahn biography and Hodges' first book, *Michigan's Historic Railroad Stations*, were named "Notable Books" by the Library of Michigan.

Gordon V.R. Holness, PE, retired as Chairman Emeritus of Albert Kahn Associates, serving for 32 years as Chief Mechanical Engineer, Treasurer, Board Member, President, and CEO. He is a registered engineer in England, Canada, and the United States, and active in ASHRAE for 50+ years, where he served on the Board and as President.

Case Allen-Kahn Kittel is the great-grandson of Albert Kahn. Inspired by his family's legacy, Case studied civil engineering at the University of Michigan which led him to become an engineer that designs and manages the construction of airport projects. Case resides in Richmond, Virginia where he enjoys canoe racing, rock climbing, flying, traveling, and photography.

Peter G. Lynde, PE, is Senior Vice President and Corporate Secretary at Albert Kahn Associates. Pete joined Kahn as a mechanical engineer in 1982 and currently serves as Director of Engineering and Research and Technology market leader. Pete specializes in the integration of building systems in complex research and industrial facilities.

Chris Meister is an architectural historian whose published work includes *James Riely Gordon: His Courthouses and Other Public Architecture*, published by Texas Tech University Press (2011) and "Albert Kahn's Partners in Industrial Architecture," published in the *Journal of the Society of Architectural Historians* (March 2013).

Kimberly Montague, AIA, is a former Principal at Albert Kahn Associates. Passionate about the creation of person-centered environments, Kimberly utilizes expertise in evidence-based design, lean principles, and sustainability to advocate for healthcare clients. By leading and presenting research, she acts as a catalyst and educator to impact the design and healthcare industries.

Jamie Myler is Research Archivist at the Ford Motor Company Archives, where he has been an archivist for over 20 years. He earned a BS and MA in History from Eastern Michigan University and a Certificate of Archival Management from Wayne State University.

Heidi Pfannes, NCIDQ, is the Director of Business Development and Marketing at Albert Kahn Associates. Trained as an Interior Designer, Heidi understands how the built environment impacts people's lives. She expanded her talents to include relationship development and leadership and is a founding member and President of the Albert Kahn Legacy Foundation.

Hank Ritter, PE, has served Kahn since 1967 in a variety of roles – Structural Engineer, Manager of Structural and Civil Engineering, Project Principal, Chief Operating Officer, and currently as an Executive Consultant. Hank's career has included many large industrial projects with a specialization in automotive stamping plants.

Robert Sharrow, AIA, is a Former Principal at Albert Kahn Associates, and previously served as Senior Vice President/ Corporate Secretary before stepping down from the Board of Directors in 2019. He was the Vice-Chair of the National Planetree Visionary Design Network, and is a founding member and on the board of the Albert Kahn Legacy Foundation.

Michael G. Smith is an architectural historian and author. He is currently writing a book on Julius Kahn, and has published several articles on Detroit architecture and the book *Designing Detroit; Wirt Rowland and the rise of Modern American Architecture*. He is a board member of the Albert Kahn Legacy Foundation.

Greg Tasker is a freelance journalist and a former entertainment editor at *The Detroit News*. His work has been published in various publications, including *Parade, Frommer's Budget Travel, and Backpacker*. He's also the author of *Five Star Trails: Detroit and Ann Arbor. Your Guide to the Area's Most Beautiful Hikes*.

Stephen White, ASLA, is Vice President, Chief Strategic Officer, and Director of Landscape Architecture and Urban Design at Albert Kahn Associates. For 23 years, Stephen has been instrumental in creating a sense of place from space in leading collaboration of the firm's master planning, landscape architecture, and urban design projects.

Gregory Wittkopp has been stewarding the collections, shaping the stories, and writing the histories of Cranbrook for over three decades, first as a curator and director of Cranbrook Art Museum (1985 – 2015) and now as the founding director of Cranbrook Center for Collections and Research (2012 – present).

Claire Zimmerman is Associate Professor of architectural history and theory at the University of Michigan. She teaches and studies mass production in architecture and the built environment. Her current book project explores industrial architecture and infrastructure in the twentieth century through the fascinating history of Albert Kahn Associates.

NOTES

1. Albert Kahn during an interview with Louis Tendler, *Detroit News*, reprinted in the Memorial Issue of the *Michigan Society of Architects*, 1942.

2. Helen C. Bennett, "You Can't Build Skyscrapers with Your Head in the Sky," *American Magazine* 108 (December 1929): 121.

3. Example projects include job numbers 148 Canada, 892 Argentina, 1225 England, 1707 Japan, 2053 New Zealand. At the time of printing we were unable to locate a project example in Africa, yet our archival materials make several references to projects in South Africa among other countries. See also the map published in "Industrial Buildings: Albert Kahn Inc.," *The Architectural Forum*, August 1938: 94-95, and "Albert Kahn: A Tribute," *South African Architectural Record*, May 1943: 104.

4. Albert Kahn, "Architect and Engineer More Closely Related Today Than Ever Before," *Truscon*, May 1935. Published by Truscon Steel Company.

5. Ibid.

6. Ibid.

7. For more on Julius and his reinforcement system, see: "The First Concrete Auto Factory: An Error in the Historical Record" by Michael G Smith in the *Journal of the Society of Architectural Historians*, (December 2019): 442-453; and "Julius Kahn; Man of Steel" by Michael G Smith in *Michigan Jewish History*, volume 58, spring 2020. Technical discussions of the Kahn reinforcement system can be found in articles by Julius Kahn that appeared in *Engineering News*, available online at www.Hathitrust.org. See: "A New System of Concrete Re-Enforcement, Designed to Resist Vertical Sheer," volume 50, number 17, (October 14, 1903): 349-52; "Some of the Causes of Recent Failures of Re-Enforced Concrete," volume 51, number 3, (January 21, 1904): 66-68; Letter to the Editor, volume 51, number 7, (February 18, 1904): 158-60; and "Shearing Stress in Concrete-Steel Beams," volume 51, number 15, (April 14, 1904): 355-58. See also: "A Reinforced Concrete System with Rigid Shear Members" by Moritz Kahn (brother of Albert and Julius) in *Concrete* and *Constructional Engineering*, volume 1, number 2, (May 1906): 79-86 and "Reinforced Concrete in the United States," by Captain John Sewell in *Concrete* and *Constructional Engineering*, volume 1, number 1, (March 1906): 67-69. A discussion of the formula developed by Julius to calculate the strength of reinforced-concrete beams can be found in "Concrete Beam and Column Design," *International Library of Technology*, by International Correspondence Schools, International Textbook Company, 1909/10, section 18: 43-46.

8. For more on concrete reinforcement in the United States War College see: "Dome and Floor Construction in the United States War College," *Engineering Record*, volume 53, number 18, (May 5, 1906): 570-71. For more on early Burroughs (aka: American Arithmometer) reinforced concrete buildings see: "The Factory of the American Arithmometer Co," *Engineering Record*, volume 51, number 13, (April 1, 1905): 382-83; "High-Speed Reinforced Concrete Construction" in *Manufacturers' Record*, volume 48, number 18, (November 16, 1905): 460; and "Albert Kahn's Partners in Industrial Architecture" by Chris Meister in the *Journal of the Society of Architectural Historians*, volume 72, number 1, (March 2013): 78-95.

9. For more on the Marlboro-Blenheim Hotel see: "Reinforced Concrete and Tile Construction" parts I and II in *Engineering Record*, volume 52, numbers 26 and 27, (December 23 and 30, 1905): 719-22 and 743-45; and "Reinforced Concrete and Tile Construction Marlborough Hotel Annex, Atlantic City, N. J." *Engineering News*, volume 55, number 10, (March 8, 1906): 251-56. For more on Albert Kahn's home see: "Domestic Architecture in Canada" *Construction*, volume 2, number 8, (June 1909): 95-97.

10. R. D. Goodrich, "Licensing of Engineers," *Michigan Engineering Society*, Thirty-eighth annual report, 1916.

11. Anthony Ripley, "Architectural Giant Attains 65 Years," *The Detroit News*, October 4, 1959.

12. Sol King, *Creative, Responsive, Pragmatic: 75 Years of Professional Practice, Albert Kahn & Associates, Architects and Engineers,* The Newcomen Society, September 1970.

13. Albert Kahn, "Speech given at dinner to Mr. Mason by Michigan Society of Architects at the Dedication of the Masonic Temple," November 25, 1926, Albert Kahn Associates Archives.

14. Albert Kahn, "Architect Pioneers: In Development of Industrial Building," *The Anchora of Delta Gamma*, edited by Alta Gwinn Saunders, volume LIII, number 4 (May 1937): 376.

15. Ibid.

16. Ibid.

17. Ibid., 377.

18. "Personal," *Detroit Free Press*, March 23, 1902, section 2, page 6.

19. Kahn, "Speech given at dinner to Mr. Mason," 1926.

20. From February 1902 to October 1903, various newspaper clippings in the *Detroit Free Press* refer to Albert and Julius' partnership as architect and engineer. *Engineering News*, November 20, 1902, refers to "Kahn and Kahn."

21. "Building for the Packard Motor Co.," *Detroit Free Press*, August 2, 1903.

22. Ibid.

23. Ibid. A 90 percent decrease sounds high; the quoted article offered no description of the type of structure with which the Packard factory's insurance costs were being compared. The plant had an automatic sprinkler system and the comparison may have been made with buildings lacking such a feature. Other features included automatic fire doors, concrete floors in the stair hall and some work areas, and corbelled brick walls to serve as a fire stop. The light weight and inexpensive construction of the buildings would also have reduced their insurance costs.

24. The patent on the Kahn bars was pending at the time and production had not begun, so the bars were constructed of individual pieces bolted together, rather than stamped from a single rolled bar as the mass-produced bars were. Architectural drawing "Factory for the Packard Motor Car Co.," Job number 201, sheet number 2, dated May 30, 1903, Albert Kahn Associates Archives.

25. "The New Packard Works," *Automobile* 9, no. 24, (December 13, 1903): 612-14; "Century and Half's Work," *Detroit Free Press*, January 31, 1904.

26. Architectural drawing "Factory for the Packard Motor Car Co."

27. Kahn, "Architect Pioneers" (May 1937): 377.

28. Albert Kahn speech to the Cleveland Engineering Society on "Putting Architecture on a Business Basis," Undated likely 1932-33, Albert Kahn Associates Archives.

29. For more information on the manor see "Willistead Manor - A bit of the history," City of Windsor website.

30. Kahn, "Putting Architecture on a Business Basis," Undated likely 1932-33.

31. Albert Kahn, "The Architect in Industrial Building," *Modern Building*, Volume 5, Number 3 (May – June, 1918): 16.

32. Ibid., 18.

33. Ibid., 19.

34. "General Library," Bentley Historical Library, *University of Michigan,* and *The University of Michigan: An Encyclopedic Survey,* Walter A. Donnelly, Wilfred B. Shaw, and Ruth W. Gjelsness, editors; (Ann Arbor : University of Michigan Press, 1958.)

35. "History," Hatcher Showcase Graduate Library History and Design, University of Michigan website.

36. Albert Kahn, Letter to William Bishop Librarian at the University of Michigan, with enclosed speech given at the opening of the U of M Library, January 14, 1920. Albert Kahn Associates Archives.

37. Ibid.

38. Job number 663 and "A Chronology of University of Michigan Buildings, 1840-1999," Bentley Historical Library, University of Michigan website.

39. In Grant Hildebrand's unpublished text (draft of *Designing for Industry*) he includes a clipping from an early letterhead noting the firm's name change to Albert Kahn - Architects and Engineers, which also listed Louis Kahn next to Ernest Wilby and J. F. Hirschman. Albert Kahn Associates Archives.

40. Job number 194 and 232, among others, show separate engineering drawings. Albert Kahn Associates Archives.

41. Job number 306, referred to as the Owen Building, was located at the corner of Wayne and Lafayette in Detroit. See also "The Trussed Concrete Building," newspaper clipping from August 14, 1909, Burton Historical Collection.

42. George C. Baldwin, "The Offices of Albert Kahn, Architect, Detroit, Michigan," *The Architectural Forum*, volume 29, number 5, (November 1918): 125 - 130.

43. Ibid.

44. Ibid., 130.

45. Edgar A. Kahn, "Albert Kahn - Architect," unpublished essay, 10. Albert Kahn Associates Archives. Also referenced in Grant Hildebrand's text.

46. Job number 843, Albert Kahn Associates Archives. See also, "Norsk Maskinindustri - Norway's first group?" The Norwegian Technical Museum website.

47. Job numbers 892, 982, 1080, 1225, 1558, and 1707 to name a few. Albert Kahn Associates Archives.

48. Construction value. King, *Creative - Responsive - Pragmatic*, 1970, 18.

49. For more information see Beverly Joyner, "Langley's history, designed and built to last," Joint Base Langley-Eustis, August 24, 2016. https://www.jble.af.mil/News/Article-Display/Article/924987/langleys-history-designed-and-built-to-last/; Carlin Leslie, "The founding fathers of Langley," *Military News*, June 21, 2017. https://www.militarynews.com/peninsula-warrior/the-founding-fathers-of-langley/article_e20f124d-80a7-51fa-b917-0a95341c22bb.html; Vic Johnston, "Do you see what I see? Two hangers on Langley trumpet architect's vision," Joint Base Langley-Eustis. https://www.jble.af.mil/Portals/46/Documents/About-Us/AFD-091215-061.pdf; Curtis, Robert Irvin, John Mitchell, and Martin Copp. *Langley Field, the Early Years,* 1916-1946. Office of History, 4500th Air Base Wing, 1977.

50. "Kahn Consultant to Soviet Russia: Detroit Firm to Aid Gigantic Communist Industrial Building Plan," *Jewish Chronicle*, January 17, 1930. Albert Kahn Associates Archives (Bentley).

51.   Ibid.

52.   Kahn, "Architect Pioneers," (May 1937): 378.

53.   "Kahn Consultant to Soviet Russia," *Jewish Chronicle*, January 17, 1930.

54.   Anatole Senkevich, Jr., "Albert Kahn's Great Soviet Venture as Architect of the First Five-Year Plan, 1929-1932," *Dimensions*, Vol Ten (1996): 45.

55.   "Ford Sells $30,000,000 in Cars to Russia and Agrees to Help Soviet Build Factory," *The New York Times*, June 1, 1929. Albert Kahn Associates Archives (Bentley).

56.   "Ford Signs $30,000,000 Soviet Deal," *The Detroit Free Press*, June 1, 1929. Albert Kahn Associates Archives (Bentley).

57.   "Detroiters Aid Soviet," *The Detroit Free Press*, August 8, 1931. Albert Kahn Associates Archives (Bentley).

58.   "Kahn Firm Sends Its Ablest: Leave New York March 29 to Aid Billion Russian Expansion; Group Feted," *Detroit Times*, March 17, 1930. Albert Kahn Associates Archives (Bentley).

59.   "Soviet Killings," *The Detroit Free Press*, undated, found with articles from May 1929. Albert Kahn Associates Archives (Bentley).

60.   Philip A. Adler, "Albert Kahn Has Faith in Soviet Trade Future," *The Detroit News*, April 24, 1931. Albert Kahn Associates Archives (Bentley).

61.   Walter Duranty, "Reds Take Blame in 'Expert' Trouble," *The New York Times*, February 18, 1931. Albert Kahn Associates Archives (Bentley).

62.   "Albert Kahn Associates Built Russian Defenses," *Warspeed Record*, 27th edition, January 29, 1943. Published by the Mahony-Troast Employees at Plant Seven. Albert Kahn Associate Archives (Bentley).

63.   "Fishers to Build 10-Story Edifice," *Detroit Free Press*, September 28, 1930. Albert Kahn Associates Archives (Bentley).

64.   Henry Jonas Magaziner, "Working for a Genius: My Time with Albert Kahn," *APT Bulletin: The Journal of Preservation Technology,* vol. 32, no. 2/3 (2001).

65.   King, *Creative - Responsive - Pragmatic*, 1970, 18.

66.   Magaziner, "Working for a Genius" (2001): 61.

67.   King, *Creative - Responsive - Pragmatic*, 1970, 18.

68.   From *Industrial Architecture of Albert Kahn, Inc.* 1939. Albert Kahn Associates Archives.

69.   Myers, Howard, ed. "Strip Mills Republic Steel Corp., Cleveland, Ohio." *The Architectural Forum*, vol. 69, no. 2, (August 1938):116 – 118.

70.   *Industrial Architecture of Albert Kahn, Inc.* 1939. Albert Kahn Associates Archives.

71.   Myers, "Strip Mills Republic Steel Corp.", (August 1938):116 – 118.

72.   Detlaf Mertins, "Farnsworth to Crown Hall: Clear Span," *Mies*, (Phaidon Press: 2014), 282-287.

73.   Albert Kahn Associates, internal document given to *Time*, Jim Crowley, March 2, 1939. Albert Kahn Associates Archives.

74.   Ibid.

75.   Myers, Howard, ed. "Assembly Building Glenn L. Martin CO." *The Architectural Forum*, vol. 69, no. 2, (August 1938):102 – 106.

76.   "Glenn L. Martin Company and the Middle River Community," The Glenn L. Martin Maryland Aviation Museum, website accessed December 30, 2019.

77.   Albert Kahn, "Architecture in the National Defense Building Program," *Michigan Society of Architects*, volume 15, number 52, (December 30, 1941).

78.   Ibid.

79.   Magaziner, "Working for a Genius" (2001): 62.

80.   Kahn, "Architecture in the National Defense Building Program," 1941.

81.   Ibid.

82.   Ibid.

83.   Albert Kahn, "Chrysler Tank Arsenal," *Michigan Society of Architects,* volume 15, number 52, (December 30, 1941).

84.   Kahn updated the plant in 1983 for the Army Corp of Engineers, including a new roof and exterior skin for better energy efficiency, new heating and cooling system, new fire protection system and a state-of-the-art energy management and control system, a forerunner to today's Building Management Systems. This was to support the production change from M-60 Patton main battle tank to the brand new M-1 Abrams tank, recalled John Cole. Chrysler Tank Plant manufactured tanks well into the 1990s.

85.   Edgar A. Kahn, "Albert Kahn - Architect," unpublished essay, 21.

86.   Louis Kahn, "Don't Let War Plants Scare You," *Nation's Business* 32 (1944): 28.

87.   Kahn, "Architecture in the National Defense Building Program," 1941.

88.   Ibid.

89.   March 29, 1943, award, Albert Kahn Associates Archives.

90.   Wesley W. Stout, *Great Engines, Great Planes* (Detroit: Chrysler Corporation, 1947).

91. "Building for Defense. . . A Million Square Feet of Floor," *Architectural Forum* (November 1941): 335-337.

92. Documentation of both projects by the Historic American Engineering Record (HAER) means that there is more information for these plants than for many of the aircraft plants by AKA.

93. George Larson, "Nebraska's World War II Bomber Plant: the Glenn L. Martin-Nebraska Company," *Nebraska History* (Spring 1993): 32 - 43.

94. Prior to this house, Kahn had worked with Higgins Industries on several projects including the design of their New Orleans factory and hanger in 1943, and several prototype houses including a Thermo-Namel house in 1947.

95. Douglas J. Harnsberger, Sandra F. Hubbard, and Janet G. Murphy, "Thermo-Con House, Building No. 172, Fort Belvoir," National Register of Historic Places, United States Department of the Interior, National Park Service, March 1997. Albert Kahn Associates Archives.

96. *The Thermo-Con Cellular Concrete System*, Higgins Incorporated, Booklet No. 72 (1947).

97. Harnsberger, Hubbard, and Murphy, "Thermo-Con House, Building No. 172, Fort Belvoir," March 1997.

98. Albert Kahn Associated Architects and Engineers, Inc., "Report on the Structural Behavior of Thermo-Con Cellular Concrete," *The Thermo-Con Cellular Concrete System*, Higgins Incorporated, Booklet No. 72 (1947).

99. "Aircraft Plants," *Architectural Forum*, *The Magazine of Building*, (March 1952).

100. King, *Creative - Responsive - Pragmatic*, 1970, 23.

101. "Aircraft Plants," 1952.

102. Ibid.

103. "Albert Kahn Organization," unpublished, November 11, 1958. Albert Kahn Associates Archives.

104. United States Steel, "National Bank of Detroit Puts Trust in Steel," *Journal of the American Institute of Architects*, (September 1960).

105. Detroit Modern Civic Center/Financial District Tour script developed by the City of Detroit Historic Designation Advisory Board staff. Michigan Modern website.

106. "Architectural Giant Attains 65," *Detroit News*, October 4, 1959.

107. "Maintaining a Detroit Tradition," *AIA Journal*, June 1971.

108. Recalled John Cole, who was the lead engineer on the project.

109. King, *Creative - Responsive - Pragmatic*, 1970, 26.

110. "Bio of the Firm," unpublished, Firm of the Year Award, 1970. Albert Kahn Associates Archives.

111. R. F. Brueck and G. E. Holmes, Press Release, Detroit Diesel Allison - Division of General Motors Corporation, January 15, 1979. General Motors Heritage Center.

112. Gordon V. R. Holness, "Designing an Air Pollution Control System for Diesel Engine Test Facilities," *APCA Journal*, vol. 3, no. 12, (December 1982).

113. Project number 2165 in Springdale, Ohio, in 1962 and most recent additions are project 2206-BK in Morton Grove, Illinois in 2012. Albert Kahn Associates Archives.

114. Gordon V. R. Holness, email communication.

115. Ibid.

116. John Cole, email communication.

117. Donald Bauman, email communication.

118. Peter G. Lynde, interview.

119. Gordon V. R. Holness, email communication.

120. "History of Children's Hospital of Michigan," blog, Walter P. Reuther Library, Wayne State University, May 20, 2013.

121. Ibid.

122. "The New Children's Hospital," Children's Hospital of Michigan Dedication Brochure, (Detroit, MI: January 1971), 4. Albert Kahn Associates Archives.

123. John Haro quoted in Colleen Troy, "90 Years of Good Work Makes Kahn Well-Known," *The Greater New Center News*, volume 53, number 25, July 8, 1985. Albert Kahn Associates Archives.

124. Kahn began working with W. K. Kellogg during the Great Depression and in the 1930s, Kahn completed a number of projects at the Battle Creek plant including a five-story concrete warehouse in 1932 and the iconic Grain Silos in 1934. Albert Kahn worked with Kellogg to expand their operations into Canada, designing a new factory in London, Ontario. The firm also designed several schools and a camp for children with disabilities for the newly founded W. K. Kellogg Foundation. See job numbers 1590, 1549, 1607, 1610, and 1619. Albert Kahn Associates Archives.

125. Job number 1617L. Albert Kahn Associates Archives.

126. According to project architect John Enkemann in an interview in June 2020.

127. Peter G. Lynde, interview.

128. Gordon V. R. Holness, email communication.
129. Robert Mauck, "The evolution of CADD in providing A/E services," *Michigan Contractor and Builder*, (June 1, 1985).
130. Ibid.
131. John Cole, email communication.
132. According to a special meeting of the shareholders on 12/30/1940, they deleted "building and contracting" from the purpose of the firm. Albert Kahn Associates Archives.
133. Michael Maurer, "Albert Kahn, IBM, EDS make data center a reality," *Crain's Detroit Business*, volume 11, issue 33, August 14, 1995. Albert Kahn Associates Archives.
134. Ted Evanhoff, "Building Factories, Not Monuments," *Detroit Free Press*, March 3, 1997.
135. "Proposed General Motors Research Laboratory/Argonaut Building Historic District, Final Report," July 20, 2005. Courtesy of the GM Heritage Center.
136. "Charles F. Kettering - Ohio Inventor," Ohio Memory, State Library of Ohio website, August 3, 2018.
137. Albert Kahn speech to Maryland Academy of Sciences, April 15, 1931, Albert Kahn Associates Archives.
138. Speech or article written by Albert Kahn, "Good Architecture," undated. Albert Kahn Associates Archives.
139. Albert Kahn, "Fisher Building," *The American Architect*, volume 135, number 2563 (February 20, 1929): 212. Albert Kahn Associates Archives.
140. Ibid.
141. They had their first meal in the house on December 19, 1889. Ellen Booth, Diaries, 1889–1891, Ellen Warren Scripps Booth Papers (1981-03), Box 1, Cranbrook Archives, Cranbrook Center for Collections and Research.
142. Henry Scripps Booth, "History," 1888–1904, Henry Scripps Booth and Carolyn Farr Booth Papers (1982-05), Box 71:2, Cranbrook Archives, Cranbrook Center for Collections and Research. A presentation drawing for the residence, published in *American Architect and Building News* 27, no. 740 (March 1, 1890), is credited "Mason and Rice Architects" and signed "G. W. Nettleton and A. Kahn, Det."
143. "Annals for 1907" in Henry Wood Booth, "Annals of Cranbrook," Henry Wood Booth Papers (1985-05), Cranbrook Archives, Cranbrook Center for Collections and Research.
144. *Cranbrook House, Bloomfield Hills, Michigan* (Bloomfield Hills: Cranbrook House and Gardens Auxiliary, c. 1977), 8.
145. "Annals for 1908" in Henry Wood Booth, "Annals of Cranbrook."
146. For a book-length discussion of why Tudoresque, and not Tudor Revival, is the preferred term, see Andrew Ballantyne and Andrew Law, *Tudoresque: In Pursuit of the Ideal Home* (London: Reaktion Books, 2001).
147. W. Hawkins Ferry, *The Legacy of Albert Kahn* (Detroit: Detroit Institute of Arts, 1970; reprint, Detroit: Wayne State University Press, 1987), 16.
148. For a discussion of Kahn's "cottage style," see Ferry, *Legacy of Albert Kahn*, 16-17. For a nuanced discussion of Kahn's eclecticism, see Federico Bucci's final chapter, "Eclecticism for Motor City," in his book *Albert Kahn: Architect of Ford* (Milan: CittàStudi, 1991; paperback English translation, New York: Princeton Architectural Press, 2002), 141-83.
149. Diana Balmori, "The Invisible Cranbrook," *Journal of the Society of Architectural Historians* 53, no. 1 (March 1994): 36.
150. The dates for the West and East Wings, which reference when construction started and when the family first used the spaces, are noted by Henry Wood Booth in his "Annals of Cranbrook."
151. Rebecca Binno Savage, "Detroit News Complex," National Register of Historic Places Registration Form, National Park Service, United States Department of the Interior, November, 2015. And William W. Lutz, *The News of Detroit: How a Newspaper and a City Grew Together*, (Boston: Little, Brown and Company, 1973).
152. "$2,000,000 Building Completed," *Building Management*, volume 18, number 2, (February 1918): 11.
153. The full inscription reads: Mirror of the public mind ... Interpreter of the public intent ... Troubler of the public conscience. Reflector of every human interest ... Friend of every righteous cause ... Encourager of every generous act. Bearer of intelligence ... Dispeller of ignorance and prejudice ... A light shining into all dark places. Promoter of civic welfare and civic pride ... Bond of civic unity ... Protector of civil rights. Scourge of evil doers ... Exposer of secret iniquities ... Unrelenting foe of privilege and corruption.
154. "D.A.C.'s New Home, Nation's Finest, Opened," *The Detroit Free Press*, April 16, 1915.
155. "Plans Ready for Detroit Athletic Club's New Home," *The Detroit Free Press*, November 23, 1913.
156. For more information see the University of Michigan Bentley Historical Library; Manning Brothers Historical Photographic Collection; Michael Hauser and Marianne Weldon, Detroit's *Downtown Movie Palaces*, (Arcadia Publishing, 2006); W. Hawkins Ferry, *The Legacy of Albert Kahn*, (Detroit: Wayne State University Press, 1989); Marilyn Casto, *Actors, Audiences, and Historic Theaters of Kentucky*, (University Press of Kentucky, 2014); Cinema Treasures, cinematreasures. org; Historic Detroit, historicdetroit.org.
157. Eric J. Hill and John Gallagher, *AIA Detroit: The American Institute of Architects Guide to Detroit Architecture* (Detroit: Wayne State University Press, 2003), 156.

158. "Cashier's House History," Erie County Historical Society, website archived, 2009.
159. "Grand Circus Park," internal marketing document, 1999. Albert Kahn Associates Archives.
160. Albert Kahn speech given December 11, 1930 at the laying of the cornerstone ceremony. Albert Kahn Associates Archives.
161. "Forty-Second Annual Report of The Grace Hospital," Grace Hospital Board of Directors, Detroit, Michigan, December 31, 1930.
162. "Forty-Third Annual Report of the Grace Hospital," Grace Hospital Board of Directors, Detroit, Michigan, 1931, 30.
163. Ferry, *The Legacy of Albert Kahn*, 140.
164. Albert Kahn Associates, copy for the *Detroit Free Press*, April 24, 1930. Albert Kahn Associates Archives.
165. Job number 599. Albert Kahn Associates Archives.
166. Samuel D. Gruber, "The Rabbi's Son Who Built Detroit," *The Forward*, January 14, 2009.
167. Jonathan D. Sarna, "The Debate Over Mixed Seating in the American Synagogue," in Jack Wertheimer, ed., *The American Synagogue: A Sanctuary Transformed* (New York: Cambridge University Press, 1987), 363-394.
168. 735 Lake Shore, along with many other Grosse Pointe residences, are listed in the book *Grand Estates of Grosse Pointe*, by Katie Doelle, Arcadia Publishing, 2020.
169. Ann Berman, "The Edsel and Eleanor Ford House," *Architectural Digest,* website, July 1, 2001.
170. Albert Kahn, description of the Detroit Golf Club, unpublished, Albert Kahn Associates Archives.
171. "Through the Years: Our Courses," Detroit Golf Club website, accessed 2020.
172. Myers, Howard, ed. "Half Ton Truck Plant, Chrysler Corporation, Detroit, Mich." *The Architectural Forum*, vol. 69, no. 2, (August 1938): 137.
173. Ibid.
174. Barbara Zaferos, "Aurora Health Care leads largest employers list," *Milwaukee Business Journal,* website, July 19, 2013, accessed May 2020.
175. Lean healthcare is the application of "lean" ideas in healthcare facilities to minimize waste in every process, procedure, and task through an ongoing system of improvement. Using lean principles, all members of the organization, from clinicians to operations and administration staff, continually strive to identify areas of waste and eliminate anything that does not add value for patients. "What Is Lean Healthcare?" *NEJM Catalyst,* April 27, 2018.
176. Who We Are," Planetree International, website, accessed May 2020.
177. "About," Aurora Health Care website, accessed May 2020.
178. Albert Kahn, article for *The Detroit News* dated April 2, 1922, "A Problem in Design: General Motors Bldg. Not Mere Construction Job," Albert Kahn Associates Archives.
179. General Motors, *General Motors Building... A Century of Progress* (1933).
180. General Motors, News Release, May 1934, 2.
181. While the majority of the displays and artwork created for the General Motors pavilion are gone, some examples do remain today. Murals and marquetry created by Miklos Gaspar that hung in the Entrance Hall and viewing gallery above the Chevrolet-Fisher Body assembly line now reside at Lane Tech College Prep High School in Chicago. A model of Edward Deeds' barn in Dayton, Ohio where famed GM inventor and vice president Charles F. Kettering developed the first electric self-starter has been preserved by the Kettering University Archives at Durant-Dort Factory One in Flint, Michigan.
182. General Motors, News Release, May 1934, 4.
183. Ibid, 1.
184. This idea is also often referred to as LEAN or Just-In-Time manufacturing. "Toyota Production System," Toyota, website, accessed June 24, 2020.
185. "University of Chicago Medicine Center for Care and Discovery Post Occupancy Evaluation," Albert Kahn Associates, June 16, 2018.
186. Albert Kahn speech to Maryland Academy of Sciences, April 15, 1931, Albert Kahn Associates Archives.
187. Gordon V.R. Holness, former President of Albert Kahn Associates.
188. Kahn, "Architect Pioneers," (May 1937): 377.
189. "Albert Kahn," *The Architectural Forum*, Volume 69, Number 2, (August 1938): 88.
190. Recollections from Ed Parks, former president of Albert Kahn Associates 1985-1992, October 1994. Albert Kahn Associates Archives.
191. For more information see "The Factory of the American Arithmometer Company," *The Engineering Record*, volume 51, number 13, (April 1, 1905): 382-383.
192. *The University of Michigan: An Encyclopedic Survey,* Donnelly, Shaw, and Gjelsness eds., 1958.
193. Michael Hodges, *Building the Modern World: Albert Kahn in Detroit,* (Detroit: Wayne State University Press: 2018.)

194. Grant Hildebrand, "Beautiful Factories," *Albert Kahn: Inspiration for the Modern*, edited by Brian Carter (Ann Arbor: The University of Michigan Museum of Art, 2001), 20.
195. "Fuller's Success Remarkable Tale," *The Sunday Herald*, Boston, January 30, 1910.
196. Patrick L. Kennedy, "A Trip Down Automobile Row," *BU Today*, Boston University.
197. "Fuller's Success Remarkable Tale," 1910.
198. Ibid.
199. Ibid.
200. Kahn Text, Spring 1989, internal newsletter in Albert Kahn Associates Archives.
201. Pierce Factory, as it is called in the Albert Kahn project list, or also called Pierce Arrow Factory, opened in 1906 and produced automobiles until 1938. In 1974, the factory and surrounding complex, which includes other buildings not designed by Kahn, was added to the National Register of Historic Places.
202. "History and Significance of the Study Buildings - Dearborn Assembly Plant," Historic Structure Report, Ford Motor Company Rouge Plant Revitalization, August 30, 2000, 7 and 21.
203. Grant Hildebrand, *The Architecture of Albert Kahn*, (Cambridge, Mass: MIT Press, 1974).
204. Grant Hildebrand, "Industrial Buildings: A New American Factory," *Architectural Record*, May 1998.
205. "The Foundations of the Hotel Pontchartrain, Detroit: A Study of the Utilization of Old Foundations for New Buildings," *The American Architect*, vol. 120, no. 2374 (August 17, 1921): 127-131.
206. Ibid., 129.
207. Ibid., 128.
208. Ibid., 130.
209. "Aircraft Plants," *Architectural Forum*, The Magazine of Building, (March 1952).
210. For more information see The Henry Ford Museum website, "Willow Run Bomber Collection," accessed June 2020, The Detroit Historical Society, website "Encyclopedia of Detroit – Willow Run," accessed June 2020, Tim Trainor, "How Ford's Willow Run Assembly Plant Helped Win World War II," *Assembly Magazine*, (January 3, 2019).
211. Albert Kahn Associates Archives, Job number 424 for Chalmers Motor Car Company. During the war years, this plant was one of Chrysler's most important, producing industrial and marine engines, marine tractors, pontoons, and submarine nets. Detroit Historical Society, "Detroit - The Arsenal of Democracy" online map, accessed June 2020.
212. Gordon V. R. Holness, email communication.
213. "A new Jefferson Ave. Assembly Plant is unveiled by Chrysler Corporation," *Michigan Contractor and Builder*, (October 25, 1986).
214. Chuck Robinson, Angelo Colasanti, and Gary Boyd, "Steel Fibers Reinforce Auto Assembly Plant Floor," *Concrete International*, (April 1991). Albert Kahn Associates Archives.
215. Ibid.
216. Ibid.
217. Jodi McFarland, "Saginaw Metal Castings Operations Timeline," MLive, April 4, 2019, accessed June 2020.
218. Ibid.
219. Albert Kahn Associates job 1430. Albert Kahn Associates Archives.
220. "Grey Iron vs. Nodular Iron," Dandong Foundry, website accessed June 2020.
221. Gordon V. R. Holness, "Retroactive Energy Conservation for Industry," *Power Magazine*, (1977). Albert Kahn Associates Archives.
222. "Building 'Floats In Air'; 'Paints Itself," *Michigan Manufacturer and Financial Record*, volume 122, number 3, (September 1968).
223. "Weathering Steel Highlights New Offices for Chevrolet-Saginaw Foundry," Press Release, August 1, 1967, Albert Kahn Associates Archives.
224. Ferry, *The Legacy of Albert Kahn*, 1987, 142.
225. "Construction Begun on New Ford Engineering Laboratory, Dearborn," *Ford News* Vol. III, No. 11 (April 1, 1923): 1, 8.
226. "Engineering Laboratory at Dearborn Completed," *Ford News* Vol. V, No. 3 (December 1, 1924): 1,5.
227. "A Place For Everyone, In Right Environment," *Ford World*, (December 1978) 6-7. And "Ford to Create Campus of the Future in Dearborn to Speed Product Innovation and Attract World-Class Talent," Ford Media Center, (September 17, 2019).

228. For full information see the "Environmental handicapped Chamber Design: high altitude simulation," *Heating / Piping / Air Conditioning Magazine*, (February 1984).

229. Gordon V. R. Holness, "Automotive Test Chambers Isolated from Noise, Vibration," *Industrial HVAC*, (1993).

230. Peter G. Lynde and Robert J. Buelow, "Development of an Alternative Metal Anechoic Wedge," *Sound & Vibration*, (October 1993).

231. To learn more, read this article: Peter G. Lynde, "Establishing an Industry Benchmark: Mercury Marine Builds Innovative World-Class Testing Facility," *Noise/News International,* (December 16, 2019).

232. Wilfred B. Shaw, *The University of Michigan: An Encyclopedic Survey* (Ann Arbor: University of Michigan Press, 1942): 1641.

233. Edgar A. Kahn, "Albert Kahn - Architect," unpublished article, 11. Albert Kahn Associates Archives.

234. Ibid.

235. Louisville became known within the firm as Appliance Park West, when, about fifteen years later, GE contracted Kahn to create Appliance Park East in Columbia, Maryland.

236. John Sprovieri, "A Century of GE Appliance Manufacturing," *Assembly Magazine*, (March 29, 2017).

237. Ibid.

238. "Making UNIVAC a Business," Computer History Museum, website, accessed June 2020. Mitch Betts, "GE's Appliance Park Still an IT Innovator," *Computerworld*, website, accessed June 2020.

239. King, *Creative - Responsive - Pragmatic*,1970, 30.

240. Ferry, *The Legacy of Albert Kahn*, 147-148.

241. Sprovieri, "A Century of GE Appliance Manufacturing," 2017.

242. Nissan won the award for B D&C Owner of the Year in the "Most Positive Impact on an Area" category. Rose Thomas, "Tokyo Meets Tennessee with mutual admiration," *Building Design and Construction*, vol. 26, no. 8, (August 1985).

243. Henry Ritter, "Nissan Motor: State-of-the-art in Steel," *Modern Steel Construction*, vol. 26, no. 2 (1986).

244. Thomas, "Tokyo Meets Tennessee with mutual admiration," 1985.

245. Ritter, "Nissan Motor: State-of-the-art in Steel," 1986.

246. Interview with John Enkemann, who was the lead architect for the power house and office building.

247. John Haro, *John Haro: Sixty Years of Architecture*, (Hancock, MI: Book Corcern Printers, 2015), 9.

248. *The University of Michigan*: *An Encyclopedic Survey,* Donnelly, Shaw, and Gjelsness eds., 1958.

249. James Tobin, "The Glory of Old Main," 150 Years at the Hospital, University of Michigan, website, accessed June 2020.

250. "Old Main Hospital Arch," Arts and Culture, University of Michigan, website, accessed June 2020.

251. Gordon V.R. Holness, "1989 ASHRAE Energy Award Winners – The University of Michigan Adult General Hospital," *ASHRAE Journal*, (March 1989).

252. Ibid.

253. Winner of an energy award in 1989 from the American Society of Heating, Refrigerating and Air-Conditioning Engineers.

254. In Michigan, for example, the legislature passed Act 1 of 1966, Section 125.1355, requiring public buildings to be designed and constructed to be accessible for wheelchair users and users with limited mobility. For more information on this project see William L. Demiene, "Handi-Access: design and planning of handicapped facilities should incorporate sensitive solutions," *American School and University*, (June 1989).

255. Heritage Newspapers, "Past Historical Sites – Ford Airport," The Internet Archive – Wayback Machine, accessed May 2020.

256. Albert Kahn, "The Architect in Industrial Building," *Modern Building*, Volume 5, Number 3 (May – June, 1918): 19.

257. "Architectural Giant Attains 65," *Detroit News*, October 4, 1959.